Brahmin in Revolt

By Leonard Baker

Brahmin in Revolt

A Biography of Herbert C. Pell

by
Leonard Baker

1972
Doubleday & Company, Inc., Garden City, New York

Acknowledgments

My appreciation, first, to Senator Claiborne Pell for giving me complete access to the papers and records of his father, Herbert C. Pell, with the only stipulation being that I write as accurate a book as I possibly could. My thanks to Richard H. Rovere and Arthur Schlesinger, Jr., who shared with me their personal memories of Herbert Pell as they knew him and their knowledge of his role in the Roosevelt years. Ladislas Farago very kindly gave me documents he had acquired from Nazi sources about Mr. Pell, and David Kahn saved me much time by scouring Nazi archives; my appreciation to them both. My thanks to Joseph Buday and Jerrell Bennett, Jr., for services as translators.

Once again I am indebted to the staffs of the Franklin D. Roosevelt Library at Hyde Park and the Oral History Research Office at Columbia University. Miss Lee Szilagyi and Ray Nelson of Senator Pell's staff put up with my impositions with much grace, and I thank them.

The following persons assisted me either by granting me a personal interview or by writing to me of their recollections of Herbert Pell, and I wish to express my great appreciation to them all: Senator Claiborne Pell, Mrs. Claiborne Pell, Herbert C. Pell III, Mrs. Herbert C. Pell, Mrs. Matilda Koehler, John H. G. Pell, Mrs. John H. G. Pell, Howard K. Travers, David Ogilvy, Richard B. Duane and the late Jeremiah T. Mahoney.

To the memory of my grandmother
Malkah Baker

Brahmin in Revolt

I THE ERA TOOK ITS NAME—THE GILDED AGE
—from a Mark Twain novel and took its political morality from no one, preferring to do without that encum-
brance. The industrial capitalist reigned supreme. He had
emerged from the Civil War with the money to control
the politics of the last decades of the 1800s. And he had no
hesitation in indulging in what Sidney Fine described as
"the doctrine of self-interest."

His money purchased him more money. Compliant legislatures, both in the states and in Washington, gave him a
protective tariff, land for his railroads, cheap labor for his
factories. And he spent his money lavishly to enjoy as
much as he could the best of the worst of times. Ward
McAllister, who most enjoyed tattling on the "Four Hundred," reported that up to the closing decades of the
1800s "for one to be worth a million of dollars was to be
rated as a man of fortune, but now, bygones must be
bygones." McAllister continued that "New York's idea as
to values, when fortune was named, leaped boldly up to
ten millions, fifty millions, one hundred millions." And
when they had it, they spent it—flashily. "One was no

longer content with a dinner of a dozen or more," said McAllister, "to be served by a couple of servants. Fashion demanded that you be received in the hall of the house in which you were to dine by from five to six servants, who, with the butler, were to serve the repast. . . ."

And what was true of New York society was true of society generally. A modern chronicler of America's *haut monde*, Cleveland Amory, tells of a Newport hostess barring from her dinner table people with less than five million dollars. In Newport a house cost two million dollars to build and many millions more to furnish. Women spent thousands of dollars on their clothes each season. The costs of the fancy balls soared into the hundreds of thousands of dollars.

But if it was the best of times for some, it was the beginning of the end of the worst of times for others. The great economic change that came to America in later decades had started. Farmers in the West were meeting, organizing, beginning to politick. Immigrants in the eastern cities were gathering in coffee houses, talking, waiting for a Robert F. Wagner and an Al Smith to emerge from their frustration and their sense of political justice to lead them.

It was at this time that a lovely young lady wandered through the streets of Chicago until she found a decaying brick building crammed between a saloon and a funeral parlor. The house had been built by Charles J. Hull, and when the young lady—Jane Addams—took it over, it became famous as Hull House. As a settlement house it became not only a hope for the poor of Chicago but also a beacon of decency lighting the way for all those who cared about their fellow citizens.

This was the time when a young man stood before a national convention of the Democratic party and warned its members that the poor would be heard. "We say to you," shouted William Jennings Bryan, "that you have made the definition of a business man too limited in its application. The man who is employed for wages is as much a business man as the corporation counsel in a great metropolis; the merchant at the crossroads store is as much a business man as the merchant of New York; the farmer who goes forth in the morning and toils all day—who begins in the spring and toils all summer—and who by the application of brain and muscle to the natural resources of the country creates wealth, is as much a business man as the man who goes upon the board of trade and bets upon the price of grain; the miners who go down a thousand feet into the earth, or climb two thousand feet upon the cliffs, and bring forth from their hiding places the precious metals to be poured into the channels of trade are as much business men as the few financial magnates who, in a back room, corner the money of the world." And he warned the politicians that "we come to speak for the broader class of business men." Then Bryan closed his address with the cry that inspired hundreds of young men in the 1890s to become the do-gooders of the 1900s. "You shall not," he shouted, "press down upon the brow of labor this crown of thorns. You shall not crucify mankind upon a cross of gold."

The Gilded Age was the apex of American wealth.

Never before had those with money spent it quite so casually, quite so lavishly. It was consequently the beginning of the demand for a redistribution of wealth. Never again would the poor remain unheard.

Few people enjoyed the Gilded Age as did Herbert Claiborne Pell. For him the Age was a world of travel, study, lavishness, sophistication, all the pleasures of the cultivated gentleman whom he epitomized. He was—and enjoyed being—a member of America's *haut monde*, the group in society which most Americans publicly criticized and privately wished to join.

But he also understood, and he was one of the few to, that the poor must be heard. "Even those of us who shared in the good things," he wrote, "must realize that the boom times benefited too few people, that the distribution of profits was unfair. The white collar man, the business girl, the farmer, the teacher and the doctor paid for all."

His is the story of a generation born to all the comforts money could buy and of those members of that generation who listened to the poor, who became their advocates, who became the enemies of those who fought the poor. From an involvement in the political turbulence created by Theodore Roosevelt, Herbert Pell moved to become a fiercely independent congressman, astute political leader, and scourge of the *laissez-faire* business world. Ultimately his life and career, like those of his friend Franklin D. Roosevelt, were engulfed in the cataclysm that threatened civilized mankind, the Second World War. Pell continued to make himself unpopular by protesting Nazi atrocities when governments preferred to ignore them.

He went into his wars armed. As a member of the Gilded Age's *haut monde*, he knew its secrets, its faults, its shames. Being a man of inherited wealth, he did not feel compelled to join the race to acquire more wealth which so attracted the Goulds and the first-generation Rockefellers and Harrimans. He could be above that contest and look upon it with disdain. And so he emerged from the Gilded Age a young man skeptical of wealth, although enjoying it, and skeptical of those who sought it above all other things. With his own social, cultural and economic background, he never could be hurt. Never in his life did he have to struggle for prestige, position or wealth. All were his by birthright and he could not be attacked successfully by petty politicians. Having more than money could buy, he himself could not be bought.

Like Roosevelt, he was a conservative. He defined that term as one "who wishes to conserve the institutions of this country, not necessarily without change, but at least without basic alterations."

It was difficult, of course, for a Pell not to wish to conserve America's institutions. The family had been involved with them for so many generations. When Herbert Pell was born February 16, 1884, in his family's home in New York City at 113 East Twenty-third Street, he was part of as illustrious a family as America had produced to that time. Among his ancestors were the Lorillards who had founded the P. Lorillard tobacco company more than a century earlier; William C. C. Claiborne, who was the first governor of the Louisiana Territory; and countless members of Congress and state legislatures.

The family tree went back even further, the family histories enjoy pointing out, to John Pell, an Englishman who served as Oliver Cromwell's minister to the Swiss cantons. Besides his diplomatic role, this John Pell is known for originating the division sign, the straight line with the dot above and below it. His son, the second John Pell, inherited much of Westchester County and the Bronx from an uncle when he was only twenty-seven. All the London dandies envied him and he even was called before Charles II to speak of his inheritance and to be knighted. Two months later, in January of 1672, Sir John Pell landed at Pell's Point in the New World to claim as much of it as he could.

Like many other young men in the New World, he added to his landholdings and became a substantial member of his community. He helped to plan the Boston Post Road and served in the Colonial assembly. As commissioner for Indian affairs for the New York colony, he learned to become a diplomat; when a local tribe challenged his land titles, he settled the argument without bloodshed by having his son Thomas marry the Indian sachem's daughter.

The descendants of John Pell were among the original landed aristocracy of America and likewise were involved in the politics of their times, sitting in the Colonial assemblies and in the federal Congress as was required of community leaders. Occasionally one found some business or other to occupy himself, but most of them were content to enjoy the serenity and the security of their landholdings. To succeeding generations they passed on their wealth (usually expanded—they were thrifty people), their social position, and the preoccupation with the arts their money allowed them.

The literary background was passed down to Herbert Pell's father, an ardent student of Shakespeare. He could discuss the plays endlessly in detail—characters, dialogue and interaction. However, the brief excursions he made into the world of business indicated he could have done very well in that world if he had chosen to enter it.

During his own lifetime, Herbert Pell accumulated a fine collection of European literature, which, late in his life, he donated to the Library of Congress. Books were important to him. He had several books that had first belonged to his great-grandfather, then his grandfather, his father and finally to himself—four generations that treasured a book enough to save it. The book ultimately passed on to the fifth generation—Herbert Pell's son, Claiborne de Borda Pell.

If it was not an ambitious family, neither was it slothful nor frivolous. The Lorillards were a different story. Herbert Pell spoke with some condescension of his Lorillard relatives who "mostly went in for games and sports." Pell criticized them for spending so much money on lavish living "and really acquiring almost nothing." He found it incredible that "they had no pictures. At a time when a Frans Hals could be had for five hundred dollars, they bought Adolphe W. Bouguereaus for thousands." He finally damned them—and revealed something of himself—

by saying that "they were very good examples . . . of the pleasant but uncultivated society of their times."

A Pell could not escape American history. He heard so much of it from his relatives in first-person narratives. Herbert Pell's paternal grandmother was the former Annie Emily Magdalene Claiborne of New Orleans, who knew both sides of the Civil War. As a young girl she had read to her family from the newspaper accounts of the great debates over slavery between Daniel Webster and Henry Clay. Her father, a congressman and member of the Mississippi State Legislature, was ostracized because he opposed secession. Her brother, a Confederate major, was killed fighting for the South. She had first come north on a steamboat and, with the other young girls, helped carry firewood for the race that began whenever two steamboats came abreast of each other on the Mississippi River. She told these stories to Herbert Pell when he was a young child, and history was always for him the fascinating story of people and never the turgid prose of the textbook.

Herbert Pell's own parents were a combination of established family and wealth. His father, the first Herbert Claiborne Pell, played with the idea of a military career for a while and actually spent several years at the Naval Academy. But he found the strict military life tiresome and resigned. Then he went to law school at Columbia University and for a career managed the family property, a task that left him adequate time for his Shakespeare studies, travel, and shuttling between Tuxedo Park and Newport.

Herbert Pell's mother was the former Katherine Lorillard Kernochan, a member of the Lorillard family whose

fortune had begun with tobacco and thrived on real estate investments in New York City. Unlike many of her
contemporaries, she was a well-educated woman who enjoyed reading and encouraged her son to read and study.
Pell's parents treated him and his younger brother, Clarence, as equals, often allowing them to choose for themselves rather than dictating to them. "They both always
went on the principle," said Herbert Pell, "that I was a
young friend and that I could be best left alone to decide
for myself. And I must say I think that is true." Perhaps
it was not.

Herbert Pell grew up in Tuxedo Park. Forty miles from
New York City in Orange County, it could have been
light-years away from the ferment that was part of American life in the late 1880s and 1890s. Tuxedo was the
private community developed by Pierre Lorillard, and its
lakes, woods and trails meandered for miles. Emily Post, a
long-time resident of Tuxedo Park, had this to say about
it: "There is a fixed idea in the mind of the general public
that Tuxedo is inhabited by a stiff-necked, snobbish, and
equally gay set of people, whose chief fear is that some
one from the outside world may evade the ceaseless vigilance of the guard at its gates and enter the citadel." She
then acknowledged: "There is a certain foundation for
this supposition."

Behind the guard at the gate and inside the citadel was a
beautiful world, all a tribute to Pierre Lorillard and his
money. The Lorillards had started buying up Tuxedo land
in the early 1800s for the valuable timber that grew there.
When the third Pierre Lorillard died, the land passed to

his seven children. One of them was the fourth Pierre Lorillard, Herbert Pell's great-uncle. Of all the Lorillard children, Pierre most enjoyed the world as a playground for himself and with his money saw no reason why it should not be. He quickly bought his brothers' and sisters' shares and determined to transform Tuxedo into an ideal community, an exclusive playground for himself, his relatives and his friends. Because, as Herbert Pell said, "It was impossible for him to do anything on a small scale," Tuxedo was conceived and built in the grandest manner.

Pierre Lorillard contacted his friends, most of whom were fellow members of the Union Club in New York City, and persuaded them to purchase shares in his Tuxedo Park Association, then nothing more than a name. In doing this he established the theme of Tuxedo—a gathering place for people who knew one another, liked one another and could afford to purchase their privacy. Lorillard was the first president of the Tuxedo Park Association, and his nephew-in-law, Pell's father (the first Herbert C. Pell), became its first secretary.

In the fall of 1885, Pierre Lorillard took an architect, Bruce Price, and an engineer, Ernest W. Bowditch, to Tuxedo and began barking commands. Legend has it that he pointed his cane and said the clubhouse will go there! Whether he did point his cane or not, the clubhouse did indeed go there very quickly. Emily Post, daughter of architect Bruce Price, wrote some years later that "Mr. Lorillard ordered homes in the same way that other people might order boots. He talked rapidly, and thought twice as fast as he talked, and he wished his orders carried out at a speed that equalled the sum of both." What Lorillard ordered that fall day was the building of a community, complete with homes, a clubhouse, roads, sewerage, water —all the accouterments of an established and comfortable neighborhood. And he wanted it ready to open the following summer.

That the deadline Lorillard set was met is perhaps a wonder of the nineteenth century; at the least, it is a testimonial to the power of money. Eighteen hundred workmen were imported from Italy. With dynamite, hand drills, picks, shovels, horse-drawn wagons and a million and a half of the Lorillard dollars, they laid eighteen miles of roads, built the clubhouse, a village consisting of residential cottages, stores, a police station, and surrounded the entire seven thousand acres of land with an eight-foot barbed-wire fence.

And what did it look like?

A newspaper reporter searching for a story arrived after Tuxedo had been opened a few weeks. He took the train to the Tuxedo Park station—"a pretty building in modernized Queen Anne style." Across the road he saw shops and cottages "in varied forms of the same general style of architecture as that of the station, or running into quaint specimens of early English, or Elizabethan." The reporter accurately concluded that Bruce Price "has not only subordinated and harmonized the form and coloring of these structures to the natural features of the landscape, but has grouped them most artistically."

The reporter was not free to roam unattended through the private property. A guard met him, found he was expected and "properly accredited" and led him to a small wagon—called a "jigger" by the Tuxedo residents—with a "canary and black body and olive plush seats." The team of horses was driven by a coachman dressed in the club's green and gold colors. The reporter was taken to the gatehouse—"what seems the buttress of a ruined Norman castle, and this impression is heightened by the ancient-looking stone gate, lodge and bridge that spans what might have been the castle moat." A private policeman stood sentry, his military uniform topped by a spiffy white sun helmet. After the reporter had been cleared at the gatehouse, his drive took him to the clubhouse, up the side of a mountain a distance of about two miles.

A turn in the road brought him to the "cottages" of Pierre Lorillard and his son. "The cottages are really magnificent villas," the reporter wrote, "one cream-colored and in the airy Italian style, the other of soberer hue and semi-Gothic aspect." He saw the other "cottages" from a distance, as each was set far back from the traffic of the occasional horse-drawn wagon on the carriage road.

"If one arrives at the splendid clubhouse at the lakeside about sunset," the reporter wrote, "the beauty of the scene cannot fail to make an impression. Standing on the piazza, about eight hundred feet above the sea level, breathing the clear cool air of that elevation, made aromatic by the autumn odors of balsamic pines, maples and larches of the surrounding forests, one looks over a sheet of water whose silvery sheen is just warmed by sunset tints and rippled by a breeze. Set like a circle of diamonds under the emerald crown of the mountain, this lake is nearly half a mile across and two miles in length. Here and there its expanse is dotted by a sail or by the slender rowing and fishing craft of the club. In the fascination of the scene one hardly notices the appearance of the clubhouse itself, and perhaps one could not say more for the natural picturesqueness of the view and for the perfection of the architect's art."

Society had its first view of the Tuxedo community on Tuesday, June 1, 1886, and for the next several decades a person's standing in society depended on whether he had or had not attended the opening of the Tuxedo Park clubhouse that day. Seven hundred guests came in special trains. At the station they were met by horse-drawn buses and little wagons painted in the green and gold colors of the Association. On their way to the clubhouse for the garden party, they passed gamekeepers dressed in green and gold and wearing Tyrolean hats complete with black cocks' feathers, paid that day to appear on the roads in their fancy costumes and wave at the guests. (Pierre Lorillard had considered everything; his money might not have insured genuine friendship, but it did prevent overt signs of hostility.) The clubhouse overlooked the lake, where there were two barges, manned by white-uniformed oarsmen, ready to take the guests for an excursion.

The garden party ended at five o'clock in the afternoon. But the wine continued to flow and the music played on. There was a dinner and the evening began with a dance. All of America's high society was present, by invitation of course. Those who weren't wished they were.

Tuxedo never hid its exclusiveness; rather it capitalized on it. One resident once wrote that Tuxedo Park became "not society's capital but its Café de la Paix. If one sat long enough on the Tuxedo Club piazza one saw everyone who was anyone in society."

But the word "society" was used in its narrowest sense. One did not see those flashier members only newly arrived to society or those panting at the gate. The residents of Tuxedo had so much money they could disdain spending it. "They were positively austere alongside many residents of Newport," wrote George Rushmore, whose family was among the first settlers. Emily Post explained that "Tuxedo people are not living from excitement to excitement. The fact that some one can and will give marvelous entertainments does not interest them in the least." Secure in their wealth, they did not have to prove it.

The community was run by the Tuxedo Park Association in much the same way that a feudal estate was controlled by the lord of the manor. The Association sold land to club members but operated all utilities and assessed taxes to pay for them. Buildings in the village itself were owned by the Association and leased to the shopkeepers who were there on sufferance. And separating the village and the park where the members played was the eight-foot-high barbed-wire fence.

Membership in the club was not impossible to achieve. A candidate for membership had to be recommended by two members of the club. Then the twenty-man governing board voted on the applicant. According to the rules, "one adverse vote in seven shall be necessary to exclude a candidate for election." That, in effect, meant three negative votes, which was actually a more liberal rule than most college fraternities applied.

Standards were high. Once a female club member brought a professional actor named Kyrle Bellow to the club, and Pell's mother returned to the clubhouse after luncheon to find "a turmoil of excitement" because of his presence. The club's board of governors hastily met in a special session and passed a rule that no actor could come to the Tuxedo Club "in any circumstances." Occasionally, however, standards were relaxed for friends. Price Collier, a Unitarian minister, had resigned from the clergy when he divorced his wife to marry a widow. The Union Club in New York City blackballed him, but his friends elected him to the Tuxedo Club.

There were standards of behavior also. At dinner the women wore long evening dresses and the men wore black tie. As a child Herbert Pell was thoroughly indoctrinated with the principle that gentlemen dress correctly. "Dress up" for him when he was a very young boy was a dark suit, with knickerbockers, a cravat and a smart cap. For the remainder of his life, he was a fastidious dresser. As a country squire in his mature years, he was garbed always in a knickerbocker suit; his may have been the only knickerbocker suits extant then in the United States. As the world traveler, he always wore a suit with a waistcoat and a large cravat. ("Waistcoat" and "cravat" were words he had learned and he always used them rather than the more popular "vest" and "tie.") Many years later, in the 1950s, when dress became relaxed, Herbert Pell, by then in his seventies, adhered to the standards of dress for gentlemen he had learned at Tuxedo. Returning to London for an extended stay in 1955, he wrote his haberdasher there to ask: "I should be very much obliged indeed if you would let me know whether the stiff starched shirt is still worn in the evening." Pell had a large number of pleated shirts without collars. "Would it be practical," he wanted to know, "to attach a modern collar to such a shirt for use with a dinner jacket?" He took the shirts to London only after the haberdasher replied that stiff starched shirts still were acceptable and also that "it would also be quite in order to wear a modern collar with pleated shirts and dinner jacket." And he not only dressed properly himself, he expected the same of others. David Ogilvy, the advertising executive, remembers this incident:

It must have been around 1957.

A *boiling* hot Sunday evening in July. New York was empty, and I was the only person dining at the Knickerbocker Club.

After dinner I went into the library to write letters, and made the mistake of taking off my jacket.

Herbert Pell, whom I did not know, came into the room. When he saw me, he snorted and snarled, "I'm surprised you don't take off your *shoes*. You would be even more comfortable," and stormed out.

Tuxedo had other standards also. There was little social mixing with the people in the village who ran the shops and did the chores that made life in Tuxedo so smooth. The manager of the Association and the overseer of the village was a man named Charles Patterson. A Tuxedo hostess conceded once that she would like to ask Charles Patterson to dinner but she really could not have a man at dinner one day who had been dancing with her housemaid the night before.

It was Tuxedo and the world it represented that Herbert Pell wrote of years later when he referred to "those of us who shared in the good things." For money never could make life better than it was in Tuxedo at the end of the nineteenth century and the beginning of the twentieth. All the comfort of the Gilded Age was known there.

Curiously, despite what money could buy, growing up in Tuxedo Park was not much different from growing up in any rural American community. The Pell children, Herbert and Clarence, two years younger, like most young children at any time were known as "general nuisances." They enjoyed teasing the older residents. And the people of Tuxedo recalled stories of the Pell boys jumping out from behind bushes to scare them, screaming like Indians or occasionally breaking a window with a misdirected ball. One Tuxedo resident tells of his father's driving up to the Pell house to be greeted by a Pell child thrusting his head out from behind a bush, yelling: "I'm the wild man of Borneo, and I can lick my weight in wildcats." From above came a cry from the other Pell child in a second-story window: "And I'm the wildcat."

Herbert Pell acknowledged being the *enfant terrible* of Tuxedo Park. In the fall of 1895, when Herbert Pell was eleven years old, he and some of his friends formed the Tuxedo Bicycle Club, known as "TBC." Pell recalled that "a good many of the grownup people said it meant Tuxedo's Bad Children." Pell controlled the club by having himself elected treasurer and then persuading his fellow members to do without a president. The club was a typical young boys' club, with a slapdash meeting house, little formality and great *esprit de corps*. One of its members had a little dog named Brownie, who was injured by a carelessly driven delivery wagon. The TBC quickly declared war on the wagon's driver and chased, shouted at and taunted him until the delivery man chose to leave Tuxedo.

A friend of the boys' was Reeves Bush, a driver in Tuxedo for the Wells, Fargo company. Bush gave the children rides on the backs of the three big brown horses that pulled his delivery wagon, and some of the children who were his special favorites were allowed to sit in the wagon and actually drive the horses. When Wells, Fargo fired Bush, the TBC declared war a second time. His successor was so taunted—the "unfortunate wretch," Pell later called him—that Wells, Fargo ultimately had to bring Bush back.

The automobile was practically nonexistent then and children were free to roam in the area. School was approximately a half-mile from the Pell house and the route took the children through the Lorillard property, where there were magnificent chestnut trees. "We would always fill our pockets with chestnuts," said Herbert Pell. "Both jacket pockets would be actually bulging with them. We would pick them up so fast that it didn't slow us up on the walk to school." In the winter the children coasted on sleds down the hill to class.

School ended at lunchtime, and after lunch, Herbert Pell and his friends were free to play Indians, to explore, to do the dozens of things that young children normally do. They played very few traditional children's games, however. Herbert Pell said he never saw marbles as a child and that he and his friends never flew kites. "We did skate in the winter," he said. "We swam in the summer, and we played lawn tennis. There were none of these modern taught games."

Ice skating was popular. A diversion for the older boys was to take a young lady skating in a chair. The girl sat in a chair with runners on it. The boy, on skates, pushed her across the lake. Herbert Pell learned to skate with such a chair. He was given his first pair of skates when he was six years old. He put them on, found an empty chair and hung on the back of it as he pushed himself back and forth on the lake. "There was no question," he said, "of a professional in tight trousers and a little round hat to teach us how to skate; we taught ourselves."

He learned swimming and tennis in the same way, by teaching himself. The boys jumped into the shallow part of the water and flapped their arms around until they could stay afloat. With tennis, it was a matter of finding a discarded racket and some old balls, then knocking a ball against a wall and trying to hit it back again.

In later years Pell conceded that the result of such

learning techniques was that he and his friends were not very good at most of their games. "But," he added, "we did have a lot of fun. I have always been sorry for the children of today who lead their life on a whistle. They don't go out on a lake to have fun; they go out on a lake to have skating lessons. They have tennis lessons. They don't wander in the woods and play as they wish; they go on hikes under the guidance of a geologist or a botanist, who gives them some instruction. Of course, the net result is that a boy of fourteen today can swim better, can play better tennis, can skate better, knows the names of a great many more trees and animals and rocks than we did, but he has reached that age without any possible exercise of his own discretion, his own decision, or the expression of his own wants."

He remembered once when he was eight years old, riding his bicycle to Monroe, which was about nine miles away over very bad roads. When he returned to Tuxedo, "I was perfectly flat—done in." While it was not a sensible thing to have done, Pell believed it was "a good thing to be let do it and learn how far I could ride a bicycle without having somebody along to tell me, 'You can't do this. You must do that. You must look out for the other thing.'" What he was learning was self reliance and what he was developing was his individuality.

Life in Tuxedo centered around the clubhouse and the lake, particularly in the winter. As a boy Herbert Pell watched workmen cut ice from the frozen lake for the icehouse. The men went on the lake and, using heavy saws, cut long straight parallel lines about two feet apart.

They then cut across these at intervals of three feet. The pieces of ice were hauled to a wooden chute and slid down to the icehouse, where they were stored between layers of hay. In the early part of the skating season, before the ice was thick enough to be cut for storage, the workmen went out on the lake and cleared paths about fifteen or twenty feet wide in the snow so club members could skate. An area also was cleared for hockey and there was a toboggan slide. "One winter," Pell recalled, "I remember horrifying the community by going down the toboggan slide from the clubhouse to the big lake on skates."

For those Association members living in the city the lake was the attraction that drew them on a winter Sunday. They boarded the Erie Railroad's 9:30 A.M. train in New York, congregating in the rear car, where, as one observer noted, there was "a group of people conspicuously different from the average passengers of suburban trains . . . there is an undefinable stamp of fashion about them." They all knew one another, and the conversation was exuberant until the train pulled in at the Tuxedo station. The club members then went by open sleigh to the clubhouse, where they changed for skating. Afterward, there was luncheon at half-past one, followed by an indoor tennis match or more skating. By late afternoon the club hall was crowded with skaters gathered before the fireplace, which burned five-foot logs. Others clustered around little tea tables for warm beverages and chats. A few minutes before six a horn blew to warn them that the sleighs were loading for those catching the six o'clock train back to the city. Like everything else at Tuxedo, Sunday was idyllic.

Herbert Pell's upbringing—the education and cultural opportunities offered to him—was the traditional one for a child of his family background and wealth. It was designed to produce a gentleman. He first attended a small school in Tuxedo, which apparently was not very effective. His teacher there was a Miss Bergman—"a little, skinny German woman." The children should learn French, she decided, but she did not have a French instructor. So Miss Bergman's young French servant girl Cecile was recruited to the cause of the education of Tuxedo Park's youngsters. The young girl lined up the students and began the lesson with "Bon jour, mes enfants." The children answered as she had directed: "Bon jour, Cecile." She was a servant and never had been called by anything but her first name and never anticipated she would be called by anything else. However Miss Bergman overheard the informality, and from then on the children answered: "Bon jour, Mademoiselle."

When Herbert Pell entered his teens, he was sent off to boarding schools, first St. Bartholemew's in Morristown, New Jersey, then to the Pomfret school. He edited the school newspaper and, in his last year, played on the football team. He described his career at Pomfret as "undistinguished." But he may have been more of a student leader than he realized or acknowledged. One of his schoolmates was Richard B. Duane, who recalled years later that "I was . . . a rather small boy, and my hero was Herbert C. Pell, a fifth former. . . . He took a liking to me; and when he wasn't playing on the team, he had me on his broad shoulders as a spectator. His nicknames were 'Bertie' and 'Padsie' because of the large pads he wore under his football jersey."

Pell did well in his history courses, but he always had been interested in history. "Mathematics—especially higher mathematics—I always regarded as perfectly worthless," he said, "although I was really good at it." Latin, which he considered equally worthless, he "was really bad at." He closed his last Latin book in the spring of 1901 and his last mathematics book in the spring of 1902. He did well in his language studies, but these were helped by his extensive traveling. He became fluent in French and nearly fluent in German and Italian.

Life at Pomfret was pleasant, as it seemed to be wherever Herbert Pell stayed. The students were left free to roam the Connecticut countryside. During recesses they ducked into a nearby orchard and stuffed themselves with apples. Putnam was only five miles away, a short ride in a rented horse and buggy, and the students' parents came for occasional visits. In the spring there were bonfires at night. For Herbert Pell life at Pomfret was much like life at Tuxedo—relaxed, easy and undisturbed by the outside world.

In 1951, almost a half-century after he had left Pomfret, Herbert Pell returned to the school for a luncheon. To his surprise he saw that every student had a daily newspaper. He was surprised, because in his days at Pomfret, of all the teachers and students, only one person regularly received and read a daily paper—Herbert Pell.

His parents' talks with him on current events had taken hold. He lived in an isolated world, but he did not allow himself to be uninformed. And as his awareness of the world around him grew, he was becoming concerned. Among his papers is this extract of a theme he apparently wrote in secondary school which shows the way his political and philosophical ideas were developing:

[The strike] was the superficial indication of a disease, which if uncured will surely collapse the greatest nation of the earth . . . the laws of property are essentially man made; they are not immutable and permanent as the laws of nature. They may be repealed and when they are abused to a horrible extent, they will be repudiated, they shall be repudiated, and they should be repudiated. . . .

Every man inherits opportunity and each has a right to be tried and woe to him who meddles with these rights. These men in the mines have no prospects. It is a terrible and onerous fact but they have no hopes. What are their lives? A mere grey desert of toil and then oblivion. What chance have they to rise and to be happy? Who will rejoice when they are glad or mourn when they are in affliction? . . .

It is the part of all men who love their country and their race to do what they can to prevent clashes of rich and poor and to cement a lasting union of those classes which together form a great nation and separated are merely discordant mobs, one little better than the others.

The idea of sympathy for the poor and oppressed, callousness by the wealthy breeding revolution by the poor, and responsibility of the haves to bring the have-nots into the economic system expressed then also pervades much of his later writing. In 1932, in an article urging the election of Franklin D. Roosevelt as President, Herbert Pell wrote that "if we wish the institutions of our country to remain permanent, we must consider these people, who in the aggregate represent a very large part of the intelligent force that guides our nation. They will not forever be content with licking the spoon and humbly observing the greater prosperity meted out to the aristocracy of wealth."

Even more than from his formal schooling, Herbert Pell's education came from his travels abroad as a child. These were not the modern quick tours with as much as possible crammed into a few days. Rather, they were leisurely jaunts abroad during which one could see and discover each new country. His first trip to Europe was in 1895 when he was eleven years old. A trip abroad, even among the Pells's wealthy friends who had traveled a great deal, was taken very seriously. There were farewell dinners—"everybody talked about the projected trip as if we were repeating the performance of Columbus"—and friends had prayers read in church for the Pells's safe return.

The steamer *Augusta Victoria*, which they crossed on, was an elegant ship for its time, but its time left much to be desired. There were no covered or enclosed decks. As a result, the experienced traveler quickly separated from the inexperienced. The experienced traveler placed his deck chair near a lifeboat or some other protection from the weather, and forward of the funnels. The inexperienced traveler with his chair at the rear of the funnels was covered with soot.

Between each two cabins was a small hole cut on the corridor side where an oil lamp swung, giving one-quarter of its light into each cabin and one-half into the corridor. All the lights were turned out at one time, which meant that small boys who went to bed early slept in the light and adults who went to bed late undressed in the dark. Meals were served at regular hours at long tables equipped with fiddles—wooden compartments, placed on the tablecloth, to hold the dishes and glasses. On the trip over the chief steward once did without the fiddles. Shortly after the passengers sat down to dinner, the ship struck a tremendous wave and the passengers were covered with plates, glasses, silverware and soup.

Herbert's parents had crossed the Atlantic many times in earlier years, but since they had not made a trip for fifteen years, they considered the *Augusta Victoria* a model of luxury. Herbert and his brother, Clarence, did not.

The first European land the Pells saw that trip was the Azores. Because the water was rough, passengers were not allowed to go ashore. But the natives were not deterred from rowing out in small boats to dive for coins thrown out from the decks of the *Augusta Victoria*. "At first they fought under water for it," Herbert recalled, "but very soon they seemed to take turns and only one dove at a time." The Pell children had only an English penny to throw over, which they wrapped in tinfoil to look like a half-dollar. "When this was thrown overboard," said Herbert, "the truce was broken and they all dove in and fought and struggled for about five minutes until one man got it and threw it to his partner in the boat."

The first European land young Herbert Pell walked on was the Portuguese Madeira islands, which his father had visited years earlier on a midshipman's cruise. Pell proudly recalled this 1895 landing, when, forty-two years later, he took up his first diplomatic post, as American minister to Portugal.

But this landing was not very impressive to an eleven-year-old boy, and Herbert remembered little of it except the oxen pulling small carts. A few days later his family went to Gibraltar, where he found the monkeys much more memorable. The first lengthy stop was Algiers, where the Pells spent two weeks. This was a new world to the Pell children. From the garden walls surrounding their hotel, Herbert and Clarence watched French soldiers drill on the Champs de Mars, and the garden itself was full of date palms and flowers they had never seen before.

Mr. and Mrs. Pell had brought along the butler, Conrad Singlinger, to take care of the children. As he escorted them through the town, they stared round-eyed at the strange-looking Arabs and spent much time in the Municipal Museum. Herbert already was satisfying his curiosity with a knowledge of history. He was most interested at the museum in St. Geronimo. The saint had been killed in a Christian massacre, then placed in a block of cement. A thousand years later, a French scientist noticed that one block in the Roman walls was overly large, and, cutting into it, found the remains of the saint which Herbert saw displayed.

Herbert also enjoyed the great tourist game of haggling with local tradesmen. These were the Arab peddlers squatting on the terrace in front of the hotel. They sold little pots, wood carvings and various other souvenirs. "We enjoyed buying some of these things," Herbert said, "and particularly the arguments and vocal bargaining which was done, as we knew almost no French, by signs complimentary and otherwise."

Staying at the same hotel was an Englishman named Logan-Logan, a name the boys found impressive. Mr. Logan-Logan had a pet fox terrier named Robert and also a pet gazelle. "He became furious," Herbert said, "when he discovered that we always talked about Robert-Robert and gazelle-gazelle."

The Pells sailed from Algiers to Naples, and then on to Rome, Florence and finally Pisa. They saw Vesuvius, Pompeii, the museums, the statues. They tarried in each city ten days or two weeks, never hurrying, never feeling compelled to see everything available, knowing they could always take another trip. From childhood on Herbert Pell always traveled in this leisurely fashion.

Then they went by train to France, arriving in Paris after stops at Marseilles and Dijon. Herbert Pell later spent much time in Paris and he observed how it had changed from the time he first saw it in 1895. The Champs Élysées then did not have a shop, and he could not remember a hotel above the Place de la Concorde. Traffic was virtually nonexistent: Clarence Pell roller-skated on the Place de la Concorde. In 1896, during their second trip to Paris, the Pell brothers had bicycles and rode all over the streets of Paris, never concerned about traffic. "Today," he remarked in the 1950s, "if you put a child on a bicycle and sent him out in Paris, you would be arrested, and properly so, for infanticide."

In 1896, however, the brothers were able to do much sight-seeing on their bicycles. Once they went to Tours by train with their bicycles in the baggage car. At Tours they bicycled off to see a castle twenty or thirty kilometers away. Then they bicycled partway back, until they tired, and finished the trip on the train. In his bicycle riding, Herbert Pell did with Parisian horse-drawn cabs what other children in cities have been doing for decades with trolley cars. Going up a hill like the Champs Élysées, he grabbed hold of the cab's mud guard, hung on and was pulled up. The exploit had a glorious danger to it, because if the driver felt the extra weight, he turned around and flicked his whip at the unpaying passenger.

Once in their travels the Pells stayed at the same hotel as the Prince of Wales. Herbert and Clarence had heard that the Prince wore the bottom button of his vest unbuttoned. Never leaving a style change like that to chance, they resolved to examine the Prince for themselves. Clarence did it. He ran up to the surprised Prince one day, studied his vest momentarily and then ran back to announce to his older brother that, rather than being unbuttoned, there was no bottom button at all!

In the following years Herbert took many trips with

his parents, all serving to increase his appetite for more travel abroad. But he did not "travel" in the usual sense. In later years he lived in Europe, becoming as much at home in London and Paris as he was in Tuxedo and later in Newport.

In 1902 Herbert Pell entered Harvard and his disillusionment was quick in coming. He had chosen the school because at the time, he said, it was the only college of prominence admitting students who did not have a background in Greek and also allowed them to omit Latin from their college courses. Herbert was in a class with eight hundred other young men, and "Out of them all," he later said, "there were not forty that had any idea of doing anything with their lives except filling their pockets." Herbert Pell's whole background to this point had guided him to living well, enjoying comforts and savoring culture. This is what his family had done for generations. Now he was thrust into a society in which, as he expressed it, "It was the great duty of a man to make money, and nothing else really counted." Money was an end in itself, not a means to enjoy life as Pell knew it. "If you inherited a million," he said, "it was a convenient fulcrum from which to pry loose another million from an unwilling community."

He found his fellow students examining the possible professions available to them from the standpoint of the financial return; professions which were not highly remunerative were disdained. Herbert Pell recalled: "Those boys who were studying architecture were looked on as deserters, those who were studying painting were supposed to be merely devoting themselves to immorality, whereas the possibility of a boy going into public life was never even considered."

He thought almost as little of his professors and of his courses as he did of his fellow students. One of his professors was Albert Bushnell Hart, a distinguished historian. Hart announced to the class that he could be taken as an authority on the Civil War because, when he was a child, his aunt had run an underground railroad, giving him the northern point of view, and "the Southern point of view I got from the slaves themselves." Pell thought the professor's background lacking and, being Herbert Pell, had no hesitation in showing his dissatisfaction. Professor Hart recommended that Pell drop the course, which he did. The story had a sequel about twenty years later when Herbert Pell returned to Harvard to give a series of lectures on government. Just before one of the lectures started, an elderly man walked in, asked to be introduced to Pell and then sat in the back of the classroom thoroughly enjoying Pell's lecture. The elderly man was Albert Bushnell Hart, who had forgotten the brash young student he "recommended" leave his course.

There were other encounters with his teachers. To another history professor, Pell suggested that "a tout at the race track with his pockets full of past performances cut from the *Evening Telegram* had a better idea of the purpose of historical study than did the faculty of Harvard." Pell conceded his remark was not polite, but, he said, "I think it was true."

Pell believed that the courses were arranged for two

kinds of students. "One was for the drunk who wouldn't study except under compulsion," said Pell. "He was forced to read at least a dozen books a year." The second group was made up of students working for marks. "But a boy who only wanted to learn for learning, to know things," said Herbert Pell, "was just left aside. I studied differently from most boys. Not caring the least about marks I never took a note all the time I was at college. I listened to the lectures and then passed the examination on my memory of them. Of course, not as well as those who had crammed for the examination, but it seemed to me much more important to know something permanently rather than to cram a lot to hit an examination which didn't interest me."

During his sophomore year, Pell became ill and later was seriously injured in an automobile accident. He was forced to drop out of college for a period. He had been elected to the Union Club in New York City and began to spend much time there, particularly in the club library. He found, or so he said, that he was learning much more at the club library than he had learned at Harvard and decided not to return.

"My family wasn't concerned at all about my reaction to education at Harvard," Pell said later. "I remember my father asked me after a while, in the spring of 1906, when I was going back to college. I told him I wasn't going back, that I had resigned. He asked me why I did it, and I told him. He seemed very justly to think that was my affair rather than his, and there was no discussion of it at all." Pell continued: "After all, what difference did it make to him whether I graduated from college or not? He didn't care. I was always left to decide what I wanted to do, I think on the very intelligent idea that anybody who doesn't make a fool of himself before he's twenty-one never will afterwards."

Pell's criticism of Harvard, obviously, was harsh. It was one of the leading schools of the time, and in the years that Pell was there, its student body also included Franklin Roosevelt and Felix Frankfurter, two men whom Harvard did not turn away from careers in public service. The fault was probably more with Pell than with his school. Young Herbert had a tremendous energy for the things he treasured and the causes he cared about, which he showed in later years. But he declined to accept that achievement in life, either in making money or in other pursuits, requires discipline. Training in immersing oneself in the uninteresting as well as in the unstimulating, mastering them and using them, is one thing a good formal education offers. Herbert Pell can perhaps be excused for not understanding this at age twenty-one. But certainly his father should have understood and urged his son to return to school. That might have been out of character for the father, however, or perhaps the elder Pell believed that his son had a strong will and could not be influenced.

Herbert Pell himself never made the mistake his father did. Herbert encouraged his own son to acquire a good formal education and watched closely over that educational process. When the son, Claiborne, was at Princeton in the late 1930s, Herbert Pell frequently wrote letters to faculty members he knew for information on his son's progress. He sought no favors for Claiborne, only information he could use to assist him. In 1940, Claiborne graduated with honors and Herbert Pell boasted of his son's achievement to his friends. And then years later, when his grandchildren were entering their teens, Herbert Pell also spoke to them of the value of a formal education. It was only in this manner that Herbert Pell acknowledged the mistake he had made when he was twenty-one.

Young Herbert, after dropping out of Harvard, took some additional courses at Columbia and New York University in subjects that particularly interested him—modern European history and American politics, the latter at Columbia from a young instructor named Charles A. Beard. Beard later became famous for his economic interpretation of the Constitution and, still later, for his charge that Pell's friend Franklin Roosevelt provoked the Japanese into attacking Pearl Harbor. Pell remembered him as a man who "really knew what he was talking about." Beard's course apparently was devoted to practical politics, a study of how local party leaders organize and gather support. As part of a lesson, he once had his students stage a mock convention, with nominating speeches, state delegations, banners, backroom parleys and the like. To preside over the convention Beard enlisted the support of a man named Tim Woodruff, who had been lieutenant governor of New York for many years but apparently not one of great achievement. Herbert Pell recalled that a New York City newspaper branded the event as a "mock convention presided over by a mock statesman."

Another reason why Herbert Pell dropped out of school

was that he could afford to. Although he had always
known that his family was comfortably off, he did not
believe any great wealth was involved and always had
anticipated that he would have to work for a living. He
had a vague idea of taking "a course in law and going
into some office." But after 1900 his father's fortunes improved and then, in 1903, an uncle died, leaving Pell's
mother the sole heir to the Lorillard money. "This of
course totally changed my prospects. . . . I realized that
there would be no necessity for me ever to be obliged
to think of the next meal." So he determined to spend
his next few years at cultural pursuits.

At one point young Herbert's father decided that his
son should have a position—"status," as he referred to it,
befitting a gentleman. They were both in Europe at the
time and the son responded to his father's suggestion by
saying he would accept a diplomatic appointment. Young
Herbert was not showing any inclination toward industry
by his offer. He knew perfectly well that the diplomatic
appointments list was heavy with names of New Yorkers
and the chances of his ever taking the foreign service
examination were practically nonexistent. But he had forgotten that his father played poker at the Gooseberry
Island Club at Newport with Senator Nelson Aldrich,
who was then a power in Washington. The senator arranged to have Herbert Pell's name put on the list to
take the examination. Young Herbert came back from
Europe, studying a book on international law on the way,
and arrived in New York on a Saturday. The examination
lasted three days, the next Wednesday, Thursday and Fri-

day. He did well in the examinations, except for the orals on the last day. Pell recalled: "They asked us where we wanted to go. Some patriot said he wanted to go to South America. He was greeted with cheers because nobody else did. They asked me where I wanted to go and I said I wanted to go to Rome. They said, 'Why?' I said, 'I have a cousin there, Princess Cenci, and I thought I would probably have a better time,' which didn't please them too much."

As soon as the examinations were over, Herbert returned to Europe. Later he was notified that he had passed the examination and would be placed on the list for appointment if he attended a summer school the State Department operated in Washington. The summers were more pleasant in Europe just then, and Herbert Pell declined. His father apparently forgot about his notion that his son should have "status."

Perhaps because he never went into business of any kind himself, Herbert Pell later felt defensive. He always spoke disparagingly of those who did, claiming that they ended up the worse for it. "All of my friends who went into business lost money," he frequently said, and he warned: "Stay out of business." When a young relative of his announced that her husband was going into business, Herbert Pell answered: "Oh, I'm so sorry." In later years, however, he allowed that it was all right to work if you actually wished to.

In his early twenties now, Herbert had developed into a handsome young man. He always had been a big person. He weighed nine pounds at birth and thirty-five pounds by the time he was two years of age. By the time he was full grown, he was massive, reaching a full six feet five inches and with a fifty-two-inch chest expansion. He attributed his large size to a nurse he had as a child who insisted that young boys should drink only milk. By that rule, Louisa, the nurse, brought up Herbert, Clarence and two of their cousins named Kent, and they all were huge. One of the Kent boys grew to be as tall as Herbert; the other Kent boy and Clarence Pell were well over six feet. With the exception of Clarence, who weighed one hundred and ninety, the boys all grew into men weighing over two hundred pounds. In addition to his size, Pell had handsome features and dark wavy hair. He also sported a large mustache.

He was aware of his appearance and capitalized on it. A contemporary of his recalled that Herbert Pell's "great size always made him a conspicuous figure in any gathering but he added to this in earlier times by wearing flowing neckties and in cool weather he was also apt to wear a large cloak which gave him a slightly conspiratorial air."

Appearance was important then, not only because of the strict standards of dress but because as a young man he was now entering society. His family connections, his background as a well-traveled and literate person, his money and his appearance all combined to open the doors to the opulent society of the Gilded Age.

Social life for Herbert, of the Pell-Lorillard families and Tuxedo Park, began when he was about seventeen or eighteen. The young men and women at Tuxedo had parties at one another's houses, usually dinner parties. "Of course," Herbert Pell recalled, "our parents were at the dinner! The idea of my giving a dinner in my house and my parents going out or being served on a tray or sitting together at the end of the dinner table as outcasts would have been nonsense. It was their house, it was their dinner, and they were naturally a part of the party and took a certain part in the conversation." And when the dinner was over the young people sat together, talking and generally amusing themselves. "It was not a question," said Pell some years later, " 'For God's sake, what shall we do—go to a movie, go to a dance, or *go* somewhere?' "

And as Herbert became older he began attending dinners in New York City, the major form of entertaining. Though less lavish than dinners in previous decades, dinner parties at the turn of the century contrasted sharply with those of later years. Herbert Pell once found a number of bills for dinners his grandmother had given in the 1870s. He figured that the food ordered for one dinner for eighteen persons in the 1870s was as much as he would have ordered for three such dinners in 1917 and four such dinners in 1951. And as for formal dinner parties in 1900, "You would horrify people by the amount that we ate."

The courses included a soup, a fish, then usually some type of fowl with salad and also a meat with vegetables. The meal ended with "a good solid dessert" and the entire meal was accompanied by plenty of wine. After dinner the young men retired for a few minutes to smoke and then returned to talk with the young ladies. The dinner, which had begun at eight, ended by ten-thirty or eleven o'clock. Protocol demanded that the men returned to the house a day or two after the party to leave their cards. Herbert and his friends avoided the extra trip by giving their cards, each with a quarter, to the butler before they left. The next day the cards turned up in the proper place.

There was no liquor, except for wine, at these parties. If any young man felt the need for liquid support before encountering the butler, the footmen, the waiters, the hostess and the young lady with whom he was being matched, then he was expected to stop in at a club on his way to the party.

There also were dances, either given at a person's house or at Sherry's or Delmonico's in New York. The dances were formal cotillions with each step rigidly adhered to. The men in their black tail coats and white ties, the young ladies in their evening dresses, presented a picture as handsome as it later was painted in fiction. During the middle of the dance, the orchestra played a march signaling everyone to go down to supper. A supper was different from a dinner; a supper was sparser. It included only soup, fowl, salad and dessert—no vegetables or meat. And at the end of the dance the young ladies returned to their homes either with maids or with their girl friends.

There were social activities in the afternoon also. One such was the Horse Show at Madison Square Garden. Ostensibly this was a showing of horseflesh to its best advantage, but there was some question of what was shown off. "The people in the boxes," said Herbert Pell, "seldom took much interest in the horses." The men dressed in uniform—black shoes, striped gray trousers, a light gray waistcoat, long frock coats, big puffed cravats with jeweled stick pins, and top hats. "Clad in these garments," said Herbert Pell, "we would walk around from box to box visiting the girls, who were wearing the best they had."

While Herbert Pell and his male friends enjoyed a certain carefree youth, the girls they knew led a more restricted life. They were being prepared for the marriage market, and the rites were difficult of passage. The chief one involved hair. Prior to the age of twelve they wore their hair long and hanging loose. Perhaps one ribbon would be used, tied in a large bow. At the age of twelve another ribbon was added, just below the neck. Four years later, when the young lady turned sixteen, her hair was "put up." "This was an event almost as solemn as the more unmentionable and painful ceremonies of savage races," said Herbert Pell. "From the time that her hair was balanced on her head, she was obviously incapable of rapid motion." For tennis, for example, in addition to having her hair precariously balanced, the girl wore a proper costume for a young lady at the century's turn—tight corsets beneath a dress that reached to the feet, and broad-brimmed hat with a veil to protect the complexion from the sun. Her appearance was the ultimate in fashion; her tennis was a bit restricted. "It was considered the height of discourtesy," Herbert Pell said, "in mixed doubles to serve hard to a girl or to smash the ball in her direction."

The young lady's education then was designed to make her a proper wife for the kind of man she met at the dances and the dinners frequented by Herbert Pell and his circle. She was learned in something called "small talk," which seemed to mean the ability to carry on a conversation without saying anything embarrassing, offensive or significant. She must be able to speak in at least one foreign language, to dance, to have some knowledge of music and to play a musical instrument. This last of course must be a refined instrument. Drums, cornets and harmonicas were frowned on. Also, girls who played billiards or poker were considered "modern"; the word was a reprimand, not a style.

A young lady's formal presentation to society meant she was beginning her career of searching for a proper husband—one with sufficient money and status to enable her to lead the life of elegance and ease to which she had become accustomed. Sometimes the search was a frantic one, depending on the market situation at the time; after all, no one could guarantee a new crop of eligible young men every year. "She was made to realize," said Herbert Pell, "that the stock went stale very quickly."

There were many balls at which these presentations took place, but none had quite the impact of a presentation at the annual autumn ball at Tuxedo Park. Eventually all such social entertainments were measured against the Tuxedo Ball. It officially admitted a girl to a select group of the *haut monde* and created an aura that never faded. It was an important line in the society column accounts of her wedding, a command to her to assume proper matronly social responsibilities, and was not forgotten when, years later, *The New York Times* printed her obituary.

The first Tuxedo Ball was given in October, 1886, the year the community opened. Not thought of then as setting a high water mark for society, it was to be, rather, a pleasant kind of party for the people of Tuxedo and their friends. It was, in fact, to be somewhat informal. The accepted costume for men at such affairs was white tie and tails, but Pierre Lorillard considered that too stiff for the kind of party he wished Tuxedo to have. Since it was his party, that first year at least, he could have his way. While in England, he had become intrigued with a costume worn by the Prince of Wales—a short black jacket. (The prince, in turn, had copied the idea from the members of the Royal Yacht Squadron, who wore short white jackets at their annual balls.) Pierre Lorillard thought the prince's short jacket perfect for the Tuxedo Ball. However, he did not test it himself, preferring, instead, to have his son, Griswold Lorillard, chance the reaction of society. The first reaction was negative. Commented one newspaper: "At the Tuxedo Club Ball young Griswold Lorillard appeared in a tailless dress coat and a waistcoat of scarlet satin, looking for all the world like a royal footman. There were several other of the abbreviated jackets worn, which suggested to the onlookers that the boys ought to have been put in straight-jackets long ago." But the press proved wrong. The Lorillards' position in society was so high that the jacket they adopted was ultimately copied all over the world and Tuxedo gave its name to the short jacket.

The ball was held in the Tuxedo clubhouse. According to a contemporary account, the cream-colored building resembled from the outside a large Romanesque villa. "Inside," this account continued, "it is a mixture of the English and Dutch—spacious yet cosy, splendid yet comfortable, tasteful without pretensions. A broad veranda, to which French windows open from all the main floor rooms, runs around the house."

All the kitchens and domestic offices were in the basement, properly out of the club members' sight. The main hall, running into a circle in the center of the house, had ceilings and walls of English oak and, at its center, was a fireplace of carved wood and tiles. The ballroom was "probably the finest . . . in America without exception." It was in an octagon-shaped wing at the end of the main hall. It had "a carefully laid parquet floor, smooth as a mirror and was seventy-eight feet in diameter, [and] furnishes space, both in shape and size, admirably for a gathering of the largest and jolliest sort." The walls and ceilings were painted in light blue and "sunset tints harmonizing delightfully with the pale olive of plush divans." There also was a stage twenty-seven feet wide "and nearly as deep as that of the Madison Square Theatre."

Perhaps because of the lavishness of the ball's site, or perhaps because of the wealth and social standing of its original sponsors, the people of Tuxedo were not obliged to demonstrate their wealth in garish displays of decoration and dress then common at large New York parties. The tasteful Tuxedo Ball became, in Herbert Pell's words, "the big fashionable dance of New York." He said that "every girl who was coming out in New York wanted to be asked up to the Tuxedo Autumn Ball. It was rather a mark against her if she wasn't." And the occasion was more than a dance, becoming a social weekend. "We all had the houses full and had dinners and all," said Pell. "A lot of boys came from outside to dance."

Emily Post said that the dance was perhaps the one time when Tuxedo "welcomes strangers, her best foot forward and with a company smile, looking not at all her usual self"—a comment that suggests what her "usual self" looked like. By teatime of the day of the dance, the hall of the club was so filled with tables that, said Mrs. Post, "not even a fashionplate figure could squeeze between. Girls and boys, girls and boys are everywhere."

Herbert Pell and the other young Tuxedo swains lined up their companions for supper at the dance's end, weeks or sometimes months earlier. One year Herbert asked a girl in June to be his supper companion for the October dance. Being assured of a partner then, Herbert made a brief appearance at the dance and then retired to the smoking room with the other "old hands" of Tuxedo. Later in the evening the headwaiter entered their den to announce: "Gentlemen, supper will be served in ten minutes." Herbert and the other young gallants rushed out to find their supper dates, their shirt collars "unspoiled by perspiration." Herbert conceded that it was a blow to the young men imported from outside who had been working on the dance floor all evening to end the night supping by themselves. "Still," he said, "the world is not made for those who refuse to foresee."

Herbert Pell's social life also included Newport, where, at the end of the nineteenth century, millionaires lived as the poor always believed they did. The homes were castles on the Rhode Island shore. Henry James, whose sophisticated study of American society followed Ward McAllister's gushing account by twenty years, reported that American society "had for half a century taken its whole relation with the place seriously . . . very gaily" and "it long remained, for its happiness, quite at one with this most favoured resort." James found that the rich began "to put things" into Newport, things "of all sorts, and of many ugly, and of more and more expensive sorts; to fill it substantially, that is, with gold that they have ended by heaping up there to an amount so oddly out of proportion to the scale of nature and of space." Which is another way of saying that they had it and they flaunted it.

It was an important training ground for young Pell. His Lorillard grandmother, Mrs. James P. Kernochan, had a summer home there, and Herbert spent much time visiting her. Because even as a teen-ager he was tall, good-looking in his dress clothes, and could converse with sophistication and intelligence, he was invited to adult dinner parties in Newport from the time he was fifteen. His grandmother often used him to even out her dinner parties, as did other hostesses on occasion. For many summers at Newport, Herbert never sat next to a girl as young as he was.

Herbert and his Grandmother Kernochan were fond of each other. After he had left Harvard and was attending Columbia he stayed in her New York house rather than commute to Tuxedo, where his family still lived. Grandmother Kernochan had definite ideas on what young people should do with their lives. She advised the young girls in the family, "Marry the life you like. The man doesn't matter after a few years." To those who spoke of love, she insisted: "No matter who you marry, you're going to regret it. Better to regret it in a Victoria than in a trolley car."

There was no doubt about the life she enjoyed. The gracious Newport house she kept required a staff of eighteen or nineteen—a coachman, a groom, two stable men, five gardeners, a chef, a butler, two footmen, a kitchen maid, a laundress who frequently had an assistant, two housemaids, and a lady's maid.

Herbert Pell learned several things at Newport. Among them, that some people did not object to taking advantage of other people's pocketbooks. When outsiders came to town for the various tennis tournaments, prices jumped enormously. During one tournament Herbert Pell took a friend for lunch at a Newport restaurant. When the check came, it was much too high. "I just wrote across the back," said Herbert, " 'You know who I am. I'm not a tennis player. Please correct this bill.' It was corrected to a third." He also noticed that when a fleet of U. S. Navy ships stopped at Newport, "the only sign the inhabitants of Newport made that they knew it was there at all was in the cheaper restaurants where coffee went up from five to ten cents a cup."

He also learned something of the difference between society in Europe and society in America. European society was much better educated. At Newport, if a dinner guest was a foreigner and could not speak English, the hostess had to be careful which young lady she seated next to him because she couldn't be certain the young lady would be able to talk to her dinner partner. "That is a consideration," said Herbert Pell, "that would never enter the mind of any person in Vienna where it was assumed that everyone could speak several languages."

He remembered a Japanese delegation that stopped at Newport when he was fifteen years old. The Japanese had been educated in Germany and could speak neither French nor English. As a result, the hostess had to scurry around Newport searching for acceptable dinner guests. And Herbert Pell, only fifteen years old, found himself sitting next to a royal Japanese princess because he was the only young man to be found who could speak German. "That would never have happened," he said, "to a man of my then-age anywhere in Europe."

The society Herbert Pell knew as a young man existed only for a brief time. For several decades it offered all that money could buy and it was sold with a mixture of taste and ostentation. Eventually taxes took their toll, and members of the servant class became rich themselves. Also, the members of society became bored with one another, telling the same stories, seeing the same people, playing at the same kind of life. And there was another change.

"Society" became less important. Matrons no longer measured their accomplishments in dances and teas but in
charity work. The yacht races never lost their thrill for
the men, but the worlds of politics and diplomacy offered
new excitements. All of this was a long time in coming,
but it had its origins in the unreal world of Tuxedo and
Newport.

The fantasy world of society has been described by
Ellin Berlin, who knew the time well and wrote of it in
a 1970 novel. Speaking of her heroine, Esther, Mrs. Berlin
writes that . . .

. . . at seventeen she was not only the most beautiful
debutante to be introduced to society, she was a re-
freshingly unexpected beauty. It was exciting, she said,
to be suddenly and simultaneously a grownup and a
success, but it was also bewildering. Oh, it was fun to
be the belle of her year. She liked the beaux who filled
her dance cards, she enjoyed the bouquets and the co-
tillion favors and the compliments they offered her, but
before the year was over, before the Tuxedo Ball came
around again, her success seemed like a childhood game
too long-drawn-out. What should have been a grown-up
world was like the spinning globe in the nursery, not
like the real world at all.

For Herbert Pell the carefree society was fun but its
gamelike quality was disappointing. At the Tuxedo Club

he learned to drink and swear. "In those days," he said in 1951, "swearing was a lot more common among gentlemen than it is today. I still do it, but I am among the few surviving swearers." As for drinking, Herbert saw at Tuxedo a "steady drinking" rather than drunkenness. "I suppose during my twenties down in Tuxedo you would normally have six or seven drinks a day—never many more, but always some."

There also was much poker at Tuxedo. At this, Herbert Pell's father was a master. An old-time Tuxedo resident has described one of these games in which the elder Pell displayed his talents:

On one side is a serving table laden with sandwiches and a waiter is hovering near to await the orders for another round of drinks. There is a sizable jackpot on the table and Mr. Pell has opened. That means to Mr. Kane that in all likelihood Mr. Pell has "Herbites," or in ordinary language, two aces, for he rarely opens on less. Mr. Kane, one visitor and Mr. Pell stay in for a round of bets and then Mr. Pell gently pushes the limit onto the table. Mr. Kane glances but it is obvious that behind the mask he is doing some serious thinking. Finally he tosses his cards into the pile of discards. Mr. Pell glances at the visitor and the visitor eagerly advances his chips. He does not know Mr. Pell as Mr. Kane knows him. He will see Mr. Pell for they have each drawn one card and he has filled a high straight. Mr. Pell lays down two aces and three twos and rakes in the chips while the visitor glances ruefully at his straight and then at the thinning pile of chips in his section of the trough.

This account concludes that "the Tuxedo crowd had a reputation of being tough to buck and they had the advantage of knowing each other's play while the visitor had to feel his way."

The senior Herbert Pell also played a lot of poker in Newport during the summers. There again his skill with the cards made him famous and the afternoon sessions each day at the Gooseberry Island Club augmented his income considerably. The Club was money. Gooseberry was a small island in a secluded bay at Newport, about one hundred yards from shore, accessible only by boat. The island was owned by about a dozen wealthy men who prized their privacy. The clubhouse itself was only a wooden structure, so badly built it eventually blew away in a storm. But it was private. Wives were allowed only under the most limited and restricted circumstances. Guests were made to understand that a visit to the island was a rare gift. Dues were substantial—three thousand dollars a year. The end product of this seclusion, exclusiveness and expense was a place where men could swim in the nude, dry in the sun and play poker all afternoon.

One of those who regularly, if involuntarily, contributed to the senior Herbert Pell's poker winnings was Nelson Aldrich, United States Senator from Rhode Island who chaired the Senate Finance Committee. Through these poker sessions young Herbert became well acquainted with

Aldrich and the business community he represented. For young Herbert it was a disturbing experience. By listening to Aldrich, reading about him in the newspapers and hearing his father's friends discuss him, he learned more about the business community than most Americans knew at the time, and what he learned he didn't like.

After the turn of the century, Nelson Aldrich was in his sixties and in his third decade as a United States Senator. A self-made millionaire, he became the political boss of Rhode Island through his vast business connections and his personal charm. Operating from such a strong base, he had considerable independence in Washington, which he used to his advantage. He was a member of a small group of United States senators who virtually controlled the Senate. They considered the government a tool rather than a responsibility. When Aldrich was up for reelection in 1892, for example, his opponents charged he had helped pass a tariff bill that benefited his extensive sugar investments. Aldrich simply ignored the charge, and was reelected.

When young Herbert Pell first knew him, Aldrich was in the process of trying to rewrite the banking laws. Experts agreed that a change was necessary, but Aldrich's proposal caused concern. Basically, Aldrich wanted a central bank for the United States operated out of New York City, owned by the major New York banking houses. The plan would have placed economic control of the United States in the hands of a few persons. His proposal never became law, owing to the opposition led first by Theodore Roosevelt and then by Woodrow Wilson. In the Wilson Administration, Congress enacted a banking law written by Senator Carter Glass of Virginia—in effect, the modern Federal Reserve System—which established a number of Federal Reserve Banks across the nation, decentralizing the banking system and putting it under public rather than private control.

But the Aldrich plan did not fail for want of trying by the business interests of the nation. "There was a great incongruity," Herbert Pell observed, "between the animal tactics of the market place and the gentle manners I saw at Newport." Behind those gentle manners Herbert Pell saw a corrupt group. "There are honest games and dishonest ones," he said, "and unfortunately business is a dishonest game." He told the story of two stockbrokers he knew who went to jail for stealing funds entrusted to them. "I would be perfectly willing to play bridge with those two men—they are playing partners against you and me—and I would be perfectly willing to walk out of the room while they dealt. I know that they would not pick an ace out of my hand and put it in their own. . . . But business is a different thing."

The young men like Herbert Pell who raised questions about the ethics of business in this time were treated with amusement. They were regarded as being fanciful and uncomprehending; they were told that they did not understand how business was done. But of course what disturbed them was that they did know, all too well.

For this was a time of unchecked *laissez-faire*. The successful man was the one who took all he could and then demanded more. "They felt that government was for them," said Pell of the businessmen. "They controlled the tariff. They controlled Aldrich. They controlled the resources of the country. Government assistance to them was proper helping of business. Government assistance to the poor was Socialism." Young Herbert Pell heard the businessmen at the Newport dinner parties and at the Tuxedo clubhouse criticize government involvement in the running of the railroads as "un-American, unethical, socialistic." But the distribution of publicly owned lands by the government to the railroads was "natural encouragement of American initiative." Pell was astonished to find that "they really believed it. They weren't playing a part. They weren't pretending that they believed this because it was to their interest. They really and sincerely did believe . . . that God in his wisdom had given them the control, and it was for the best possible good of all that they should keep it."

As a young schoolboy Herbert Pell had written the theme expressing sympathy for the striking miners who "have no prospects . . . no hopes" and had written that their strike indicated a disease that if uncured "will surely collapse the greatest nation of the earth." These earlier impressions could only be strengthened by the environment he lived in after he had left school. His family had a sense of responsibility, often becoming politically involved and usually showing the reciprocal medieval concern for the tenants who worked their lands. With that kind of background Herbert Pell could not accept that he or anyone else had the right to take all that he could and do it not only with the government's blessing but with its cooperation.

Herbert Pell enjoyed traveling and in most of the ten years after he left college he spent much of his time abroad. For a trip young Herbert would pack a bag full of shoes "because American shoes were so good," underclothes, for the same reason, "and as few outer clothes as possible." These he purchased in London and stored there. Without bothering about advance reservations, he boarded a ship at the New York City docks, found the purser and ordered a stateroom, for which he paid cash. Eighty-nine dollars bought him first-class accommodations on the French line; ninety-five on English ships. As none of the rooms then had private bathrooms, the steward scheduled bath hours, suiting the passengers' convenience as much as possible. When it was Pell's turn to bathe, the steward knocked on his stateroom door. Pell then went down the hall in wrapper and slippers to the hall bathroom, bathed and then returned to his room to dress.

Getting off the ship was as easy as getting on. When the ship neared Europe, Herbert told the purser where he wanted to disembark, usually either Cherbourg or Southampton. Herbert would walk down to the customs shed to find his bag waiting for him there. He remembered that at Cherbourg the customs officers sauntered by asking what he had to declare. *"Rien à déclarer"* was the answer. And the customs officer's answer to that was *"Bien, Monsieur"* as he marked the still unopened bag as having passed customs. "You went from one country to another," said Herbert Pell, "just as you do from New York to Paterson, without comment or observation." Europe itself was as nonchalant about its visitors. He was never asked to register at the small country hotels where he stayed, often being called simply "Monsieur Renault" after his car. "You traveled quite alone, quite unobserved and without being interfered with in the slightest—without any formality."

Herbert Pell traveled to Europe by himself for the first time in 1908, when he was twenty-four. His brother, Clarence, was on an around-the-world tour and his parents had gone to Egypt to see him. When they arrived back in Rome, they were surprised to find their other son, Herbert, waiting for them. The three journeyed to Paris, where the parents bought their son his Renault. They then went on to Cannes together. In the spring Mr. and Mrs. Pell returned to the United States while Herbert stayed on. He had his Renault body changed from a limousine to a three-seater and used the car for the next half-dozen years.

Even his sports car was always driven by a chauffeur. Herbert Pell paid his driver three hundred francs a month, or about sixty dollars. One time Herbert's cousin, Pierre Barbey, accused Herbert of overpaying and boasted that he had a perfectly good chauffeur and paid him only two hundred francs a month. But when Pierre's chauffeur was arrested as an escaped homicidal maniac, Herbert Pell reflected: "It pays to get a good man to drive your car."

Pell claimed that a chauffeur was necessary because of the difficulties of driving. A tire usually lasted only six hundred miles and changing it was not only dirty, but a thirty-minute job. There never was much traffic: "If you passed three cars in a morning you would feel that you were in a traffic jam." But driving along the dirt roads was a dusty business. Pell's car was an open one, without even a windshield. He wore a hat, goggles and a veil over his nose and mouth to keep out the dust. Rutted roads were a constant problem. "If you fell into these ruts with your car," said Pell, "you could drive along with your arms folded for a mile before you could jerk yourself out of it and you would very likely fall in again in a little while."

On one winter trip, Pell and the chauffeur had spent so many hours pulling the car out of sloshy ruts that "I looked like a terra cotta statue." The tires were badly torn and Pell thought the best thing to do was send the car ahead on a flatcar while he finished his trip to Rome by train. When he finally arrived at a hotel there, he was covered with dried mud and was "a perfectly filthy object." He asked for a room and how much it would cost. "They looked at me and thought fifteen lire a day was about as much as they could get out of anybody who looked like that," said Pell. He took the room. When he asked for his baggage, which had been sent ahead, the hotel clerks, suddenly realizing that he was Herbert Pell, "were perfectly taken aback because they had expected to rob this American millionaire for probably about fifty lire a day."

The cars were not only a haphazard convenience for their passengers, they splattered unwitting pedestrians. One time in Italy Pell drove by a regiment of bersaglieri soldiers, considered the fastest in the world. They did not ride or walk but ran all day at a steady dogtrot. When Pell came by, they were taking a short break for their regular lunch of a small lump of cheese and a tumbler of wine. Pell told his chauffeur to slow down to a crawl to avoid covering their meal with a brown cloud. The soldiers responded to his courtesy by cheering him loudly as he went by.

Herbert Pell moved through Europe in a leisurely fashion. He never hesitated to stop where something caught his interest, refusing to establish an arbitrary schedule. In a typical trip he left Paris in the afternoon and arrived at Fontainebleau for the night. Because "you're a fool to be in Fontainebleau and not take the occasion to go over the castle again," he stayed overnight, not getting away until late morning. Sens was a good stop for lunch, particularly because there was an interesting cathedral there he had enjoyed previously. In every town he searched out the history of the community and was particularly interested in its old homes, its churches and castles and its ancient legends.

He roamed through France and Italy this way, driving for perhaps fifty miles or so, and then stopping to examine some relic. "It was," he conceded, "a very pleasant way to live."

During the winters he spent a couple of months at Cannes, passing time by playing lawn tennis and golf. Sometimes he drove over to Monte Carlo with friends. He considered the gambling tables a bore and spent much time wandering around, searching out small shops that offered jewelry pawned by "unlucky young women who apparently did not know that thirty-seven is a larger number than thirty-six." Years later, in 1951, he recalled those early visits to Monte Carlo and said that "the wheel in those days did a very big business. There were a good number of rich Russians and a very large number of English—people who had big invested incomes, largely invested in government securities and who got some spiritual effect out of risk. Their private lives were so secure that a little risk was probably a desirable condiment." And he added in 1951: "They don't go there so much now because there is plenty of risk at home."

Traveling as he did, he became familiar with smells. Adopting the philosophy that the best way to defeat an enemy is to join him, Pell recommended that "in the first meal you take south of Lyon, order something with a good deal of garlic in it."

But he also became interested in the more pleasant smells of Europe. In France, in a town called Grasse, he stopped at a perfume factory known as Bruno Court. Its perfumes were made from local flowers using time-consuming, traditional methods. Pell saw petals of violets dropped into alcohol, where they remained until they yellowed. Then they were replaced by new violets until the alcohol absorbed the perfume of the flowers. For another perfume, jasmine was laid out on a thin layer of beef fat, which absorbed the jasmine's scent. The fat was then mixed with alcohol and separated again to transfer the perfume of the jasmine.

Herbert Pell spent much of his time in Europe visiting museums but for sessions of only an hour. He believed that a person could appreciate only so much art at one sitting and that an hour was the outermost limit: "Anything else will just spill over the edge." His first approach to a museum was with a professional guide. The next day he returned alone to study what he had been shown and to judge it in view of his own background and tastes.

In 1908, Herbert Pell was elected to the Travellers Club in Paris. This became his home when in Paris and his headquarters in Europe for many decades. It was pleasant living for a young man. But young Herbert did not search out the gay and daring haunts of the students; although he arrived in Paris with good looks and money, he did not try the new Bohemian life that was attracting wealthy young Europeans. The Travellers Club was eminently respectable. Several evenings a week were spent reading and his partying was confined to gatherings of established Parisian society. "I never in my life went to Maxim's in the evening and only once or twice to Montmartre," he said later, "I did not hunt for gay little places where students go. . . . I have occasionally been to the so-called wild and gay establishments but found them distinguished by the three unpardonable sins: bad service, poor food, and high prices."

Most winters during those carefree years of his twenties, Herbert Pell continued to spend several months at Cannes, playing tennis in the morning and golfing in the afternoon. Numerous young and attractive ladies as well as the top rim of European society were there. And because Cannes did not offer what a later generation called the "swinging" attractions of the larger Nice or the gambling tables of Monte Carlo, there were—in Herbert Pell's words—"no sharpers and deadbeats" to mar their world.

One morning Pell was playing lawn tennis with the local professional. After about a half-hour of playing, the professional had to leave but introduced Pell to the Count Guy de Levis-Mirepoix and suggested that, being evenly matched, they could have a good game together. Herbert Pell and the Count subsequently played tennis together frequently and became good friends. The Count's family was part of a closed world rarely visible to Americans—"the old nobles living on the left bank of the river who never went out into the rich society of Paris and knew very few foreigners." Through the Count, Pell was introduced to this society and was welcomed into its company whenever he was in Paris. He was quite taken by its members. "Their conversation was intelligent," he said, "I never saw one of them overcome by drink. There wasn't a woman who was unduly flirtatious, although all were charming. . . . Their houses were run simply, much less gorgeously than the English; excellent cooking, but the servants were not as neatly dressed; their gardens were not as manicured as the big English gardens." Like most of his old neighbors at Tuxedo, these Parisians had status and wealth and were not compelled to prove their position with ostentatious displays. They lived a quiet life, enjoying occasional parties but reveling more in intelligent conversation and charming company. They were people of culture and taste—the kind of people Herbert Pell liked.

A pleasant excursion from Cannes began with a drive over to the Gorge du Loup, the site where the Loup River roars down a canyon, cuts under the road and plunges down to the sea. Driving in March, back about 1910, meant traveling a road where there was usually no other automobile traffic, the wind coming across the fields, carrying a delightful aroma from the olive orchards. Herbert Pell found a small restaurant where one ate trout on a balcony, looking out over the plain between Cannes and Nice, the Mediterranean on one side and mountains on the other.

The view from the mountains was breathtaking; one supposedly could see across to the island of Corsica. Herbert Pell never saw Corsica from the shore, but he never prized the view any the less for it.

From the Gorge du Loup, he drove down to a little walled town called St. Paul du Var, located in the middle of a rich valley. There were acacias, eucalyptus, cactus, oranges, olives and flowers whenever there was enough land for a seed to grow. The return trip to Cannes was through Antibes, where Herbert found an old Roman fort to explore. Sports, cultured companions, travel, study—such were his years then.

Herbert returned to the United States usually in the late summer, spent several months in New York, Tuxedo or Newport. Always then there were parties, and his time in the United States was primarily spent socializing. His friends at home envied him his travels and some of the men were jealous of what they considered his revels. They assumed he was on a continuous spree, living like a drunken sultan.

Young Herbert's father heard many such comments about his son's exploits and one year determined to see for himself just what he was up to. He sailed to Europe to join his son and, if necessary, to chaperone him or, at the least, to reprimand him. Young Herbert suspected that his father really made the trip because he enjoyed sailing across the ocean and looked for any excuse to do so. But whatever the cause, the father arrived in Naples, where he was dutifully met by the son. There was no sultan's harem and no cause for reprimand, so the two Pells decided on a motor trip through Sicily.

Their automobile was one of the first to touch the island and wherever they stopped, a crowd of twenty or thirty people gathered around them to examine their strange-looking machine. The Sicilian roads were more primitive than the Pells had anticipated. Their journey to the Temple of Segesta ended with the father and son riding donkeys for the last stretch. Then their car broke down altogether, forcing them to finish the journey in a two-wheeled peasant's cart, a crowded railroad car and a closed carriage. They offered a lift in their carriage to a soldier going their way. But their offer did not represent kindness so much as the hope he would protect them from brigands who might try to rob them.

On the trip, they saw an accident with a peasant's donkey cart. The animal became nervous, moved backward and was jerked down the roadbank. The cart crashed to the ground, its shafts pointing to the sky, holding the donkey an elevated prisoner. Young Herbert jumped down, cut the girth with his knife, and caught the donkey as the animal fell free. He carried him up the hill to deposit him in front of the small, frightened Sicilian owner. All that milk his nurse Louisa had made him drink as a child apparently had positive results; Herbert had developed into a young man of enormous strength.

Of all his travels in Europe in those years, one jaunt stood out as being particularly pleasurable, the one he would choose to repeat if he had only a week or ten days traveling in Europe. It was through the Roman ruins of Provence with the city of Avignon the focal point. On the way to Avignon he passed through Orange, where the road went under a triumphal arch. Young Herbert found moving beneath that arch a most impressive experience, knowing that he joined people from thousands of years who had gone under that arch—Roman legions marching to conquest or peasants leaving the countryside for the Neuville. In Orange itself he enjoyed trying out a Roman amphitheater. He stood on the stage and spoke in an ordinary tone of voice and the acoustics were so fine that his friends standing at the very last row heard him perfectly.

At Avignon he stayed at a small hotel run by three charming elderly ladies. He went there first with his father and mother, and then later when he traveled alone, he continued to return. In Avignon he spent his time examining the old walls that surrounded the city, the Palace of Popes and the many interesting houses there. He studied the frescoes on the palace walls, the architecture and even the building techniques used in their construction. He not only saw, he learned and felt.

And on he went, exploring Roman arenas, ancient aqueducts. "I don't know another part of the world," Herbert

Pell once said, "where you could spend a week or twenty days traveling more really comfortably, see more, and enjoy yourself better than in the south of France." He learned that the old homes and castles were not destroyed by time but by men. In a new home he saw an ancient fireplace; the owners had taken it from an old castle because stealing old stone was easier than having new stone cut.

When in the 1950s Herbert Pell reminisced about that trip, he realized that he never could make it again. The south of France he had loved as a young man no longer existed. The triumphal arch still stood, but automobiles had become too wide to go beneath it so the road was curved around it. The small hotel at Avignon had been replaced by a larger and more modern one, lacking the warmth the three elderly ladies had brought to its predecessor. Herbert Pell had seen in the years before World War I a Europe that had existed almost untouched for hundreds of years but that was about to be touched—brutally—and that would never again be the same.

Herbert Pell had sufficient funds to begin collecting books and works of art. Although he had purchased books enthusiastically since his first trip to Paris at age eleven, he was much more cautious about art. When he was twenty-four he went through Italy, touring alone for about three months, and bought nothing. "I knew that I wanted pictures and bronzes," he explained, "but I did not trust my taste or my judgment." During his second trip he did purchase a few things, but it was not until his fourth trip to Italy that "I really put my hand in my pocket."

While he was in Italy a friend of his sent him a letter of introduction to Charles Loeser in Florence, which really began Herbert's career as a student of art. Loeser had graduated from Harvard with the class of 1886, in itself coincidental. Herbert Pell was to have a great deal of association with members of that class although they were twenty years older than he. In addition to Loeser the class of 1886 included a man named Howard Taylor, who managed Herbert's first campaign for Congress; Alanson Houghton, a friend in the House; and William Randolph Hearst, who would make a grab for political power in the 1920s and be blocked by Franklin Roosevelt with Herbert Pell's assistance.

Charles Loeser's father owned a large dry goods store in Brooklyn and had the sense to realize that his son would not be happy in business with him. He settled a small allowance on Charles, enough to keep the young man going while he lived in Florence studying art. And that became Charles Loeser's career, studying Florentine art. He was not an artist himself. Nor was he a broker; he did not collect commissions for bringing together a buyer and an art work. He only studied art, all his life. He liked Herbert Pell; after all, Pell was one of the few people who really appreciated what Charles Loeser was doing.

Herbert went to a museum in the morning alone. He returned to his friend Charles, reporting on what he had seen and explaining why he did or did not like it. In the afternoon Charles accompanied Herbert to the museum, explained what he should have seen, what mysteries had been hidden by the artist from all except the most diligent investigators. "The result was," said Herbert, "that I really got to know a certain amount."

Charles's income was not sufficient to afford a car and so he was happy to have found a friend like Herbert Pell who had a car and enjoyed driving. During the summer months the two men and the chauffeur drove through the towns near Florence, discovering carvings in churches, beautiful and previously unknown paintings in old houses, both men broadening their experiences.

But it wasn't all studying art. Once they drove down to Siena for the Palio, a horse race. The race was around the town's center square, and Herbert Pell, who never did anything second-rate, rented an apartment with a balcony on the square, directly over the point that was both the starting and finishing line. He would not have a good view; he had the best view in the whole town. The horses represented the different parts of the ancient city-state, and before the race they were taken into the local church to be blessed and prayed over. On the day of the race itself there was a magnificent parade. First came the jockey, resplendent in the uniform of his district or *contrada*. Then came the horse itself, wearing only a bridle and without a saddle. Next came the captain of the *contrada*, dressed in armor and waited on by four men, one holding his helmet, another his sword, the third his shield, and the fourth looking obsequious. They were followed by the men of the *contrada*, wearing medieval costumes and carrying spears. There was a similar procession for each horse, each procession preceded by two little boys carrying the banners of the *contrada*, waving and tossing them about.

After the procession for the horses, came the *carroelio* —an open carriage with the flag of Siena (a banner with a picture of the Virgin Mary) painted on the side, and representatives of the three largest sections of the city. This was presided over by the captain of all the people of the city. The entire procession moved slowly around the square to the cheers and shouts of the townspeople. The Palio was a descendant of the medieval festival, when the peasants' dreary existence was broken by pure joyousness.

The race itself with the horses ridden bareback was also medieval. "It was as crooked a race as could be imagined," said Herbert Pell, "and every jockey had been bribed and cross-bribed; bribed to win, bribed to lose, bribed to overthrow some jockey whose success was feared." The year Herbert Pell and Charles Loeser saw the race, there was one horse that had won several times in the past and was the favorite. Almost as soon as the race started, the jockey on that horse was straight-armed by another jockey, stopping his winning streak. The jockeys also carried heavy whips, which, rather than using on the horses, they used on one another. It was that kind of sport. Herbert did not recall which *contrada* won that year, but he remembered the people from the victorious district taking over the square for joyous dancing.

During these years when he was in his twenties he became a club man. The Travellers in Paris was a perfect place for him; it was quiet, and had a good library and was home to other men of culture and refinement. It also was a place of dignity. So Herbert Pell began to seek out other clubs in other cities. "Wherever Herbert Pell was," said a friend of his, "there was a club." And so there was. In New York at this time, the prestige clubs were the Union and the Knickerbocker. "Membership in either," explained Herbert Pell, "really meant that a young man had been selected by the elderly gentlemen who managed it as a person who would be a credit to the organization." Herbert belonged to both. He was very much aware of what club membership meant at that time. He said:

I remember one time crossing the Atlantic. There was a foreigner aboard with whom I scraped up an acquaintance. We would sit in the smoking room talking, but that was all. In those days we carried cigarettes, usually in gold cases. After the second or third day out, I offered him a cigarette, which was marked "Union Club." He took it and smoked it. He then asked me if after dinner I would join him and his wife at coffee. The fact that I was a member of the Union Club to a Frenchman meant that I was a person who would be suitable for him to present to his wife.

Pell did not deny the exclusiveness of his clubs; he enjoyed it. "One goes to a club," he said, "not because of whom one will see but because of whom one will not see." Snobbishness? Yes. But snobbishness of a particular kind. As Ellin Berlin wrote of this period: "The members of the old families aren't snobbish, at least not in the usual way. They are merely completely unaware that there are any people to know except themselves and those they choose to accept."

The life Herbert Pell led in Europe—its elegance, its charm, its satisfaction of the soul—compelled him to stay there, to become another with Charles Loeser, devoting his life to the study of art. For that life was a seducer, luring good men from the reality of the future to the fiction of the past. And Herbert Pell had been seduced by it for ten years.

In the United States, however, the reality of the future was being acknowledged. Theodore Roosevelt became President and began wrenching the government from the hands of the rich and those who would be richer and return it to people who could not buy their leaders. Muckraking reporters forced the American people to acknowledge the conditions in the stockyards and the sweatshops. And educated men were learning they could join the great game of politics and play it for keeps. These were new and exciting times and Herbert Pell came home. His Gilded Age had come to an end. Mrs. Berlin has written of that time, "Every generation must have a golden age to remember but looking back on the one my generation had, I think it was more golden than most. I realize—I've read it and been told it often enough—that all sorts of things were wrong with the prewar world and I can't argue. Still, growing up in America then was more tranquil; it was something we knew how to do. The rules were fixed, the setting was firmly there and would not be removed by the stagehands. The curtain was never going to come down. This year was like last year and next year would be the same. We knew where we were today and nothing could change tomorrow."

Those who emerged from the Gilded Age had confidence. They believed in the past, were determined to make the future as glorious as that past, and believed themselves capable of such achievement. This was what the discerning and sensitive ones had acquired, a faith and a self-confidence and a willingness to use both.

2 HERBERT PELL RETURNED TO THE UNITED States in the summer of 1912, just as the Progressive campaign of Theodore Roosevelt was getting underway. In contrast to others of his class, Pell always had admired Roosevelt. It would have been difficult for someone who knew and hated the business leaders as Herbert Pell did, not to have admired the man who was taking their measure. But in the drawing rooms of Tuxedo, Pell heard the shocking story that one of the club members, an otherwise perfectly respectable gentleman named Harry Hooker, was for Roosevelt. "If they had said Harry Hooker had smallpox," said Pell, "they wouldn't have been more shocked."

Shortly after his return, Pell happened to meet Harry at the Tuxedo clubhouse. "Well," he said, "I hear you're voting for Roosevelt."

"Yes," said a nervous Harry Hooker, "but I don't talk about it here."

"Like hell you don't," answered Herbert Pell. "We're going to begin right away."

And with that vow Herbert Pell became an Orange County committeeman for the Progressive party ticket.

One of his friends in Tuxedo—"an older gentleman who had seen me brought up, a very nice, cultivated man, very pleasant"—decided to give young Herbert Pell some advice. This old gentleman accepted that Pell supported Roosevelt. He was broad-minded enough not to be astonished by heretical politics; another matter bothered him. "But, Bertie," he said in a troubled voice, "don't you know that there's no money in politics?"

Pell ran the Progressive campaign in Tuxedo and journeyed up to Goshen for the county meetings. The party people then had much enthusiasm, great faith in what they were doing and very little political experience. Only one committeeman ever had been on a political committee before. The committee chairman was an able person, but he operated a cider mill and "his big hard days of work were just at the time of the campaign." They were a new kind of people for Herbert Pell to be associating with. There were doctors, lawyers, teachers, small businessmen and plain working people. He even began to meet some of the people who lived in the Tuxedo village, meeting them, that is, on other than an employer-employee basis.

Devoted as the residents of Tuxedo were to the Republican cause, the workers in Tuxedo were equally stout partisans of the Roosevelt-Progressive ticket. They had come from Europe as immigrants twenty-five years earlier to build Tuxedo and expecting to find the streets paved with gold. The streets were paved with macadam, but these workmen did learn that the political process was the means for assisting themselves and their children. They had problems being for Roosevelt, however. If it were known, they would be out of a job as well as a house. Tuxedo still was run that way. The Association owned all the property and leased it only to those workmen whose labor and politics were acceptable. It was not feudalism, because the men could quit anytime they chose, but it was as close to feudalism as society dared come in a democracy.

The Progressives in Tuxedo went underground. Pamphlets were distributed at night, but no one acknowledged having passed them out. Signs appeared on poles, but no one confessed to having hammered the nails in. And when pressed, the Tuxedo Progressives shrugged and said it was the work of Herbert Pell. "Everything was charged to me," said Pell. "No county committeeman in the world has ever done as much work as was credited to me in that campaign."

Theodore Roosevelt lost the election, but the Progressives won. They had learned how to organize, how to involve the nonprofessional in politics, how to enunciate an ideal and then rally the people around it using the existing political system. The Progressives won because they became a political force, and from that moment on any political group ignored them at its peril.

Pell liked politics. Because of his parents' interest in public affairs, his own vision of how a society should be open to all, and his awareness of how the wealthy in America were operating the government for their own ends, it was natural that he should. And he seemed to be successful at it. He had done a good job as committeeman. He was personable and treated men with respect whether they lived in Pierre Lorillard's old house or cut the hedges surrounding it. And he also had a certain independence that people admired. He didn't need politics. As wealthy and as sophisticated as he was, as capable of enjoying the culture of Europe and the pleasures of its aristocracy, he could make it perfectly clear that he anticipated no personal benefits from politics.

In 1914 the Democrats and the Progressives combined in some counties of New York State to field candidates for the state constitutional convention. Pell was nominated first as a Progressive and then also as a Democrat. Still he lost. The Republicans in Orange County were much too strong politically, no matter how many endorsements the opponent might have. That was the first time Pell's name appeared on a political ballot.

Herbert Pell was now thirty years old. He had lived almost ten years in Europe, was tall, handsome, literate, rich and, as far as the women were concerned, a very good catch. He had had his romantic interests but had never considered any prospect very seriously until he met Matilda Bigelow—a beautiful woman, thin almost to fragility, with long dark hair. She had grown up in Europe under the watchful eye of a protective mother. Returning to the United States in her late teens, she had a certain skepticism about the ways of its society. When a young gentleman friend asked her to go dancing with him, she replied that her mother never permitted her to go dancing with a man, just the two of them. The man suggested that he bring his mother along. He would ask his friend Bertie Pell to make it a foursome. "Just talk to him about automobile tires," the friend advised, "and everything will be okay."

And so it was that Matilda Bigelow, not quite twenty, found herself standing next to this giant of a man and could think of nothing else to say except: "I understand you like automobile tires?"

Pell had once talked of investing in tires and was amused that his idle chatter should come back this way. And he was very much taken with the young lady who could be so serious about such a silly thing. The next day he sent her a copy of *Anna Karenina* and an orchid corsage. Matilda was thrilled with the flowers; they were the first a young man had given her. She was going to Boston for a party at the Saltonstalls' and took them with her. She wore them until they were frazzled and then she pressed them.

They were married November 3, 1915, a Tuesday. The event was an important social occasion. He of course was from the Pells of Tuxedo and of the Lorillards of just about all over. She was a Bigelow, whose family also was socially prominent and whose mother's family, the Dallases, had long played a role in American history, providing a Vice President and an early Secretary of the Treasury. The noon ceremony took place at the Church of the Heavenly Rest in New York City before more than one hundred guests from the *haut monde*. Matilda was given away by her brother, Anson Bigelow, who was a midshipman at the U. S. Naval Academy at Annapolis. She wore a dress of white satin over a many-tiered underskirt of white chiffon. Straps hung over the shoulders to hold in place what *The New York Times* described as a "tremendous long plain train of silver cloth." Her veil, an heirloom dating back many generations, was banded flat on her black hair just above the forehead, held in place by orange flowers; the veil fell in a mantle over her train. Her only jewelry was a stomacher of emeralds and diamonds, a present from the bridegroom.

Life as Mrs. Herbert Claiborne Pell was an awakening experience for the young girl whose mother never would allow her to go to a dance unchaperoned. He traveled from city to city as other people walked from block to block. His friends were from as high a society as her acquaintances were, but then he was making new friends now. Those workmen in Tuxedo and a Tammany Hall politician named Jeremiah Mahoney also were becoming part of his world. Once after he and Matilda had been married several years, he invited Mayor John Hylan of New York to their house for dinner. Matilda was so shocked at the prospect of a politician's dining in her house, and a Democratic one at that, that she refused at first to come downstairs. Only after much coaxing did she ultimately perform her role as hostess.

But there was much pleasantness for the two Pells. They read together often. A particular favorite was Mary Roberts Rinehart's *Bab—A Sub-Deb*, which amused them with a young girl's adventures in society meeting, as she said, the "other sex." Herbert Pell felt awkward on a dance floor but greatly enjoyed dinner parties. His wife made a gracious home for him. The dinners were served expertly and made a backdrop to the conversation that the Pell house became famous for. The talk was of history, art, sometimes of politics, often of the war engulfing Europe. His home was an extension of the society he had known as a child.

It was for many years a pleasant marriage. Herbert Pell enjoyed showing his young wife the castles and cathedrals of Europe that he knew so well, and he was amused at her reactions. "It's so musty," she once said to him when they were in Westminster Abbey. "Is it the living or the dead?" They enjoyed the theater and one week they saw eight plays. During one show there was a tense point when the villain was about to strike the hero over the head. Matilda, who always was carried away by good drama, could contain herself no longer. She jumped up from her seat and cried out to the hero: "Look out!" Herbert Pell enjoyed the incident enormously and frequently told the story. On November 22, 1918, their only son, Claiborne, was born.

When the United States entered World War I, Herbert Pell wanted to enlist, but weak eyes made him unacceptable for military service. He fretted about his inactivity and tried to inveigle some of his friends to fix him up with a noncombatant's position, but without success. Finally in the summer of 1918 he decided to run for Congress. The decision was a carefully calculated one. He chose the Seventeenth District in New York. Not yet famous as the Silk Stocking District, it was carved out then, as it seemingly would be ever after, by a Republican state legislature to elect a loyal Republican to Congress. Pell by this point was a registered Democrat. He figured that if he put up a good fight, he could then appeal to his old neighbor and Harvard friend Franklin D. Roosevelt, the Assistant Secretary of the Navy, for a job in the Navy Pay Corps. "By that time," he explained, "they were getting down a little bit further and, although my eyes were not good enough to distinguish a submarine two or three miles off at sea, they were amply good enough to tell a one dollar bill from a two."

The Silk Stocking District was a long, narrow strip of Manhattan from Fourteenth Street in the south to Ninety-ninth Street in the North, built around Fifth Avenue. It jutted out from the Avenue only when its gerrymandered lines could include some expensive apartment buildings to add more Republicans. It was the kind of congressional district that made a Democrat forget about the problems of moving to Washington.

Although Pell originally had entered the contest lightly, he had a fighter's streak when aroused, as the campaign succeeded in doing. He also had a couple of lucky breaks. One was his opponent. Originally it was a man named George Blinn Francis, but Francis was shortly bumped from the ticket. It seems that the Republican governor of New York and his state chairman, a lawyer named Frederick Tanner, were having a dispute. To settle it, Tanner was ousted as state chairman and, as a sop, given the GOP nomination for Congress in the sure Silk Stocking District. Francis out; Tanner in. It was so certain a Republican district that several of Herbert Pell's friends suggested he confess political truth. "Mr. Pell," said one of the Democratic leaders to the young politician, "when we nominated you we knew you had very little chance of election, but now running against the State Chairman I can assure you, as a friend, that you have no chance of election and that you should not spend much money."

If the prediction wasn't encouraging, it was honest. But Tanner believed it too and barely campaigned.

There were some other pieces of luck, luck being in Herbert Pell's philosophy "seeing opportunities and seizing them." His first opportunity came when the Republican organization charged that he was a carpetbagger. The previous year he had voted in Tuxedo and had, in fact, never voted in the Seventeenth Congressional District, which he now so presumptuously sought to represent in Congress. When the GOP trotted out these facts, Pell acknowledged them as true. And then he added that if the worst thing the Republicans could say about him was that he had a place in the country, then he must be pretty good. And while the pros were trying to find their way around that, Pell also pointed out that his family had been New Yorkers for generations and that he himself had been born very near the district, on Twenty-third Street.

He also had some luck with his running mates. One was Robert F. Wagner. Wagner had been a poor German immigrant who had gone to law school and then worked in politics to help fellow immigrants. In 1918, Wagner was running for New York State Supreme Court. By this time, he was so popular that he did not have to campaign. But

Wagner was a consummate politician, one who learned not to count his victories before his votes. He waged as vigorous a campaign as New York had seen. He spoke before any district club, religious group or ladies' association willing to hear him. He walked the streets shaking hands, put up posters and distributed circulars. He waged an expensive and arduous campaign, one that insured him not only victory but a victory of major proportions, which also helped any Democrats on the ticket.

Another running mate was Al Smith. As the Democratic candidate for governor, Smith headed the ticket. He began his campaign talking about people who were unfortunate, about how the state had an obligation to them, how the people acting together could help them and nobody paid much attention. Several weeks before the election an asylum upstate caught fire and a number of helpless inmates were injured, forcing the people of New York to think about the ineffective fire regulations and the crowded conditions that had prevented the victims' escape. They began to remember some of the things Al Smith had been saying. And they began to listen. Being on a ticket with Al Smith was part of Herbert Pell's luck also.

Pell knew Al Smith at this time and liked him. "He had probably the best knowledge of the government of the state of New York of anybody. . . . He knew the laws of the state; he knew the people; he knew the districts and their needs." Al Smith then, so Pell thought, was "a progressive, beer-drinking Irishman." Much later, or so Pell charged, Smith "took to Scotch whiskey and reaction."

Of course Herbert Pell had the required number of endorsements from prominent Democrats. One was from Franklin Roosevelt. It read:

My dear Pell:

As you probably know, I returned from France a couple of weeks ago, but have been laid up with pneumonia since then. I have just heard that you are running for Congress in the Seventeenth District. May I tell you how very glad I am, and I sincerely hope that you will be elected.

But with all his "luck" and his endorsements, Pell's chance for victory depended primarily upon himself and how good a campaign he waged. His problem was to locate whatever Democrats had gone undetected by the Republican gerrymanderers and still remained in the district. Meeting them at district clubs, private homes, the bars where the pols hung out, he persuaded them that he was worthy of their support. They came along. The local leaders were backing him and they persuaded the party faithful to come out on election day along with their brothers and uncles and anyone else they found.

Pell also had the problem of winning new votes to the Democratic column. In this he showed a remarkable ability to turn adversity to advantage. Prohibition was a major issue at the time. Pell opposed it while his opponent, Tanner, favored it. For his support of prohibition, Tanner received the plaudits of the Anti-Saloon League. This was one of those organizations which made a lot of noise but was actually not very effective. "Pay no attention to it," the Democratic pros advised Pell. But Pell figured if his opposition to prohibition might be used against him, it also could be used for him. At Pell's request, one of his friends wrote the Anti-Saloon League for advice on voting. The response came back: "Mr. Pell has refused to answer our questions but Mr. Tanner's answer is satisfactory to us." Anybody that the Anti-Saloon League did not like must be a friend of the liquor store owners, of the tavern keepers and of all those who believed that imbibing occasionally was not a matter requiring federal intervention. Pell made certain that they knew who their enemy was. He had photostats of the Anti-Saloon League's response made up and circled the League's endorsement of Tanner in red pencil. These went out to all the liquor stores and taverns in the district. "You can imagine how many liquor dealers there are between Fourteenth and Ninety-ninth streets," recalled Pell, "and every single one of them got a copy of this photostat with an annotation, 'If he's satisfactory to them is he satisfactory to you?'"

Tanner was not satisfactory to them and on election day Herbert Pell squeaked through to victory by seventeen hundred votes out of approximately forty thousand cast. If it was not a stunning victory, it was a triumph of a Democrat in the Seventeenth. Only three Democrats after Herbert Pell have equalled his feat of winning election in the famous Silk Stocking District.

Being Herbert Pell, the first thing he did when he got to

Washington was join a club; he chose the Metropolitan. The more he learned of Washington society, the more he appreciated having the sanctuary of his club to repair to or hide out at, as it turned out to be. "Washington," he said, "is almost the only society where you can go out to dinners and find the women less intelligent than the men." Of all the cities where he had been invited to fancy dinner parties—Paris, London, New York, Boston, Tuxedo, Newport, and later, Budapest and Rome—Washington was the only city where the women were duller than their husbands. "Sometimes," he said, "I would be sitting next to contemporaries of my grandmother, a large number of them with a total lack of education and no experience in the world, whose one qualification was that when they were twenty they married a coming man and never advanced with him."

The men, in contrast, were much brighter than he had found in New York society. So eventually he turned down all dinner invitations and dined at the Metropolitan Club with his cronies from Congress or with men of importance passing through the city. "That," he said, "was rather pleasant." Among his dinner companions were John Dwight, a former Republican whip of the House, and Alanson Houghton, a Republican House member from Upstate New York of Charles Loeser's Harvard class. One night at dinner, as the three discussed various politicians, Dwight turned to Pell, saying: "Well, Pell, it's none of my business as an ex-Republican politician to give any advice to a rising Democrat, but I will tell you this: 'When you're dealing with a Republican, you take his word.

When you're dealing with a Democrat, you can take his word. But don't forget, Pell, that when you're dealing with a Reformer, you're dealing with a crook.'"

In his own political career, Pell found that advice to be true. He never was tricked or deceived by any regular Republican or Democrat. The regular politician was always perfectly straightforward and honest. He had to be because the politician's stock in trade is his word and if he becomes known as a liar, he does not succeed in his profession. "The only dirty tricks that were ever played on me," said Pell, "were played on me by the so-called pious elements. They're the only people who have ever lied to me and the only people who have ever betrayed a confidence."

Like a visitor in the gallery who comes to watch briefly and then leaves disappointed, Herbert Pell was not impressed by Congress. "I always rather resented Mr. Truman referring to that Republican Congress in his time as the worst in history except those that immediately followed the Civil War," he said. "I always thought the Congress I belonged to stood very high on that list." He was in Congress when the World War I peace treaty came before the Senate for approval. As a member of the House, Herbert Pell had a privileged position, able not only to hear the formal debates but also to witness the behind-the-scenes maneuvering. He was convinced that the Republicans opposed the treaty primarily to hurt Woodrow Wilson and the Democratic party led by Wilson.

He also was skeptical of the diligence of fellow House

members. One day one of them was making an impassioned speech and "at the top of a particularly effective howl," the member's false teeth shot out. Unperturbed, he picked up his teeth, inserted them into his mouth and continued with his speech as if he had not been interrupted. "I think I was the only person in the House that observed the phenomenon," said Pell. "No one was particularly listening to the speech."

On another occasion, after a two-hour debate that was supposed to have centered on a naval bill but had seemed to touch everything else, Pell rose to address the House. "I'm going to speak on the Navy Bill," he began. A colleague shouted: "It's a good thing. We haven't heard a word about it yet."

Many years after his tour in Congress, Herbert Pell claimed he never expected to spend more than one term in the House. "I was like Eliza standing on a lump of ice," he once said; "the one thing I knew was that I couldn't stay where I was." This, he said, explained why he voted as he did. Perhaps. It may also be that he was just not the kind of man to bend his convictions, even if his refusal meant his defeat—as it did.

Certainly while he was in Congress he worked hard and did all the traditional things New York members do if they hope for reelection—helping constituents, visiting the district, trying to get his name mentioned in *The New York Times*. He spent Monday morning to Friday afternoon in Washington and the weekends usually in New York City, often visiting and speaking at as many district clubs as he could. He was an effective and a popular speaker, generally discussing the various pieces of legislation before the House. But his success as a speaker may not have been due to his choice of subjects or his ability to sway crowds. Rather, it may have been because he never spoke more than fifteen minutes. "If you're going to get your audience up in fifteen minutes," he once said, "you had best leave them there and don't try any monkey tricks. And if you can't get them up in fifteen minutes, you won't be able to do it in fifteen weeks."

In Congress he favored women's suffrage, saying: "I am certain that American women have sufficient character to preserve their virtue, even in the fascinating atmosphere of a polling place."

He supported a minimum wage bill for government employees, conceding: "Passage of this bill will, of course, cost the government a certain amount of money directly, but there will also be a very considerable economy if it is passed. . . . Where we employ men at a very low wage . . . it is quite obvious that the man will, as soon as he can get anything better, go away, and the Government thereby loses a partly trained man."

He supported appropriations for the American Printing House for the Blind, saying: "Anyone who ever saw a blind man reach for these books would realize how they are treasured by the blind when they get hold of them."

He opposed a reduction in the appropriation for the Navy, warning: "If there is one thing made more clear than another by this war, it is that the second best navy is about as good as the second best poker hand—a bad thing to bet on, and you are ruined if you are called."

None of these political positions hurt him in his district. Other positions, however, did. When the American labor movement supported a proposal that Pell believed would lead to the nationalization of railroads, he did not hesitate to speak out against it. "Government ownership," he said, "will certainly bring politics into the administration of railroads. It will certainly result in the management being either a bureaucracy or a political machine."

But losing a few votes on a labor issue was piddling compared to what his stand on the soldiers' bonus cost him. When the First World War ended and America's soldiers came home, politicians vied with each other for the "soldier's vote." Like politicians before them and after them, they tried to buy it. The measure was the bonus proposal. Any person who had served in the military during the war would receive a cash bonus—beyond his salary and separation pay. A strong case can be made for the government to have taken some action of the constructive kind taken after the Second World War and the Korean War which enabled millions of young men to go to college, start businesses and buy their own homes. But handing out a few dollars indiscriminately as proposed after World War I was not that kind of constructive action.

No member of Congress wished to speak against the bonus. The "soldier's vote" was considered too important. Not only was each veteran involved, but every veteran had relatives, all of them potential voters.

On Saturday afternoon, May 1, 1920, before a sparsely filled House chamber, Herbert Pell rose to speak. The few members in the chamber who were listening to him were shocked as he began: "I intend to vote against the bonus." No one hearing him then or thinking about it later disagreed with his following statement. "I am doing this," he said, "in the full realization that it means the end of my political career. I can tell you frankly that it is a painful thing to commit suicide, but I do not think that honor will permit me to follow any other course." He continued:

> Of course, I shall vote for the most generous treatment possible for men that have been injured in the service of the United States, and also for proper care of the dependents of those men who have been killed, but I cannot bring myself merely for consideration of political advantage to vote for a bill which would impose a tax of $20 a head on every man, woman and child in the country.

Pell's position frightened the other members of Congress. "They felt," he said, "that they could get in trouble if they were seen too much in my company." Pell ran for reelection, fighting as hard as he could, speaking to whatever group would hear him, walking the streets of his district, listening to the droning complaints of the party professionals. From the beginning, however, he knew he was going to be defeated.

His opponent was Ogden Mills, actually an old family friend. Herbert Pell's mother had been a bridesmaid at the wedding of Ogden Mills's parents. Pell considered his opponent able and an excellent student of the political process and he knew him to be very rich. One day during the campaign, Herbert ran into Mills at the Knickerbocker Club and the two men dined there together. Pell began to explain the way Washington operated, giving advice on how to be a successful congressman: "Get a good secretary and have someone down there to watch out for a comfortable office." Mills laughed. "Why," he said, "you talk as if I'd won the election." And Herbert Pell answered: "Well, you know as well as I do, you're going to."

As the race neared its end the fact became clear that much more than who represented the Seventeenth Congressional District was at stake. In its lead editorial on October 26, 1920, *The New York Times* pointed out that Pell was the only New York City congressman to vote against the bonus bill and one of only two city representatives to vote against the bill extending the federal government's hold on the railroads. The bonus bill had passed the House but had not come to a vote in the Senate, meaning Congress would take it up a second time. "Many members of Congress," said the *Times*, "will be guided in their attitude toward bonus measures by the success or failure of Mr. Pell in this contest. If he is beaten, Congressmen who conscientiously believe the bonus proposals are wrong in principle and who think they would impose unjust burdens upon the taxpayers will simply throw up their hands and say 'What's the use?'" As for the bill releasing the railroads to private ownership, "He voted for it, as he voted against the bonus bill, in obedience to his convictions of the public interest. It is a fair question to ask whether businessmen to whom a Congressman's sound record has been most satisfactory, who . . . asked support for the railroad bill to protect the savings of millions of wage-earners, will turn against him on Election Day." The *Times* then said:

It is to the last degree important, as we have pointed out, that his courageous and conscientious action should not be punished by defeat. Will the voters of the Seventeenth District forget all about the service Congressman Pell rendered to the country by that vote against the bonus and give their support to his opponent, thus warning many other Congressmen that it would be dangerous to follow his example?

The *Times* concluded that Pell's defeat would be "a pretty glaring example of the fickleness and unreasonableness of electorates."

If the *Times* was correct about what Pell's defeat would show, then the voters were indeed fickle and unreasonable. Mills beat Pell. Many years later Pell claimed that his vote against the bonus did not effect the outcome of the election. There were other factors. Nineteen-twenty was a Republican year; Warren G. Harding led the ticket against James Cox with Woodrow Wilson's postwar plans the issue. And, of course, the district had originally been designed as a safe berth for a Republican. Still, Pell's stand against the bonus bill had an impact on the outcome and probably was the determining factor against him. His later disavowal was undoubtedly the gesture of a gracious gentleman not wishing to call his former constituents "fickle" and "unreasonable."

His stand against the bonus not only was courageous, it also was prophetic. In January, 1921, Congress was meeting, with Pell a "lame duck" member, when the Republicans announced their plans to pare the government's spending. There was nothing in their budget to cover the costs of a soldiers' bonus. Pell was not surprised. In a speech to the House, he said:

I voted with a small minority against the bonus bill on the theory that it might possibly become a law, although frankly I never thought that it would. It was inconceivable that any political party would seriously suggest the passage of an important measure in the way the bonus bill was passed, if there were any intention whatever that it would become a law. It was quite clear that the impassioned orations on the subject of the soldier boys were intended merely for political effect.

The bill promised that an enormous sum would be scattered among those men in the hope of attracting their support on election day. At the time I thought, and I realize now that I was right, there was no intention whatever that this promise should be kept. . . .

It is a disgrace that men who have lost their health in the war should be the victims of stinginess parading as economy rather than the objects of willing and grateful generosity. Tubercular and insane men, ex-soldiers and sailors of the war, instead of getting the best and tenderest care from a sympathetic people, proud to call them fellow countrymen, are being lodged in jails and barns, because now after election two million or three million dollars cannot be found by a Congress which before election voted for an indiscriminate bonus of two billion dollars scattered broadcast to every man, sick or well, who had ever seen a uniform. Is it because the tubercular will soon be dead and off the voting list and the insane have not the franchise?

After all the cheap gestures of last spring, is this cheeseparing to be an indication of the policy of Congress? These men do not come here asking for billions of dollars. They do not ask to wreck the Treasury of the United States, but they do ask for this small sum and we deny their request. Is this to be our attitude toward the soldier?

Is it to be said with truth that before election the American Congress will promise anything that any man who ever wore a uniform may want, and that afterwards we are going to save a beggarly sum at the expense of men who have suffered in the defense of their country, merely because their votes will not be needed in the near future and because they themselves are unorganized?

Herbert Pell was correct in charging that Congress had bowed to an organized pressure group and that its members had hoped to buy votes by supporting the bonus bill. It was a kind of cheapness that has been engaged in by Congress on many other occasions. And such cheapness produces tragic results. Ultimately the bonus that members of Congress lacked the courage to defeat became more and more mired in trickery. Rather than vote the ex-soldiers any money, Congress issued them bonus certificates that could be redeemed in 1945; let another Congress worry about finding the funds to pay them. This sneaked by in the boom times of the 1920s but was not acceptable in the depression years of the 1930s. In 1932 the veterans, many of them unemployed for months and with starving families, began the "Bonus March" to Washington. Riding the rails, crowding into old jalopies, walking, they came to the nation's capital to demand that their bonus certificates be redeemed immediately. But by 1932 Congress did not want their votes and the nation was treated to the grotesque and horrifying scene of General Douglas Mac-Arthur and Major Dwight D. Eisenhower leading a charge of mounted United States cavalry against a group of dirty, hungry and disillusioned men who once had fought for their country and believed in their government.

Pell had few illusions about his congressional service. He said later that there was only one thing that "wouldn't have happened in Congress if I hadn't been there"—the immigration bill establishing quotas limiting the number of specific nationals allowed to enter the United States. Toward the end of the Wilson Administration, Pell was in the House late one night when he learned that the quota bill was about to be brought up for a vote. He did not believe in national quotas, although he was willing to limit immigration. "What I wanted," he explained, "was a simple law providing that anybody could come into the United States that wanted to, provided he could pass the physical examination for entrance to the United States Army. Now if we find that brings in too many people we can jack up our qualifications. . . . We could make any qualifications we want, but have it a quality test of the individual."

In the 1920s such a belief was not popular politically and Pell had no chance to stop the quota bill. This particular night, however, he did seek recognition and raised the point of order that a quorum of the House membership was not present and the House could not conduct business. As the members could not be roused from their homes or found elsewhere late at night, the House adjourned until the next morning. The bill was brought up the next day and was passed. The Senate then passed it and it went to Woodrow Wilson for his approval. Because of the one-day delay caused by Pell, however, Wilson was able to "pocket veto" the bill. If it was at the White House ten days without his signature, it became law. But it was at the White House only the last nine days of his term.

After Harding became President, Congress passed the immigration bill again and it did become law. But Pell's point of order had delayed enactment of the quota system for three months. "There must be thousands of people today in the United States who wouldn't be here if it wasn't for me," he said later, adding: "I don't know the name of one."

Pell made a farewell speech in the House the day before Woodrow Wilson left the White House. Although it is about the First World War and Woodrow Wilson, it later could be said that it was about the Second World War and Herbert Pell.

The one chance [he said] seriously to make an effort for world peace seems to be passing away from us, but I hope that it can come back and that in the apotheosis we will see the great dream made real. The American people can not suddenly be turned into broad-minded idealists, guided only by a sense of justice—that was Wilson's mistake—but neither can it suddenly be made to turn its back on the great humanitarian thoughts that are the foundation of this country and turned overnight into sordid grubbers, inspired by nothing but selfish commercialism and private or partisan profit—that is the mistake of his enemies. Mistake for mistake, there can be no doubt which is the nobler. . . .

It is not probable that a group of partisans will be able for long to deny to the world what it has wanted for ages and seen and almost reached so recently; but, of course, it is possible. . . .

I should regret to feel that the sacrifice, the energy, the unselfishness called out by the war had all been wasted and that nothing but the hatred and the loss remained. Ten million men have died, for what? Nothing or something? Who can tell?

We will soon learn whether or not they are right who think that they can safely disregard the aspiration for which so many lives were given on the ground that dead men cast no votes.

Wilson will be the hero of this drama—not perhaps in the flesh, although I hope it will be, but certainly in that great thought that his enemies do not even comprehend.

He hadn't bid farewell to Washington completely, however, even when his personal equipment had been moved from Washington to his home in New York. "Coming from the House office building," he said, "introduced cockroaches into the house in New York which had to be exterminated at some cost."

If Herbert Pell could not win and hold an elective position, he was not quite ready to leave politics. It had taken hold of him and he was not interested in breaking loose from its grasp. After leaving Congress, he toyed for a brief period with something called the Constitutional League. Its purpose was to be "for" something. Organizations claiming to be "100 per cent American" were multiplying, each being against one thing or another. "I organized a society called the Constitutional League, which wasn't against anything; it was simply pro-American."

What it tried to do was best explained in a form letter Pell wrote to prominent persons asking their financial support. The letters began with an invitation to a lunch designed to raise funds and explain the work of the league. Then he wrote: "The League was organized to meet the radical propagandist on his own ground. We believe that the American system of government, if correctly explained and properly understood will commend itself to all classes. It is obvious that the way to meet a campaign of propaganda is by argument rather than by force and abuse." Pell then claimed that more than three hundred newspapers had published articles originated by the league "illustrative of the opportunities which are open to the poorest man under the American system of government." The league also had sent out a million copies of the Constitution. The letter ended with an appeal for one hundred dollars and the claim that "this work is unique." That particular letter was sent to Franklin Roosevelt, who replied that he had hoped to attend the luncheon but must instead be present at an important conference. Apparently a number of other prominent persons also had important conferences, because the Constitutional League did not have a very long life.

The summer of 1921, Herbert Pell was in Tuxedo wondering how to return to politics when he read in the morning newspaper that the Democratic state chairman had resigned. "I promptly went upstairs," said Pell, "took off my white shoes and trousers, put on brown ones and took the second train down to New York. I presented myself to the proper Democratic authorities. . . ." The "proper" authority in this instance was Jeremiah Mahoney, a Tammany sachem. The triumvirate of Mahoney, Robert

Wagner and Al Smith represented a unique American political phenomenon. Born poor, they had pulled themselves up the economic and educational ladder until they had the poise, the intelligence and the bravado to rise as high as any man can aspire. And while they did achieve success for themselves—Smith particularly became wealthy—they primarily assisted others. They were truly generous men who instead of giving a percentage of their income or their time, devoted their careers to others. Politics was their game, honesty their watchword and the American people were their beneficiaries.

Mahoney and Pell had met about 1906 or 1907 when both men were in their early twenties. Socially they were not close friends; their backgrounds were too dissimilar. But an interest in politics drew them together. Mahoney had been instrumental in helping Pell win the nomination and then the election in 1918 to Congress.

When Herbert Pell, dressed in his brown suit, walked in to see Mahoney about the state chairmanship, he walked into a dispute with Al Smith, one that was never settled. Smith had his own candidate for the state chairmanship, his former secretary, a man named George Van Namee. Van Namee had all the attributes for a state chairman— he was experienced in politics, honest and capable—but he faced one serious drawback. Tammany did not like him. Actually it was not Van Namee that Tammany was against; Tammany and Smith were on the outs at this time and any candidate advocated by Smith would be turned down by the Tammany men. Pell, in short, presented himself at the right moment, the moment when there was need for a compromise candidate.

The state committee convened at the Hotel Commodore in hopes of finding a man suitable both to Al Smith, who had been governor of New York and as a top vote-getter was one of the powerful Democrats in the state and to the Tammany chieftains. In addition to the Tammany men, there was present John McCooey of Brooklyn, Ed Flynn of the Bronx, Norman Mack of Buffalo, William Kelley of Syracuse, and Franklin Roosevelt from Dutchess County. It was a larger turnout than usual; the smell of a fight between the two party factions had brought out all the troops.

To this group, Jerry Mahoney presented as his choice for chairman Herbert Pell. With the exception of Roosevelt, they all laughed. After all, as they pointed out to Mahoney, Pell was a member of the Harvard, Union and Knickerbocker clubs as well as being a socialite who flitted from Tuxedo to Newport. Roosevelt didn't laugh because the description fitted him almost as well as it did Pell. But Mahoney insisted that Pell's background made him just the type of person they needed. Pell, he said, had a fine reputation, had an active interest in politics and, more important, was not aligned with any particular faction. Roosevelt may have cinched it for Pell by saying: "Bertie. Bertie. Bertie. I know Bertie. We were at Harvard together. He's not such a bad fellow."

So the group unanimously elected Herbert Pell chairman in a meeting described by *The New York Times* as "characterized throughout by perfect harmony." In accepting the chairmanship, Pell promised, as all good politicians should, not only to work for his party's victory but "to see that the party deserved it." The *Times* editorially considered his election a brilliant choice: "If Herbert C. Pell, Jr., the new chairman of the Democratic State Committee, makes as good a political manager as he was a Representative in Congress, the Democratic Party of this State has had a considerable piece of good fortune. He is a man of real intelligence." The *Times* editorial then recalled the two votes—against the bonus bill and for private ownership of the railroads—that had caused it to praise Pell previously, and concluded that "under such leadership the Democratic Party of New York should follow honorable methods and commend itself to intelligent and public-spirited men and women."

When Herbert Pell took over the chairmanship job he was thirty-seven years old. As in his twenties, he was strikingly handsome with dark wavy hair, a large mustache and an almost-Roman face. He wore a *pince-nez*, had his clothes tailored in London, could dine in French, Italian and German as well as English. He knew European art and European literature better than most professors. He was more at home in the salons of the European capitals than he was in the saloons on the East Side of New York City. He preferred wine to beer and cigarettes to cigars. He had never worked a day in his life, was a member of the group known as "high society" both by his parentage and by his marriage. He had dabbled in politics. Although showing himself a man of integrity in Congress, he had not demonstrated great political acumen or creativity.

And yet there was something else about him. A comment that Pell once made about Franklin Roosevelt serves equally well to describe Pell himself. "Franklin Roosevelt, to a certain extent," said Pell, "started off a little outside of the money-making community. That is, he started out to watch it as I did and he was not an integral part of the machine. He was an observer. He had a certain indignation at the attitude of the business people. . . . There was a feeling on the part of Franklin Roosevelt and certain others like him, that these people had gotten a good deal too big for their breeches. We see them and they bulge *too* much. . . . This collection of knaves setting themselves up as if they were gentlemen, as if they were the best in the country!" And then it erupted from Herbert Pell as he dwelt on the corruption that flourished under the Republican administrations of the 1920s: "Am I to look up to Doheny and Sinclair? Am I expected to bow to Rockefeller? By God, I won't do it! . . . I'm not going to accept the idea that they are natural leaders of the country." When his anger had cooled, he added: "I think there's an awful lot of that feeling in men like Roosevelt and Wilson." There was an awful lot of that feeling in Pell.

Men like Franklin Roosevelt and Herbert Pell, and Theodore Roosevelt and Woodrow Wilson before them, had been brought up to be gentlemen in the true meaning of that word. While there always was a sense of personal ambition in what they did, there also was an understanding that what had been given to them in the sense of the good and bountiful life demanded a response by them to society. They had been given and they must repay. It is an interesting facet of American politics that this kind of person could mix so smoothly with the Al Smith—Bob Wagner—John Nance Garner types. This second group knew the problems of the poor as only those who have personally experienced poverty can know them. America brought together the rich who felt compelled to assist and the poor who demanded assistance. With the exception of Theodore Roosevelt, who fathered it, they built the modern Democratic party into the most powerful and most responsive political tool the nation had ever seen. Through wars, depression, civil disturbance and the threat of aggression, the Democratic party that these men created provided the leadership to which the American people rallied.

In 1921, Herbert Pell did not see his problems in such grandiose terms. In fact, his primary problem was the simple one of money. When a party has the aura of victory about it, finding campaign contributions is easy. But the Democratic party in New York State in 1921 had no such aura. Its biggest vote-getter—Al Smith—had been defeated for a second two-year term as governor in the Harding sweep of 1920. Another gubernatorial contest was coming up in 1922 and Smith probably would have to wrestle William Randolph Hearst for the nomination, a match that would split the party. To top it off, Smith did not like the state chairman. Herbert Pell had not been his choice and Smith was not used to having his choice turned down. Also, Pell was not "Smith's man"; Smith was not able to control him. Pell, the man responsible for drawing up a budget, learned that all this meant that campaign contributors considered the Democratic party a poor risk.

Pell persuaded a small group of Democrats with a little money to pledge one hundred dollars each; raising fifteen hundred dollars that way, he set himself up in an office with a stenographer. But that money didn't last long. He gave up the office and moved the Democratic party's state headquarters into the dining room of a Democratic club on Fifth Avenue. Every time the club gave a party, Pell had to lock up the state committee records in a rolltop desk. But the committee creaked into action. What little movement there was, actually, was Pell's. He crisscrossed the state, making speeches. But he was not only speaking of the glories of the party, he was addressing himself to its responsibilities. He understood that the party must improve itself. It deserved no votes for its name; it must earn them. "I do not urge anyone to vote the Democratic ticket merely because it is the Democratic ticket," he said in one typical speech. "The voter should select each candidate according to his qualifications. It is our duty to nominate the best man for public office; it is the duty of the public intelligently to judge fitness. . . ."

Armed with a secondhand mimeograph machine (the Red Cross had gotten its best days), Pell launched a publicity campaign against the Republicans. For two hundred dollars Pell hired an accountant to go over the state budget and examine the Republican claims of big savings. Like most political claims, the Republicans' were exaggerated. According to the budget, there was a considerable saving to the state in the cost of distributing automobile license tags. Examination showed that the Republican efficiency simply was transferring the cost of distributing the tags from the state treasury to the various county treasuries. There were other similar efficiencies. Salaries had been trimmed, the Republicans claimed. But examination showed again that there was less trimming and more transferring. Herbert Pell as Democratic state chairman charged the budget was full of trickery. The New York *Sun* replied with a strong editorial criticizing him for his outburst. He shot back that two years earlier the *Sun* had praised him editorially and now it was criticizing him. "Of course," Pell later reflected, "that brought publicity which we wouldn't have gotten if it had just been put out as a single statement."

For Herbert Pell the day-to-day dealing with the professional politicians was an enlightening experience. Contrary to the stories he had heard, the politicians were honest. A group of party leaders, primarily from the New York City area, met at least once a week in a group known as the "War Board" to draft a party platform for the 1922 state convention. There were the Irishmen Jerry Mahoney, Jim Foley, John Delaney, and there was Maurice Bloch, an assembly leader, representing the Jews—all coming together to meet at the table presided over by Herbert Pell, whose family had been in America so long he could forget that its members were immigrants once, if he chose to. This was ethnic politics in its true sense. It told the minority members that they could be represented in the councils of government, that they could work through the system, that there was a place for them.

This group of politicians learned that the city was going to tear down a spur from the old Sixth Avenue elevated, running from Fifty-third to Fifty-eighth streets. "There was a certain amount of talk that it might come down," said Pell, "but not much was known by the public. We knew, every one of us, not only that it was coming down, but we knew when the demolition was to start." And knowing that the elevated was coming down everyone of the group could have cleaned up financially by buying the property along the elevated's path at a low price and then selling high once the track was removed. "But not one single one," said Pell, "bought a square inch. Not one of us."

This honesty on the part of the professionals stood out because it was in contrast to the dishonesty around them. Once when Pell was state chairman a lawyer representing a large railroad came to see him. The railroad had wanted access to a dock in the city and had applied to the Dock Commission. Almost immediately after the application had been filed, a man came to the lawyer's office, represented himself as an employee of the Dock Commission and asked the lawyer for ten thousand dollars. If the railroad wanted access to the dock, it had to make that kind of illegal payment. The lawyer asked Pell what he should do. Pell told him not to pay. Shortly after, the lawyer returned to see Pell. The Dock Commission "employee" had come a second time to the lawyer's office and demanded the ten thousand dollars immediately. The lawyer admitted he was ready to pay. "I told him," said Pell, "to tell the man to go to the devil. He didn't want to do it. I told him that if he didn't do it, I would expose the whole story." Against that position, the lawyer had no choice; he refused to pay the money. The next day the railroad's application was granted as a matter of course. The Dock Commission "employee" turned out to be merely a hanger-on who had learned of the pending application and tried to use his information to pick up some fast money. The shocking part, thought Pell, was not that a two-bit crook tried to shake down a giant industry for money, "but that the heads of great American corporations are always ready to give it."

Herbert Pell had been taught that gentlemen went to the Tuxedo Park balls and wore white tie and tails and gambled for high stakes at the Gooseberry Island Club. Now he learned that the Democratic politicians were gentlemen of the very highest order. These were not the politicians he had met in Washington when he was in Congress, men who dealt with issues of foreign policy and domestic problems with nationwide significance. These local men dealt with the neighbor who needed a job, with the twelve-year-old youngster who had gotten into trouble with the police, with the widow who had no money to buy food for her children. They dealt with the politics of the most basic sort, helping people to live. There was Charles P. Murphy of Tammany Hall. According to the newspapers and to most histories of the period, he was a tyrant who ruled the Democratic party in New York with a whip made of patronage. Pell found him "a truly remarkable man." Pell does not recall Murphy's ever dictating to or even instructing any of the Democrats in Congress or in the state legislature. He listened to Pell, discussed matters with him and eventually the two men reached conclusions agreeable to both. "I almost invariably found that his advice and suggestions were good," said Pell.

Pell and Jerry Mahoney became close friends for life. When Pell later left politics, Mahoney became attorney for his business affairs and the two men saw each other frequently through the years. Pell also made friends with a big, bald-headed man named Jim Farley, who was then a Democratic county chairman. Pell came to Rockland and made some speeches to the local party faithful to help Farley over some of the hard times, and Pell earned himself a friend for life. "Jim never forgot that little service I made when he was county chairman and I was state chairman," said Pell. "Long after he was national chairman and I was nothing at all, he was ready to help."

But the professional politician with whom Herbert Pell came closest at the time and the man whom he admired the most was the commanding figure of that group of Democrats—Franklin Delano Roosevelt. There was much similarity between the two men. Both came from families representing America's landed aristocracy, and from that inheritance both had developed a keen sense of responsibility and a healthy skepticism of the rich, whom they had seen close up. Both had come from Upstate New York; their parents had been close friends. And the two men had been at Harvard together. Also, the two men enjoyed the rough-and-tumble New York politics. Neither man could be comfortable wearing a derby as Al Smith did, and "The Sidewalks of New York" was a little too sentimental for their tastes. But each enjoyed the camaraderie, the back-slapping good fellowship of clubhouse politics. Even Republicans concede that Democrats have more fun, and the fun begins at the local level. The men shuck their jackets, loosen their ties, tilt their chairs back, blow some foam off their beer and get down to work. To men like Roosevelt and Pell this New York City politics was a completely alien world. Although their backgrounds were such that they could never become a permanent part of such a world, they could not deny its attractiveness. They were neither the first nor the last to learn that New York is a nice place to visit even if they didn't want to live there.

When Pell became state chairman, Roosevelt already was a national figure. His distant relationship to Theodore Roosevelt had brought him early prominence. His role as Assistant Secretary of the Navy during the First World War and then as the Democratic vice presidential candidate in 1920 had added to his reputation as a political comer. There was no question, of course, that Pell wanted his old friend on the state party's executive committee. In September of 1921, Pell wrote to Roosevelt, who was vacationing at Campobello Island:

My dear Frank:

I should be very much obliged indeed if you would accept a position on the Executive Committee. I am writing this as an official invitation to confirm the conversation we had some time ago.

I hear from the Colliers that you are quite ill, but I sincerely hope that you will be in good shape again in the very near future.

An answer came back about ten days later addressed to "Dear Mr. Pell." It read:

Mr. Roosevelt while well on the road to recovery is still forbidden by his doctors to attempt to answer any correspondence but your note of Sept. 1 has been read to him and he asks me to write for him accepting your offer of a place on the Executive Committee and assuring you that you could count on him at all times to do everything he could to help the Democratic cause.

Mr. Roosevelt hopes to leave for New York in a few days but it will be some time I am afraid before he will be allowed to undertake any active work of any kind. As yet the doctors have not allowed him to sit up in bed even as they do not want to take any chance of a setback until he has made the very trying trip to his home.

Franklin Roosevelt had been struck with infantile paralysis and would be a physical cripple for the remainder of his life. The carefully and coldly calculated decision of his aide and personal kingmaker, Louis Howe, was to hide the seriousness of Roosevelt's illness. He was a potential

Presidential candidate and nothing must threaten that position. This became apparent in the stories that Howe managed to persuade the newspapers to run. On Friday, September 16, *The New York Times* ran a story on its front page announcing that Roosevelt had returned to New York the previous day suffering from poliomyelitis "which for more than a month has caused the loss of the use of both legs below the knees. Mr. Roosevelt was taken to the Presbyterian Hospital, Seventieth Street and Madison Avenue, where it was said that the attack was very mild and that Mr. Roosevelt would not be permanently crippled." The story quoted the Roosevelt family physician as saying "definitely . . . he will not be crippled. No one need have any fear of permanent injury from this attack." That was the first story the *Times* had run on the illness of the former Vice Presidential candidate. The second story ran the next day. It was one paragraph long and appeared on page 13 and said that Roosevelt's "condition showed improvement." That was the last story the *Times* ran on the Roosevelt illness.

Herbert Pell, greatly concerned over his friend's illness, was relieved by the positive reports in the press. The secrecy built around Roosevelt's present condition to protect his political potential had, of necessity, to close out the New York Democrats; even more than the public they would be quick to write off Roosevelt if they learned he was a permanent cripple. Wanting to make certain his friend did not feel left out, Pell sent him a letter in October inviting him to a meeting of the party's executive committee at two thirty. The letter also invited Franklin

(1) As a young man Herbert Claiborne Pell *(left)* enjoyed the best that the Gilded Age offered. He was related to the wealthy Lorillard tobacco family and grew up in Tuxedo Park, the development outside New York that epitomized American wealth at the turn of the century. (SENATOR CLAIBORNE PELL)

(2) This picture was taken on one of Pell's frequent trips to Europe. (SENATOR CLAIBORNE PELL)

(3) and (4) After attending Harvard for a while, Herbert Pell dropped out of college to pursue his cultural interests at his own speed. Not having to work, he traveled extensively in his twenties. As these pictures show, he was both a serious and a dashing young man. (SENATOR CLAIBORNE PELL)

(5) In 1915 Herbert Pell was considered a good "catch." He married Matilda Bigelow, a beautiful young woman from a socially prominent family. They had one child, Claiborne de Borda Pell, now the United States Senator from Rhode Island. (SENATOR CLAIBORNE PELL)

(6) Herbert Pell took great interest in his son's upbringing, even after he and Matilda were divorced in 1927. (SENATOR CLAIBORNE PELL)

(7) In 1918, Herbert Pell ran for Congress. A Democrat seeking to represent the Republican-dominated Silk Stocking District in Manhattan, he surprised everyone by winning. (SENATOR CLAIBORNE PELL)

(8) Shown at work, Pell was the picture of the elegant congressman. (LIBRARY OF CONGRESS)

(9) Denied reelection, Herbert Pell stayed in politics and became chairman of the New York State Democratic party. He is seated next to another young New York Democratic politician, Franklin D. Roosevelt, at a meeting of the state chieftains. (SENATOR CLAIBORNE PELL)

(10) Pell with F.D.R. and Al Smith. Although Pell was never very fond of Smith, he supported him as long as F.D.R. did.

(11) By the mid-1930s, Pell was in his fifties, remarried and out of politics entirely. He still traveled, now made his home in Newport, and watched with great pleasure the rising political career of his old friend Franklin Roosevelt. He occasionally wrote articles, but primarily he lived the comfortable life of a retired gentleman. (SENATOR CLAIBORNE PELL)

Roosevelt to a luncheon with Pell an hour earlier. When the letter came to the Roosevelt residence, someone—most likely Louis Howe—attached a note to it saying: "Mr. Pell had better wake up & hear the birdies!"

Franklin Roosevelt obviously thought so also, but he would not use that kind of language. He dictated a letter to "My dear Bertie." It read:

> I am awfully sorry but October 11th is rather too early a date for me to attempt to attend a meeting of the Executive Committee. I hope before long however to be back in the game.
>
> I am going to ask Mr. Howe to see you sometime and learn all that is doing in politics as I have got rather out of touch since I was taken ill.
>
> I regret also that I cannot enjoy the lunch which you so kindly suggest on that day.

Herbert Pell replied that he had never believed that Roosevelt was well enough to attend the meeting and that he was very happy to hear that Roosevelt would be back soon. "It will be a real pleasure to me both as a personal friend and as chairman of the state committee to see you well and strong in the near future," Pell said.

Franklin Roosevelt never became "well and strong" in the conventional sense; he barely was able to walk again. But his toughness showed through, overcoming his affliction. He did actively participate in the executive committee during the coming years and he carved himself a role in state politics. First it was as a nonparticipant who was willing to use his reputation where he thought it would help a candidate. In 1922, Al Smith wished to run for governor of New York again. He had been elected to a two-year term in 1918 and defeated in 1920. But Smith did not want to appear to be actively seeking the nomination; he now felt he should be the statesman loyally responding to his party's call. Roosevelt obliged. He wrote a private letter to Smith inquiring if Smith would be embarrassed by a public letter asking him to accept the gubernatorial nomination. Roosevelt knew the answer, but he wanted to go through the proper motions. Smith answered privately that he would not be embarrassed. Roosevelt's second letter then was a public one to Smith asking him to accept the gubernatorial nomination if the Democrats offered it to him—for the good of the party and the state. Roosevelt's national political eminence and his stature within the state Democratic party assured his public letter wide publicity. Smith then answered publicly and this too received wide publicity, allowing how for the good of the party and the state he would make the sacrifice and run again for public office.

By 1924, Roosevelt was ready to take the second step on the road back to political prominence. He reappeared on the public scene, making the famous "Happy Warrior" speech nominating Al Smith as the Democratic candidate for President at the national party convention. At this time Roosevelt became a great letter-writer, using the correspondence as a means of developing contacts with Democrats on a national scale. After the 1924 election, when the Democrats, led by John W. Davis, were beaten so badly, Roosevelt wrote a letter to every person who had been a delegate to the Democratic nominating convention. He asked their advice on party organization, explained his own ideas for strengthening the party nationally. And then he expressed his ideas on what the philosophy of the Democratic party was and how it should be made into a national party.

Something must be done [he wrote], and done now to bring home to the voting population the true basis and sound reasons why the Democratic Party is entitled to national confidence as a governing party. There is room for but two parties. The Republican leadership has stood and still stands for conservatism, for the control of the social and economic structure of the nation by a small minority of handpicked associates. The Democratic Party organization is made more difficult by the fact that it is made up in chief by men and women who are unwilling to stand still but who often differ as to the methods and lines of progress. Yet we are unequivocally the party of progress and liberal thought. Only by uniting can we win.

It is not, I take it, a matter of personalities or candidates, but a matter of principles. If in the next three years we stop wasting time in booming or opposing this man or that for a nomination four years away, and devote ourselves instead to organizing for party principles, for the taking advantage of our opponents' errors and omis-

sions, and for presenting our own logical and progressive
program, we shall gain the confidence of the country;
and find it far easier to choose a representative and
successful ticket when the time comes. . . .

Roosevelt's loyalty in these years when he was working
for the rejuvenation of the Democratic party was to Al
Smith. This was apparent to all at the 1922 state convention in Syracuse when the contest for the gubernatorial
nomination was between Smith and William Randolph
Hearst, the newspaper publisher. Some men start their
careers with a vision of themselves and then gradually re-
shape that vision to something beyond themselves. Franklin
Roosevelt was such a man, beginning his political career
with a vision of himself imitating his cousin Theodore's
career but then gradually altering his vision to see, instead of his success, the task that had to be done. Hearst,
in contrast, began his career with a vision beyond himself.
His newspapers, in the style of journalism he stole from
Joseph Pulitzer and then molded with his own brand to
make "yellow journalism" synonymous with the Hearst
press, were aimed at something more than the glorification
of William Randolph Hearst—at first. They informed and
entertained, and led and fought for the people who had
been ignored by the establishment press. But eventually
Hearst could not limit himself to others and began to use
his influence and power to further his own ambitions.
And his ambitions were political; undoubtedly he hoped
to be President, more Emperor, as he saw it. His first step

was to become governor of New York. And the target date was the 1922 convention. It was here that he was stopped by Franklin Roosevelt and Herbert Pell, who were backing Al Smith.

"Who will be the next Democratic candidate for Governor?" a reporter asked Herbert Pell in March of 1922 when the state chairman was in Syracuse for a conference.

"I don't know," answered Pell, with a shrug of his shoulders. "The Hearst boom, so-called, never got much of a start."

His remark was worth a couple of laughs. It was well known that the Hearst "boom" was running as well as Hearst money could push it. His men were traveling through Upstate New York drumming up support for their boss. Hearst believed he had the New York City Democrats pretty well lined up behind him because he controlled the city's patronage through Mayor Hylan, who was beginning to act more and more like the publisher's stooge. Hearst needed stronger upstate backing and thought he could insure it by buying two newspapers, one in Syracuse and the other in Rochester; thus was editorial support assured.

Hylan showed his support for Hearst by writing a letter to Herbert Pell, which Hylan conveniently made available to the press, suggesting that Pell organize the party along lines acceptable to Hearst. Pell played at being confused by the Hylan ploy. He acknowledged receiving it but professed not to understand the mayor's intention. He said he had heard nothing from Hearst as to what was "acceptable" to him and, of course, could not say how he would react to a proposition prior to its being made to him. "Obviously," he told the press, "being the head of a regular party organization, I cannot engage in the formation of a nonpartisan or a bipartisan movement." Mayor Hylan had spoken of "purifying" the ballot and what, the reporters asked, did the state chairman have to say to that?

"Unquestionably it is the duty of every citizen to vote for the principles in which he believes."

"Did you draw from the letter the inference that either Hylan or Hearst would be nominated?"

"I have my own personal choice, of course, but I cannot give it."

Then Herbert Pell thrust the political knife as deeply into the Hearst candidacy as he could. "The Republican newspapers," he tossed out casually to the reporters, "seem to be working as hard as they can to nominate Hearst." The inference of the remark was clear: the Republicans figured Hearst was the easiest Democrat to beat.

The Republican newspapers may have been correct. Hearst had had his day, years earlier. There was now little support for him beyond what he could buy. In July, for example, his organization scheduled a women's luncheon for him in Westchester County. But the luncheon, although widely publicized, had to be canceled; not enough women wanted to attend.

Then came the correspondence, private and public, between Roosevelt and Smith, which set Smith up for the gubernatorial nomination. Mayor Hylan tried to counter this alliance by sending a second public letter to Pell, this one urging the nomination of Hearst as the one man who could unify the Democratic party in the state and perhaps lead the party nationally in 1924.

This letter came a few days before the convention opened in Syracuse on September 28, a Thursday. On Tuesday the Tammany contingent boarded the Empire State Express at 8:30 A.M. for convention city. Leading them was Charles Murphy and following were John McCooey of Brooklyn and others of the party faithful. And on whom were the leaders going to bestow the political nod? Murphy winked back and said: "You never can tell."

The Tammany people actually had a problem. Hearst was cutting a wide swath through their city because of his control of Hylan, but they doubted strongly that he could win a statewide election. Smith, in contrast, was a popular vote getter. He probably would have been re-elected in 1920 except for the Harding sweep and had the best chance of recapturing the state house for the Democrats. That he was not very popular with the Tammany boys, much preferring to establish his own power lines in the state rather than deal with the Tammany organization, was a factor that Murphy could overlook if he saw sufficient Democratic candidates riding to victory with Smith.

The traditional political solution to the problem the Democrats faced was to compromise: nominate Smith for governor and Hearst for United States Senator. What could be sweeter, the politicians asked. Everyone is happy! Wednesday, the day before the convention opened, Hylan and the other Hearst men let out the word that their man was willing to settle for the Senate nomination. The compromise seemed ideal. The ticket would be headed by the most popular candidate the Democrats had and the second most important spot would be filled by a man who controlled much of the press in the state and who would spend wildly to insure victory. But they all reckoned without Al Smith.

Smith hated Hearst. They had been political rivals for years. Smith distrusted Hearst's motives. He personally didn't like Hearst and, a devout Catholic, he was repelled by Hearst's extramarital activities. But more than that was involved. In 1919 the Hearst papers had accused Smith, then governor, of being in league with the milk trust. As a result, the Hearst press charged, the children of New York City starved for milk. Smith could not tolerate a man who had accused him of starving children. The leaders of the Democratic party begged him to reconsider his personal hostility toward Hearst. If he consented to joining a Smith-Hearst ticket, victory was assured, they argued. Furthermore, Smith owed it to the party, to the state, to the nation and to anyone else they could invoke in the smoke-filled hotel rooms.

But Smith was adamant. "Say," he answered, "don't you think I have any pride?" He was not joining a Smith-Hearst ticket. That was final.

Next the politicians went to Smith's closest political associates—Franklin Roosevelt and his wife Eleanor—to beg their intercession. But the Roosevelts were firm in supporting Smith, "They would recognize no possibility of anyone else," Herbert Pell recalled. "Eventually it was their firmness that got the nomination for Al Smith. If it

had not been for them, in my opinion, he would certainly
have been beaten and instead of going on to be four-times
governor of New York and candidate for President he
would have been today almost as forgotten as John Dix."

Pell himself liked neither Hearst nor Smith. His refusal
to jump on Hearst's manufactured bandwagon had helped
keep that wagon in the shed. Of the two men, however,
Pell preferred Smith and he joined Roosevelt in backing
Smith at the 1922 convention. And so the professionals
had to give in to the Smith faction led by Franklin Roosevelt with Chairman Pell's support. Roosevelt could have
swung his support to whomsoever he chose and won for
himself, if he had so desired, the publicity machine of
William Randolph Hearst. But Roosevelt was loyal to his
old friend Smith and continued loyal for many years, until
at last there was no reason to be. Hearst withdrew as a
candidate for public office. His personal political career
was finished. He spent the remainder of his days watching
the financial and professional disintegration of his newspaper empire, playing at being a theatrical entrepreneur and
pretending that he still wielded political power.

Al Smith was elected governor and the state Democrats
were started on a victory splurge that lasted until Thomas
E. Dewey was elected governor in 1942. One issue that
troubled Smith in that campaign and for several years
after was prohibition. America had gone legally dry and
illegally wet. With his derby hat cocked at an angle and his
association with New York City famous for its speakeasies,
Smith was believed by the nation to be a "wet." That
perhaps would not have concerned him except that he

hoped to be the Democratic party's candidate for President, possibly in 1924 and certainly by 1928, and was trying to play down the wet image.

Herbert Pell, however, did not see prohibition that way. In a speech once to a group of "drys," he said: "If any of you believe that Prohibition is a good thing or that Prohibition is the most important issue before the people, you will do well to vote against us because we will do nothing for you. You can hope for nothing from us." Pell believed that prohibition was wrong, but this was not only a statement of principle. It was a shrewd political ploy. He had given the Republicans to the Anti-Saloon League. Most Americans, at least in New York State, which was his concern, were tired of prohibition and looked forward to its demise. From Pell they understood that the Democratic party was the political means of ending it. "The Democratic Party in this state," he said, "is not committed to a wet policy. Our State platform merely demanded the right for the individual states to say what constituted an intoxicating beverage within the bounds of reason." That made the ending of prohibition not only a fight between the wets and the drys but also a struggle for states' rights. The Democrats would have their liquor and their Jeffersonian principles—an unbeatable combination.

But prohibition was a gnat compared to the ogre that hung before the politicians in the 1920s. This was the Ku Klux Klan. An anomaly of American life is that the American people can respond to the best displayed before them but also respond to the worst at times. The Klan represented the worst as it appealed to the vilest of man's prejudices, and the 1920s was a time when it was most popular. It controlled political fortunes, both of men and of parties. Few dared defy it. While a New York City politician might have been safe from it, a New York State politician appeared at its mercy because of its hold in Long Island and in other areas. Against this background, Herbert Pell responded to a request for a statement from the *Pittsburgh Courier*, a Negro newspaper. Writing in his official capacity as chairman of the Democratic party in New York State, Pell said:

Freedom of speech and the political equality of all citizens are part of the civic creed of every decent American, and we may be sure that any group or organization which is attempting to organize for political action along racial or religious lines is fundamentally opposed to the best principles of Americanism. An organization appealing to prejudice and hate in the long run cannot have a good influence, no matter for what purpose it may be organized or what class of men its members may be, and no such organization can expect anything but serious opposition from the Democratic Party, the principles of which it attacks.

I do not take much stock in the extreme theories of race which have been promulgated in recent years. Of course there are congenital distinctions between men, and probably between races, but I can not believe that any one race today is made up entirely of supermen, while none worthy of preservation exist in any other, and I certainly do not believe that it requires a hundred armed nordic supermen to overcome one unarmed individual belonging to a race destined to succumb. Nor do I believe that the laws and institutions developed by the American people in a century and a half are incapable of being operated by my countrymen in such a way as to produce justice and to maintain order.

The Klan represented hate for the minority, but it was more than hate. Arthur Schlesinger, Jr., has written that "rural America was digging in for its rearguard stand in the twenties" and "the Klan was the cutting edge of rural protest." It was the means used by farmers and small-town residents to display their fear of what they saw coming —the blacks, the Jews, the Catholics, the immigrants, the factories, the urban sprawl, the turbulence of modern society. And as they displayed their fear, they ignored their problems. Problems are countered by being met rather than being cursed, but this was not understood in the 1920s.

Too strong for any political party to buck, the Klan in 1924 came closest to meeting a national challenge at the Democratic convention. The convention platform was intended to strike against extremist groups but unoffensively. They were to be described but not specifically mentioned. This was so the Democrats from the small towns and rural communities could go home and claim to their hooded friends that the Democratic party was against everybody but them. There was a motion at the convention to identify the Klan by name, but it failed by one vote. That single-vote deficiency was the height of liberalism and decency that year achieved by the national Democratic party.

Locally it was a different story. Herbert Pell hated the Klan. It represented everything he understood America to be against. At the national convention he had wanted to speak against the Klan. As one whose ancestors, on both sides of his family, had come to America long before the Declaration of Independence, he believed himself eminently qualified to attack the Klan. But Franklin Roosevelt by this time already had become the state's most prominent Democratic leader and he was controlling the delegation as the leader of Al Smith's forces. He vetoed Pell's proposed speech. The fight over the Klan apparently was going well without adding any additional oratory, and Roosevelt perhaps did not consider it wise for a strong anti-Klan speech to come from a Democrat backing a Catholic for President. Pell's speech probably would not have swayed the crowd. He was a good speaker, but only a Democrat of national stature and respect could have influenced the convention. One such was William Jennings Bryan. Many of those attending the 1924 convention remembered when Bryan had called forth a new generation of reformers with his cry against "a cross of gold." But this year the man who had led the fight against the excesses of the Gilded Age was a part of its remnant. "My friends," he told the Democrats, "it requires more courage to fight the Republican Party than it does to fight the Ku Klux Klan." The Democrats, as a result, lost both fights.

Pell watched the shenanigans and the cowardice at the

national convention with a sense of shame and concern. His shame was for people who had not stood up when they were needed. His concern was for the party's future. It could not duck issues and expect people to support it. When he had been named state chairman, he had understood his responsibility was to lead and he said then that "I do not urge anyone to vote the Democratic ticket merely because it is the Democratic ticket. . . . It is the duty of the public intelligently to judge fitness." He would allow his fitness to be judged.

Long Island at this time was an area of small farms and a few resorts. With the exception of some wealthy New Yorkers who owned estates, it was home to a largely rural population that looked to the past rather than concern itself with the future. The Klan was particularly strong on Long Island, and a center for it was the community of Smithtown on the North Shore. A local newspaper editor, Lawrence Deutzman of the Smithtown *Messenger*, wrote to Pell to ask him the Democratic party's position on the Klan. The Deutzman letter was the opportunity Herbert Pell had been waiting for. Using the stationery of the Democratic state committee and signing his name as state chairman, Pell wrote:

In answer to your letter, I tell you that there can be no doubt as to the stand of the Democratic Party in relation to the Ku Klux Klan or any other organization gotten up to promote religious or racial prejudice in this country.

The Ku Klux Klan violates the fundamental principles of the American Government by its fight against tolerance and by its interference with and open contempt of the constitutionally organized courts of law. Its claim to be the special guardian of the interests and traditions of our country is gross impertinence. A flag, which has flown boldly and openly before the world for a century and a half, does not require the support of men too weak, too low, too despicable, or too cowardly to show their faces.

Deutzman had been particularly active in fighting the Klan, and Herbert Pell knew that his answer would be prominently displayed in the Smithtown newspaper and probably in other Long Island papers. To assure even better publicity, Pell sent copies of his letter to every paper in New York "so there could be no possible doubt where we stood—where I stood."

There could be no question that the Democratic Party in the state at its convention would have to denounce the Klan by name. Herbert Pell as its chairman had assured that. And the party following his lead at the September convention leaped with enthusiasm to its responsibility. "We unequivocally condemn the Ku Klux Klan," said its platform.

[The Klan] seeks to subject the sovereign State to the will and wishes of its own invisible empire. It further seeks to create intolerance by secret appeal and masked attack against particular classes, based on race, religion or color. Its objects and its activities are diametrically opposed to the fundamental principles upon which our Government was founded and to the liberal principles of the Democratic Party. We decline its cooperation. We spurn its support.

The New York Republican party could not bring itself to do as well in 1924. It opposed in its platform "any organization, whether it be called Ku Klux Klan or by any other name," that challenges the doctrine of tolerance. "Moreover," it continued, "we condemn any candidate or party that endeavors to make political capital out of such an issue, and, while posing as its champion, betrays the cause of liberty by a direct appeal to racial and religious groups." Even that statement, more an attack on the Democratic party for acknowledging that the Klan existed than an assault on the Klan, came reluctantly. *The New York Times* reported that the Klan plank in the Republican platform was "contrary to the wishes and judgment of at least one-half of the delegates to the convention. . . . This plank was inserted in the platform by a narrow margin of one vote in the Committee on Resolutions, after one of the hottest fights in Republican state convention annals." The chairman of the convention was Ogden Mills. He favored the plank and realized that as weak as it was, it still might get voted down. He rammed it through the convention by shutting off debate and calling for a vote, then declaring that the plank had passed before anyone could challenge his count of the shouted chorus of ayes and nays.

That Republican convention nominated Theodore Roosevelt—"Little Teddy," the son of the late President—as its gubernatorial candidate. Whatever it was his father had, Little Teddy missed it completely. When Herbert Pell heard that the Republicans had named Roosevelt, he hurriedly told his fellow Democrats who were just gathering for their convention. "They broke out in cheers," he said. "When they entered the hall they felt that we could win only by a miracle," Pell continued. "They left looking as if the miracle had happened. It had."

The year 1924 was a Republican year nationally. Calvin Coolidge, the Republican candidate for President, did well in New York, winning the state by a million votes. Ordinarily that should have been enough to carry the GOP gubernatorial candidate to victory. But Smith beat young Theodore Roosevelt by 140,000 votes, a particularly impressive victory in view of the Coolidge sweep. Pell described the Smith victory as "the most remarkable phenomenon of vote-getting strength in the history of American politics." It wasn't all that, but it was a brilliant showing.

By his victory, Al Smith was "Mr. Democrat" in New York State. Never a Tammany man, he was a political loner who built an organization out of personal loyalties. Men like Franklin Roosevelt supported him for his accomplishments rather than for his associations. But because he was a loner, there always was trouble between him and the state organization headed by Pell, dating from Herbert Pell's being named state chairman over Smith's man.

Pell made clear through the years that he was his own man. In 1918 Smith had moved the party's headquarters from New York City to Syracuse because he was wooing upstate Democrats; he believed the New York City Democrats would back him no matter where the party headquarters were. But when he became chairman, Pell moved the state headquarters back to New York. In the following years Smith and Pell had different goals. Smith was interested primarily in being elected governor, operating the kind of administration he wanted in Albany, and smoothing the way to win his party's Presidential nomination. Pell wanted a gubernatorial victory for his party; but more, he wanted to build a statewide party.

Smith was gobbling up campaign contributions for his own races and drying up funds for other Democratic candidates, or so Pell believed. Also, Pell began to suspect that Smith was being too cozy with the Republicans. In exchange for needed votes in the state legislature, Smith did favors for the Republicans, not an unusual practice among politicians both then and now. Pell believed, however, that Al Smith carried it beyond normal levels. Rising young Democrats were bypassed by Smith in patronage matters; Smith dealt with the Republicans instead. Pell also was disturbed by what he considered Smith's pussyfooting on issues like prohibition and the Klan. On the other side, Smith had some justification in believing himself to be the state's Democratic party. He had led the ticket and could claim that most Democrats would have been defeated without him. Jeremiah Mahoney many years later remarked that Al Smith was a more practical politician than was Herbert Pell.

Certainly if practical politics means being on good terms with the party's most powerful politician, Pell was not practical at all. He made clear to the Democratic leaders that he was dissatisfied with the way the 1924 campaign had been run. Pell argued that Smith should have given more of his personal support to Democratic candidates running for the legislature and other local offices. He attributed the Democratic defeats in the Syracuse and Rochester mayoralty elections to Smith's lack of interest in those races.

The dispute between Smith and Pell came to a head over the nomination for mayor of New York City. John Hylan, still Hearst's errand boy, had to be toppled as mayor. Smith wanted James J. Walker, or Jimmy Walker as he later became known in Tammany legend. Pell wanted a man named John Delaney. "I had opposed Jimmy Walker for mayor," said Pell. "I didn't want him at all. Along with McCooey I worked against him."

Shortly afterward, Pell resigned as state chairman. He had no choice. He could not stay as chairman against the wishes of Smith, and Pell had done very little to win Smith's favor. "I was not getting on very well with Al Smith, who was becoming more and more conservative," said Pell. Whether or not Smith was more conservative, he was the leader, and Pell was out.

While conceding the dispute with Smith, Herbert Pell also offered an additional explanation. "I didn't want to be too much of a specialist," he said. "One of the things that impelled me to resign was that some episode happened in France, and I immediately wondered how that would affect the French vote along the St. Lawrence River. I thought that if I was getting to think so much of politics, I had better get out because all my life I've hated the thought of being a specialist about anything."

Some years later Herbert Pell offered another description of himself which might have more bearing on his quitting the state chairmanship. Writing to his son, Claiborne, in 1943, he said: "My worst quality was, of course, an almost uncontrollable unwillingness to work except sporadically." Herbert Pell had announced his resignation as state chairman in December of 1925, and it took effect the next month. He was forty-one years old at the time. Most men by that age are well on their way to achieving what will be the success of their lives. Herbert Pell, however, chose to stop short, to end his career as a politician before he stepped on the road to success. Whether it was because Smith was too conservative or because Pell objected to being a specialist or because of his unwillingness to work consistently, he stopped short. He did not care enough about success to engage in the prolonged hard work that the achievement of success usually requires. Never before had it been required of him, not as a child at Tuxedo, not as a student at Harvard, not as a young man of the world. And he could not develop it as a mature man. So he was a connoisseur, even a dabbler. Unlike most persons, however, he would have a second chance to prove himself. And this next time he seized his opportunity and tenaciously pursued it.

Shortly after Herbert Pell resigned as state chairman, his father died. Herbert spent the spring clearing up the estate, summered at Newport and then sailed in the fall to join his mother in Italy. Before sailing for France on the French liner *Paris*, he was chatting with some newspapermen. Herbert Pell had been around politics and reporters too long to believe he was speaking off-the-record when he said that Ogden Mills is "the most unselfish candidate either party has nominated for fifteen years." Now Mills had set his sights higher; he was the Republican candidate for governor of New York—to oppose Al Smith. Although Pell added to the newsmen that he disagreed with Ogden Mills's politics, that was largely ignored in the light of his accolade. Al Smith never could forget that Herbert Pell always had been Herbert Pell's man rather than Al Smith's. Some years later Pell wrote a letter to Smith. Smith replied:

Dear Herbert,
I read your letter along with a number of others. My mail is very heavy and my work equally so and I find it difficult to be able to answer or even acknowledge all of the letters.

The relationship between two of the most prominent Democrats of the 1920s in New York State had come to an end; both men apparently preferred it that way.

Herbert Pell had been active in politics for almost fourteen years, ever since that day in 1912 when he returned from Europe and heard at the Tuxedo clubhouse that Harry Hooker was for Theodore Roosevelt. This excerpt from a speech of his is a commentary on what he had learned in those years:

Today the average office holder owes his place to an organized group of political workers which, regarding politics as a business usually interlocked with other businesses, has taken up, as a private enterprise, the labor or governing abandoned by us to attend to our own affairs. This group, which is usually called the machine, did not reach its entrenched position in America through conquest, as so many seem to infer, but simply and solely by the default of the people. The ordinary citizen, through his apathy and lack of interest in public matters, has abdicated his sovereignty, and without a general vigilance and a much more serious and sustained interest in the commonwealth than he now has, he will never regain it. As long as the American people frankly show that they do not want to govern themselves in their own interests, they will be ruled by volunteers working for their personal advancement. Somebody is always ready to control the State, and, if the citizens don't want to do it, there will always be men delighted to take on the job for a consideration. Short spurts of popular excitement will never be worth much; they may start good work, but they never can see it through. . . .

3 AFTER SPENDING SOME TIME VISITING HIS mother in Italy, in 1926, Herbert Pell went to Paris, where his wife, Matilda, joined him. On February 26, 1927, in accordance with their mutual agreement, Matilda Bigelow Pell filed a petition for divorce in Paris. A month later the divorce was granted. On Friday, June 3, 1927, *The New York Times* carried the following society item:

Mrs. Matilda Bigelow Pell . . . was married yesterday afternoon in the Madison Avenue Baptist Church . . . to Lieut. Commander Hugo W. Koehler, U.S.N., who is stationed at Newport, R.I.

Although they had been acquaintances for several years, their marriage yesterday came as a surprise to many of their friends. When a rumor circulated a week ago that Mrs. Pell would marry a naval officer she forcefully denied it. The couple obtained their marriage license at the Municipal Building only a few hours before the ceremony. . . . Following their honeymoon, Commander and Mrs. Koehler will live in Newport.

A little more than two weeks later, on Monday, June 20, the *Times*, which seemed to be giving its society pages over to the Pells, carried this item:

Relatives of Mrs. Bigelow Tilton and Herbert Claiborne Pell have been informed by cable of their marriage in Paris on last Saturday. No previous announcement had been made of the marriage plans of the couple.

The bride, who is the former Miss Mildred Bigelow, daughter of Mr. and Mrs. Poultney Bigelow of this city and Malden-on-Hudson, visited this city last winter after an absence of six years in Europe. As Olive Bigelow she has acquired an international reputation as an artist. Her paintings were exhibited last Winter in New York, and they have been shown at art exhibitions in London.

The present Mrs. Pell is the granddaughter of the late John Bigelow, Minister to France under Lincoln and Johnson. Recently she has been making her home at 44 Gloucester Square, London. She is a niece of Mrs. Guest, the wife of the Hon. Lionel G. Guest of that city. She has two daughters, Miss Mildred Tilton, the elder, was presented at Buckingham Palace last Summer and later made her debut in London. She spent the Winter studying music in France. The other daughter is Pyrma Tilton. Mrs. J. Francis A. Clark of 903 Park Avenue and Newport and Mrs. Ward Melville of Brooklyn are Mrs. Pell's sisters. . . .

Herbert Pell's first wife and his second wife were cousins, giving rise to the family joke that Herbert Pell "only marries Bigelows."

Whatever the cause of the divorce, and it was undoubtedly many causes rather than one, Herbert Pell and his first wife always had considerable respect for each other in the following years. Pell was amiable and friendly with his wife's second husband and was kind to the son they later had. As Hugh Koehler grew up, he began collecting stamps, and Herbert Pell often thought to send him one from some far-off place. And young Hugh often wrote to his mother's first husband, whom he referred to as "Uncle Bertie," and always included his best wishes to "Aunt Olive."

Matilda had legal custody of Claiborne, but the two parents shared in his upbringing. He was now entering his teens. He often visited his father and his stepmother and his schooling was a matter of great interest to Herbert Pell. When Claiborne was old enough for boarding school, Herbert sent him to St. George's in Newport. To be near his son, Herbert Pell had his summer home there reconditioned for the winter, had it heated throughout, and lived there a couple of years while his son attended school. These were the depression years of the 1930s and private school tuition was very low or in some cases nonexistent. "The boys would pay very frequently by notes of their parents, redeemable sometime in the future, which may or may not have ever been redeemed," Herbert Pell recalled later. "Of course the boy whose bills were paid when they were presented was a valuable character. Thus I was able to do a great deal more with Claiborne than I would have in normal times."

Claiborne came to visit his father in the big Newport house every Sunday afternoon for lunch, usually bringing about four of his friends with him. Lunch was turkey and ice cream with chocolate sauce, the kind of lunch young schoolboys like. Then Herbert Pell and the boys withdrew to the library, as was customary for gentlemen after the main meal of the day, for conversation. They talked about the boys' lessons and about Herbert Pell's personal experiences: he was now entering his fifties and knew the European continent intimately. But often he steered the conversation around to education and the purpose of the schooling the young men were undertaking. He would "try to impress them with the fact that what they were studying at school was not simply acquiring a key to college, but that it was worthwhile."

After St. George's, Claiborne Pell went to Princeton, where Pell's friends on the faculty kept him advised of his son's progress. Edward S. Corwin, professor of political science, wrote: "I now have reports from your son's instructors on all of his courses. I find that he is getting on very well in his history, his English and also in his work in this department; but that he is doing indifferently in geology and rather poorly in philosophy. . . . Maybe he had better leave philosophy alone after this." And Robert G. Albion, assistant dean of the faculty, reported: "Claiborne is doing a good job this term; his attendance record is excellent, and he received only one minor warning in history."

When his son was at Princeton, Herbert Pell was a diplomat, living abroad, and he spoke to his son through the medium of long, carefully written letters. They are models of the now-middle-aged gentleman advising his son on the proper standards of behavior. In one letter he says:

> I have no fear of you drinking to excess. You are not the type of person who would naturally enjoy that sort of thing. Neither was I and I had plenty of opportunity. The real risk is that at college and during a good part of your twenties, you will find a large number of the young men with whom you are thrown will be pretty sound drinkers and terrible time wasters. I spent a great deal of this time abroad and when I finally settled in this country I was nearly thirty and by that time the heavier drinkers had already dropped so far that I would not choose them as new friends or particularly desire to renew their acquaintance. . . .

In this letter Herbert Pell acknowledged that a person who drinks a lot can appear attractive but insisted that "it is absolutely certain that eventually his weakness of character will make you regret that you have chosen him for a favorite. Of course you should not abandon an old friend however desirable it may appear to do so but it is unwise to select a new one knowing that abandonment will in the future appear desirable."

In another letter, Herbert Pell sent Claiborne his allowance, and then said: "It is possible that you will want more when you are at college. I know that you are careful and economical but I do not want you to feel that you are unable to keep up with your friends. You should treat them as often as they treat you and live and dress in a way that will not be conspicuous either way. . . ."

Herbert Pell went on to explain the value of having sufficient funds. "If you are not able to keep up with your friends," he wrote, "you will either be a sponge which is unpleasant or else find yourself unduly limited in the choice of your companions. If you are too lavish, you will find yourself nothing but a hero of suckers who will leave you as gulls will leave a piece of floating swill when a more succulent morsel appears." He continued in that letter:

> In your intercourse with people I am sure that you will never deny your convictions but there is no reason for an intelligent man to fight for his whims and it is very important to remember that everything must be taken in its due order. There is much more good accomplished in the world by those who work for small changes which can be attained than by uncompromising Utopians.

And following that advice, Herbert Pell added: "That is one of the reasons I am supporting Franklin Roosevelt instead of Norman Thomas."

Herbert Pell was, of course, instructing his son in the art of being a gentleman. It was the art of learning self-restraint, camaraderie and, ultimately, accomplishment.

Herbert Pell never ceased to be proud of his son. To Claiborne's mother he wrote in 1940: "I have just received Claiborne's telegram saying that he is graduating in the second group with honors. I was more pleased than I can say." And to a friend Herbert Pell was also the boastful father. "Claiborne will be twenty-two in a few days," he wrote. "He is not quite as tall as I—about 6'3" and considerably lighter than I was at his age. He is handsome and has just graduated from Princeton. . . . He graduated with honors, that is to say Cum Laude. His thesis was one of fifteen out of three hundred selected for exhibition, and he also received a certificate from their school of public affairs, which is a very difficult thing to do. I hope he will go into government service at some time, and I shall probably commission him as a courier and send him off on some trips."

When Herbert Pell had retired from politics in the 1920s, divorced and remarried, he had settled down to the life of elegance he had known so intimately twenty years earlier. "I did very little politically," he said. "I lived in Newport and traveled, usually going away in the summer during the social season." And he traveled exceedingly well, as always. In 1927 he had a car, a Minerva, built in Belgium by the d'Itieren company. The cost was about ten thousand dollars and the car was at the time considered the best touring car in Europe. That was eminent status in the late 1920s, which were, as Pell described them: "the culminant period of the millionaire epoch."

Although he was not personally involved in politics during those years, he cheered from the sidelines. When Franklin Roosevelt was nominated for governor of New York in 1928 and began his climb to American and world leadership, Herbert Pell wrote him a congratulatory note: "I give you my most heartfelt good wishes, reinforced by a small contribution which I am enclosing." Roosevelt was appreciative. "My dear Bertie," he answered. "It is delightful to get your letter just before this campaign closes and I only wish that you were here to take part in the excitement of this close race."

Roosevelt was elected governor of New York in what turned out to be not a close race after all, an election that made him—because of New York's high rank among the states and among the delegations belonging to the electoral college—a presidential candidate in 1932. From Paris, Pell wrote to his old friend of his inaugural address. "The extracts . . . are most interesting . . ." said Bertie Pell to Franklin Roosevelt ". . . and it is a real pleasure to see how strong a position can be made by a man of courage and intelligence. Of course, I am more of a radical than you. . . ."

Pell admired Franklin Roosevelt and Theodore Roosevelt and Woodrow Wilson "not for their innovations but because what they did was the only possible way of preserving the old system. These three men represented an effort to keep the American system as a going concern. . . ." Herbert Pell, who had been brought up in the days of the Gilded Age when wealth made right, who had seen firsthand the economics of those such as Nelson Aldrich and the politics of Washington and New York, had developed a pessimism about the future of the American free enterprise system. He understood that the threat to its existence came from those who benefited from it, when they abused it. The Republican administrations in the 1920s had been the keystone of this abuse. The Teapot Dome scandals—the whole atmosphere in Washington of political deals over poker hands was corrupting the system. Herbert Pell came to believe in Franklin Roosevelt because Roosevelt best fitted this description of the type of President America needed:

> Not only an administrator, but a leader—a pathfinder, a blazer to the trail to the high road that will avoid the bottomless morass of crass materialism that has engulfed so many of the great civilizations of the past. It is the privilege of Democracy not only to offer such a man, but to offer him as the surest leader to victory. To stand upon the ramparts and die for our principles is heroic. To sally forth to battle and win for our principles is something more than heroic.

The words are Franklin Roosevelt's, part of his 1924 "Happy Warrior" speech nominating Al Smith for the Presidency, but they describe the kind of national leader Roosevelt himself became much more than they described anyone else.

Pell also had become a believer in what a later generation described as the "new politics." In this kind of politics the call transcended the old traditional cries, to appeal, instead, to the voter's intelligence. In 1929 he advised his old colleague Jerry Mahoney:

The more I consider public affairs in this country, the more I realize that the effort to maintain a liberal party is as certain to fail here, as it failed in England and in every other country during the last few years. I need not say that I, personally, regret this very much, but we must face facts.

The old idea that the government should maintain order and justice, favoring none and recognizing no favorite class, is I regret to say, over, and any political organization which fails to realize this is certain to lose strength year by year.

However powerful we may be at the present time, especially in New York City, we cannot hope to be a factor in the nation or even in the state or city, unless we appeal to intelligent people, facing actualities. Personalities will get us nowhere. Pleasant and popular political dramatists hardly count and are usually afflicted by the artistic temperament that makes the life of a grand opera impressario a burden.

There were also notes to and from Franklin Roosevelt: "Dear Bertie; Thanks for your nice note. We are all going strong!" And there was the indignation of an experienced politician and mature citizen over developments in his state and nation: "I am very strongly of the opinion that the Democratic Party has disgracefully mismanaged the prohibition situation in New York State" by allowing the Republicans to avoid the onus of having been the dry party, Pell wrote. "There is a grand cheer to destroy our Navy in the United States in the interest of the income tax payer and of the Evangelicals, to do away with any possible defense that we might have in case of war. But when it comes to taking our part in any organized effort to preserve peace, to maintain justice and to help international relations, we refuse it with scorn. It all seems crazy to me."

By 1931 he had become a permanent resident of Newport and from there he began to support the Presidential candidacy of Franklin Roosevelt not only, he told Roosevelt, "because you are an old friend but primarily as a citizen of the United States who does not want to be forced into the Socialist organization but who unquestionably will go there if a tame Democrat is nominated." When Roosevelt was nominated, Pell quickly came forth with ideas. To James Farley, the former Rockland County Democrat once befriended by State Chairman Pell and who now managed Roosevelt's campaign, Pell wrote a long letter. "May I suggest that it would be a very good thing if [Roosevelt] would call together the Legislature of the State of New York and recommend in the State a three year moratorium on principle payment for all mortgages now recorded. I am not advocating this primarily as a political move, although it could not fail to be successful in that direction." Pell continued that the country was being "crushed by bank mortgages which are being ruthlessly foreclosed." He added that "I own some mortgages, but I do not feel that it is decent to oppress unlucky fellow citizens overwhelmed by the Hoover crash." The letter was answered politely, as were all his letters; likewise his appeals in Rhode Island for Democratic support of Roosevelt and his articles in the *North American Review* calling for Roosevelt's election were all politely appreciated. But Herbert Pell basically was out of politics. He had made the choice in 1926 with his retirement and his lengthy stays abroad. Obviously, although he apparently never acknowledged it, he missed the political arena. Whatever he later said about leaving politics because he did not wish to become a specialist, he was having second thoughts in the early 1930s when Franklin Roosevelt moved into the Presidency.

If he was not involved in that race for the White House, however, he well understood its implications. Walter Lippmann, who should have known better because of his association with Roosevelt through the years, had opposed Roosevelt's candidacy because, Lippmann said: "Franklin D. Roosevelt is no crusader. He is no tribune of the people. He is no enemy of entrenched privilege. He is a pleasant man who, without any important qualifications for the office, would very much like to be President." Herbert Pell did not make Lippmann's mistake of underestimating Roosevelt. Shortly after the Roosevelt election, Pell wrote:

> The election was the acceptance and not the repudiation of leadership. The confidence of the people who have elected him has raised Franklin Roosevelt far above the demands of any individual who has assisted him. And of one thing we can be definitely sure: during the next four years he will be President of the United States, the responsibility will be his, and he will not dodge it. He will deserve the credit of his success and he will accept the blame for failure.

Pell's involvement in the Democratic party in the 1920s and his support of Roosevelt in the 1930s was an attempt to fight the business community, which backed and controlled the Republican party. The story of his fight is, in a small way, an economic history of some of the American years. He summed it up in an article for a magazine called *Yankee* in which he said:

> Many years ago, the German government refused to admit American pork products on the grounds that they were trichinous. This question was finally settled by the establishment of adequate inspection at the American packing houses. From that time on, no trichinous meat was sent to Germany, and there was no loss to the

American meat packers, for it was all sold to the people of the United States. This incident and the embalmed beef of the Spanish War, and the enormous use of unwholesome and unpleasant preservatives finally caused the public indignation which resulted in the Pure Food & Drug Act during the Administration of Theodore Roosevelt. . . .

Everyone remembers 1920; everyone remembers how in that year "the only party fit to govern"—controlled by the "best minds"—turned over the country, lock, stock and barrel to Big Business. And what a country it was—untouched by the destruction of war, burdened by a lower debt than any of the great nations—with the finest manufacturing equipment that had ever existed— the only country on a firm financial basis, able to take over the reconstruction of the world. In 1914, we owed thousands of millions to the investing nations of Europe; in 1920, we were the bankers of the world. The universal financial center might have been New York; we could have controlled political and economic conditions over all the earth.

All of this was handed to the leaders of business on a silver platter, and what did they do with it? In less than ten years, they had destroyed the entire structure. Hostile Barbarians, Huns, or Vandals, sacking a captured commonwealth, might have taken less time, but they could not have accomplished the job more thoroughly.

It is obvious that the worthless securities pumped out from Wall Street would never have been issued had the great concerns which shamelessly put their names back of them had the slightest regard for the interest of the investor. But it must be equally apparent that if the leaders of finance themselves had any confidence in the permanence of their own organization, they would have preferred to build up a legitimate business which might have lasted for a century. No man can be so stupid as not to realize that a million dollars a year for the rest of your life is worth more than five millions in cash.

The business leaders did not act as if they were settled in Wall Street, but as if they were camped there. . . .

In the 1920s, Herbert Pell watched as the Wall Street banking houses unloaded hundreds of millions of dollars' worth of German bonds on a gullible American public. "They were issued to the bank at a low price," said Pell, "and the bank sold them to the public at a profit. That was all the bankers saw in it." During those years, Pell traveled frequently in Germany ("I was a tourist looking for beer and pictures") He saw houses going up "to be rented for no more than the cost of paint and janitor service—huge rows of them built with American money." To Pell it was obvious, and later events would prove him correct, that there was no possibility that the German bonds held by Americans would have any permanent value. "All that information," he said, "was quite as much within the reach of the American bankers as it was in mine. But . . . they sold the bonds with no sense of responsibility." And then in 1929 "the whole structure collapsed partly because they had been dishonest, but mostly because they had been short-sighted and stupid."

His great disgust with American business leaders in the 1930s led him to charge that "they are not fit custodians of other peoples' property." He was writing to John W. Davis, the 1924 Democratic Presidential nominee, whom Pell much admired. Pell insisted that he had given instructions to the managers of his estate "that in no circumstances are they to invest one dollar in the stocks and bonds of any American corporation." Perhaps he exaggerated in that statement or later changed his mind, because Herbert Pell did not tamper with the rather extensive estate he inherited. Much of that was in stock of the General Electric Company and Pell kept up a running feud with that company for thirty years. By selling his GE stock, he might have forfeited his right to indignation.

The dispute began in 1930 when he read a newspaper story reporting that the General Electric Company had contributed to the "special educational fund" of the American Tariff League. The fund and the league only served to propagandize against liberal organizations. Pell quickly wrote to the company officers asking "definite assurance" that General Electric had made no such contribution. He explained that he did not feel that the company had the right to contribute stockholders' funds to a political organization. The answer from the company secretary, W. W. Trench, was abrupt: "We have never considered that in contributing to the American Tariff League we were in any sense making a contribution to a political organization. . . ."

Pell found the answer disturbing. He could see no reason why the company should contribute "to the work of organizations which have nothing directly to do with the business of the company," he wrote back to Trench. He added that "it is absurd to ask anyone to imagine that the officers of the General Electric Company did not realize at the time that this contribution was made that it was an indirect gift to the Republican organization and that it would be used for the advancement of Mr. Hoover's campaign." Herbert Pell was correct: the General Electric officials knew perfectly well they were making a political contribution with their stockholders' money.

Through his own holdings and the holdings of his various relatives, which he managed, Herbert Pell controlled General Electric shares totaling in the tens of thousands. He tried several times to win a seat on the company's board of directors to help reform it from within but was consistently rebuffed by the company's officers. During the following years there were many company officers, including Ralph J. Cordiner, board chairman, who told a company management conference early in 1960 that "when we speak of business ethics in a free and competitive system, therefore, we are talking primarily about self-discipline." Whatever discipline was needed then—self or otherwise—apparently was lacking. It was revealed at the time Mr. Cordiner was talking about self-discipline that General Electric and other large manufacturers of electrical equipment had bilked the public of hundreds of millions of dollars by price fixing. Prosecuted by a Republican administration, the companies pleaded no contest.

Herbert Pell, now a few years short of eighty, continued to be astonished at the rapaciousness of American industry. Still arguing for American business to reform itself, if it wished to save itself, he wrote a letter to Robert Paxton, president of General Electric:

I am neither a small nor a new stockholder of General Electric. I find myself representing about forty thousand shares, much of which has belonged to my family since the early nineties when it was bought on the advice of old Mr. J. P. Morgan.

The stock has gone up and it has gone down—from time to time it has been added to but never since 1908 when I received from my mother the gift of a few shares, has a single one been sold by me.

I have observed the Company under the Morgans and under my friend Owen Young—much less attentively but with equal confidence under their younger successors.

I have been shocked and horrified by the latest news. It seemed impossible that such things could take place in an organization run for so many years by acquaintances and by friends of mine whose predecessors I was brought up to respect and whom themselves I trust today.

What does it mean?

Was my old friend William Travers Jerome, once District Attorney of New York, right when he told me towards the end of his life that the Criminal Code is the ethical standard of American business? And not even that?

I have always felt a certain pride in the General Electric Company. I have looked with satisfaction on its laboratories. . . .

The General Electric Company is not of course an eleemosynary institution but to me, and I believe to most of my fellow citizens it is something more than just another company organized for profit. It has for years been an incorporated institution from which its stockholders indeed profited greatly, but more than that it has been a monument of American achievement in which all of our fellow citizens took pride; it has been a model and a sign of our triumph—it is a product of the American system of which we boast so much and which we compare so proudly with the structure of communism and with the petty capitalism of other countries. It is inevitably the consequences of the American character and of the American spirit—Let the world wonder. . . .

Pell's discouragement over the years with the standards of the business community was not the idle rumbling of a spectator. He was a wealthy man who benefited greatly from the profits earned by American capitalism. In a few cases the businesses of which he complained were run by his relatives or by his very close friends, and in many cases by people he had known most of his life. Their background was his—Tuxedo, Newport, the Riviera, the dances at the old St. Moritz. He was part of them, part of their community and of their life cycle. Politics had brought him together with Al Smith and Jerry Mahoney, but when politics ended for him he returned to Newport, where he felt more comfortable.

And because he was so much a part of them, had benefited so greatly by them, he wanted to see the free enterprise system by which they lived preserved. But he understood, much better than those who abused the system, that the threat to its existence lay not from its enemies outside—no matter how great the cry during the 1920s and the succeeding decades against the "Reds"—but from within. The danger was from those leaders of the established system who refused to live up to their responsibilities. By his criticism Herbert Pell became a "rebel," although a mild-mannered and gentlemanly one.

Pell had once said he supported Roosevelt rather than Norman Thomas because "there is much more good accomplished in the world by those who work for small changes which can be attained than by uncompromising Utopians." Like Norman Thomas, the perennial Socialist candidate for President, Herbert Pell gradually became an "uncompromising Utopian." His criticisms of the established order's favoritism toward business became more strident. In 1933 when he was invited to attend a National Anti-Crime Conference, he answered that "you are going at the problem in the wrong way. . . ." He explained: "The law will be respected in America as soon as the law makes itself respectable. In a democracy, the law will treat all classes substantially alike and until it ceases to show lenity to the rich, it can never be effectively vigorous against the poor."

The next year, in an article for the *Harvard Graduates' Magazine,* he wrote: "The general feeling among the businessmen seems to be that the proper standard of business ethics is the criminal code, and that as long as a businessman has succeeded in keeping out of jail, he has done all that can be expected."

That year was marked by the congressional investigations of Wall Street revealing, again, greater depths of corruption than the American public had believed probable. Legislation to curb the worst abuses appeared in the offing, but business leaders cried for the chance to reform themselves. "If we wait for business to reform itself," argued Pell, "we will, I fear, wait indefinitely. What has been revealed to the community by the Senate investigations must have been known for a long time to the leaders of American business. They were in a position where they could easily prevent, control or reform their own practices and those of their associates. And yet they did nothing at all."

Pell's indictment seemed harsh then but not so today. One of the most prescient observers of American life, Denis Brogan, recently recalled this period in American history. "Looking back," wrote Sir Denis, "It was the complacency of the American ruling class which struck me most deeply. I remember a great corporation lawyer in Chicago telling me in 1934 that between 20 million and 30 million people would have to go back to the land and become subsistence farmers. I wondered whether, in fact, the great corporation lawyers and the great bankers who had made such a mess of things might not themselves be better employed back on the land."

To the members of the business community, comments like Herbert Pell's were damning, not of them but of him. Over the cigars and brandy in the libraries of the Union and Knickerbocker clubs their old acquaintance Bertie Pell became in their eyes a "radical," a "Socialist" or worse. But of course the name callers had not paid attention to what he said, only to the fact that he could not enjoy their corruption. "I am not a radical," Pell insisted. "I believe that honest capitalism is the best system for the United States, but I am being slowly convinced by the leaders of business that honest capitalism is a myth." The establishment, by its failings, had succeeded in turning one of its own against it.

The early 1930s, however, were principally years of leisure for Pell. The depression had crimped his traveling style somewhat and he also wished to spend time in Newport while Claiborne was at school there. He turned to writing. In addition to a number of letters to the editor, which appeared in many newspapers, and covered most topics of the day, he tried writing light verse. He did a series of short poems about English history and another series about American history. Franklin Roosevelt liked them. "Why don't you consider getting someone to illustrate them in water color," he said to Pell in 1935, "and have them published for children?" Despite Roosevelt's enthusiasm, Pell was unable to find a commercial publisher.

In this period he was an occasional guest lecturer at Harvard, as well as a member of the Board of Overseers Visiting Committee on Government. He served along with Walter Lippmann, Mark Sullivan and his old political opponent and family friend Ogden Mills.

He took an active interest in the affairs of Newport. He advocated to the Chamber of Commerce, for example, that something be done for "your poor fellow citizens, the workers of Newport. . . . I know of no place that does so little for its workmen." He also was concerned that the workmen could swim only "in the oily filth of the harbor at Kings Park . . . [and] they must put on their bathing suits at home." In the spirit of a proper gentleman he asked: "How is this for a decent woman, who has no car?"

He was disturbed that property values in Newport had fallen so drastically. "My own house on the corner of Narragansett and Bellevue avenues was built by a man called Osgood in 1887. The place cost Osgood well over $300,000. Ten years ago it was sold to me for $20,000." He spoke of the need for a restoration of Newport to the grandeur it had known in the Gilded Age when "Newport was the synonym for everything that was magnificent. . . . Newport was famed throughout the world. No foreigner of distinction would have felt that his visit to the United States was complete unless he had spent at least a few days at Newport." He was of course now almost a senior citizen, just entering his fifties, still tall and handsome. His hair was graying and his mustache was trimmed back somewhat to make it less flamboyant and more befitting a middle-aged man. He seemed very happy with his attractive wife Olive. His experiences as a traveler, as an elected member of Congress and as a working politician as well as a self-educated student of the arts gave him a broader frame of reference than that of most of his contemporaries. And like most middle-aged citizens, he was listened to with great respect and largely ignored.

In 1936 he returned briefly to politics, to assist with Franklin Roosevelt's second Presidential campaign. With his background as a gentleman, Herbert Pell had become shocked, perhaps more than others, by the malicious stories he heard circulated about the President. "I have often been asked the difference between the Republican and Democratic parties in the United States," he said. "In many cases they overlap, but there is one distinction that I would like to suggest at the present time." He then recalled the long history of personal attacks made against Democratic officials and their families. In his own lifetime he had witnessed the nasty gibes at Grover Cleveland and also at Cleveland's wife—"one of the most charming ladies who ever occupied the White House." He recalled whispering campaigns against Al Smith's wife and against the wife of New York City Mayor Hylan. "Since I began to take a serious interest in American politics," he said in 1936, "there have been three Democratic presidents and six Republican. I have no recollection of any unpleasant stories or gossip directed against the wives of the Republicans. All of the Democrats, who have occupied the office of Mayor of New York City, Governor of the State, or President of the United States have been consistently subjected to the cheap and filthy humor emanating from the gutter outside the Stock Exchange. We all remember the mud that was thrown at Mr. Wilson and at both his wives." He continued that "we can at least say of our fellow Democrats that they have never attacked the character of women in our political campaigns, and there has rarely been a Democrat installed in any high office who has not had to suffer from this dirty thing." He concluded: "Is it possible that the Democratic organization . . . has always been the party of gentlemen?"

Despite this history of slander, Pell was particularly shocked in 1936 by the stories being circulated about Roosevelt. They concerned his personal life, his family relations and his general health. One day when Roosevelt was at Hyde Park, Pell drove up to see him and suggested that Roosevelt do something to curb the gossip. "He had the reaction that any gentleman would have," Pell recalled, "he wanted to do nothing, to pay no attention to the stories." Pell argued that Roosevelt was not only a gentleman but that he also was President as well as a candidate for reelection and was obligated to take some action. If Pell was so certain something should be done, Roosevelt responded, why didn't he do it himself? So he found himself the Vice Chairman of the Democratic National Campaign Committee with the job of trying to end the whispered rumors about F.D.R. His approach was to send a letter to every county committeeman, to all the candidates and to as many Democrats in prominent positions around the country as he knew about. The Pell letter asked for any information about stories derogatory to Roosevelt. Pell then said he would answer each story with the truth.

Some of the stories Pell received were quite remarkable. One claimed that Franklin Roosevelt was not really Franklin Roosevelt at all. Rather the man occupying the White House was an American Indian who had been adopted while a baby by a director of a western railroad on a tour with his wife. Another story was that Roosevelt had not graduated with his class at Harvard. Pell checked and discovered that the story was true. Roosevelt had entered Harvard in 1900 and should have graduated in 1904. But he actually graduated in 1903, taking his degree in three years instead of four.

Some of Roosevelt's recent biographers make the same error, reporting that F.D.R. graduated in 1904. When Roosevelt was a Harvard undergraduate, the university president, Charles W. Eliot, believed that college should be completed in three years. Roosevelt and a number of other students then did fulfill their requirements for a degree and graduate in three years. After graduating in 1903, Roosevelt stayed on at Harvard for another year, taking five additional courses as a member of the Graduate School. He did not take an advanced degree for his extra year's work, however.

Most of the stories attacking Roosevelt were found to originate with the Republicans. Although they could not be traced to the party leaders—it was doubtful that the party candidate Alf M. Landon even was aware of them

—they were traced to Republican party underlings. The stories spread the most widely were the vilest and they involved the President's health. These stories suggested Roosevelt was not physically capable in 1936 of being President, not capable really in body or mind because of the infantile paralysis that afflicted him. Herbert Pell had a prepared answer to these stories which he sent out to all Democrats requesting it. The answer is an interesting glimpse of Franklin Roosevelt as he finished his first term in the White House. It read:

The rumor which you describe about the President's health is quite untrue. You may remember the same sort of stories were told four years ago when he was first running. I remember I met a good many by the use of what is known as a fool's argument; that is, a bet. I offered to put up any reasonable amount that Franklin Roosevelt would outlive his term, and also Mr. Hoover. No one was willing to take this bet, but I suggest that if you offer anyone two to one that Mr. Roosevelt will live out his term by two years, barring assassination, you will have as good a bet as anybody can want, and if you can not find any sort of a guaranty of your bettor, I shall be very glad to relieve you of a good deal of it. The other day I saw the President and I have never seen him in better health. His arms could do credit to a blacksmith. His digestion is perfect, and he sleeps well. I have known him for over thirty years and have seen him fairly frequently. He has become continuously stronger since his original attack of infantile paralysis. The history of this disease shows that those who recover from it do not suffer in their general health, especially if, as in this case, it is possible to take continual exercise. I remember very well the shock to all his friends when he was originally stricken, and the great admiration we all had for his courage in meeting the situation and not retiring to invalidism, as would have been so easy for a man in his circumstances. About two months ago I saw Mrs. Roosevelt [his mother] and she told me the whole story, which was exactly as I recollected it. Mr. Roosevelt was in Campobello on the Bay of Fundy and had been swimming in the bitterly cold water of the Bay. He then ran home, apparently in a bathing suit. When he arrived at the house he found the New York mail had come, and without changing his clothes immediately after the run of over a mile which followed his cold swim, he sat down to read his letters. The next day he was not well, and the day after was down with infantile paralysis, which reached its worst point very soon and left him with his legs paralyzed.

At that time he impressed the casual observer as a much smaller man than he is today. A great part of this development comes from his continued exercise, which must be taken with his arms and body. He is not a fat man and gives me the impression of being in far better condition than most of my friends who are about his age.

You are at perfect liberty to show this letter to any person you wish; publish it in whole or in part; explain that it comes from an old friend of the President who is perfectly ready to stake his money on his opinions.

Despite the nasty stories or perhaps in part because of them, Franklin Roosevelt won a stunning victory over Landon, the sunflower candidate from the sunflower state of Kansas. The popular vote was almost 3 to 1 in Roosevelt's favor and the electoral vote was 523 to 8 in his favor.

Pell voted in Newport, which by this time had become his year-round home. That spring his gardener had planted some sunflowers on his property to hide some waste material. By election day these sunflowers had dried up. Birds had eaten the seeds out of them, and the few remaining leaves were withered. That night as Newport's wealthy Republicans sat around the dinner tables at the exclusive Clambaker Club agonizing over the election returns, tall, handsome Herbert Pell, looking elegant in tuxedo and black tie, perfectly waved graying hair and *pince-nez*, walked purposefully from table to table. On each, Pell deposited one seedless and withered sunflower. Then, with a courtly bow, he withdrew.

After quiet years at Newport, Herbert Pell found he enjoyed politics and wanted to be a part of the politics of the late 1930s. Although he had spent too much time abroad and living in Newport to have developed close working political relationships with the Democrats who operated the party machinery, he could not keep his hands out of politics. In 1938 he wrote a couple of "position papers" for James Farley, still the Democratic party leader. The papers did not have great influence on the development of the party's philosophical position in the late 1930s. In this respect, Pell was not a creator but a codifier.

I do not believe that the regulation which is necessary today would have been a good thing a hundred years ago but we must be considerate of the present, [Pell wrote in one of these papers]. You can not go through a city, you can hardly go through a village without finding one-way streets and stop and go lights at important corners. Thirty years ago the introduction of such a system would have been ridiculous tyranny.

When I was a boy you could drive up Fifth Avenue in New York, pull across the traffic and stop on the left side of the road. This was perfectly right at that time but we all recognize today that it would be impractical. To do away with traffic regulation would not promote liberty, it would destroy traffic. The only reason that we did not hear talks about the constitution founded by their fathers when traffic regulation was put in is that nobody had a financial interest in the preservation of chaotic traffic. I know that my great-grandfather could break through the woods as he pleased whereas I am compelled to keep to the right side of a cement road. I can not turn off and dash over the hills, I must stick to the road, but I get there a great deal quicker than he did and this is possible because of regulation and because of public expenditures which would have been beyond the means as they would have been beyond the necessities of the time.

It is true that the foundations of a house are necessary—without foundation no house can stand, but this does not mean that we must carry the foundations without doors or windows up to the roof. As conditions change we must meet them.

He wrote another paper for Farley in 1938 which also shows what the Democratic party was trying to accomplish then and why Herbert Pell supported the changes the New Deal was affecting on the money markets and the world of finance. Designed as an appeal to the American voter to support the Democratic Party, it read:

I do not fear the future. I am not among those who look back into my own memory or into a history book to find my inspiration in a golden age that is past. The country has developed and it will continue to develop. You are told by our opponents to look back for all that is good in America. I tell you to look forward. There is no ship so certain to go on the rocks as one that keeps the look-out in the stern gazing regretfully at the wake.

Eighteen years ago the people of this country elected Senator Harding President of the United States mainly on his cry of "Back to Normalcy" and nine years ago in '29 you began to reap the bitter harvest.

Remember that even the worst watch will not go backwards; the energies, the hopes and the wishes of great people will flow continuously. It may be possible to canalize them but the effort permanently to suppress that glowing and continuous force can result in nothing but the most disastrous of floods.

It was said of a great President, Grover Cleveland, when I was eight years old, "We love him for the enemies he has made." Who are the enemies of the present Administration? From Whitney in Sing Sing to Blackmer in Paris, you will not find one of the great leaders of exploitation who profited in the carnival who is not ready if I may use the phrase of one of their leaders, to "gang up" against the Administration.

A group of prominent lawyers of the type of those who directed the late Liberty League in referring to the separation of powers under the Constitution said, "This venerable and beneficent policy President Roosevelt has undertaken to reverse, and in its place to set up a policy of autocratic force. He has shown that a President who has the will to usurp legislative functions, to exalt the power of the Executive above the Constitution, and to commit our Nation to violations of international justice, easily finds a way."

It is perhaps worth reminding you that these eminent attorneys made this statement in 1904 and not in 1938, that they refer to Theodore and not to Franklin Roosevelt. I can remember when the same groups which are now abusing the President were talking of Theodore Roosevelt as the "lunatic in the White House." We were told that he was always drunk, we were told that he would ruin the country, and that he was engendering class feeling which would inevitably lead to a revolution.

Has there been any revolution since the time of Theodore Roosevelt?

For what are we being attacked? For spending too much money? If our opponents were in power, where would they begin to economize? In the face of every great nation of the world straining its assets to prepare for a war which almost all consider to be inevitable, would they leave the United States defenseless? If so, let them say it, and let them say it all over the country.

Four hundred years ago there was unemployment in England. King Henry VIII solved the problem by hanging 10,000 "lusty beggars." The British have progressed far since those days. Do our opponents want us to revert to such a policy? It is all very well to say that in the long run things right themselves but in the meanwhile every one of the victims of circumstances must be provided, one way or another, with three meals a day, and if possible his self-respect must be maintained by giving him work.

It would be cheaper to feed them in kitchens than to employ them. It would be cheaper still to let them starve. Which of these alternatives do they want? Are we to imagine that a Republican Administration will call down manna from heaven at no cost to anybody on earth with which to feed the multitude? If any of them have discovered that miraculous secret, let him announce it and once I am convinced of his truthfulness, I shall be his most enthusiastic supporter.

I repeat of Franklin Roosevelt the words that were said in my childhood, "We love him for the enemies he has made." Is there a single man in this town, in this state, or in this country, who is known for hard bargaining with the unfortunate, whose name is recognized as that of an enemy of labor, who is also not an enemy of Franklin Roosevelt? Is there a man of smirched business reputation who is not his enemy? Let that be a great reason to you for being his friend. What is it they fear? If it is the effective regulation by the Federal Government of the admission of stocks and bonds to the exchange let them say so. If it is keeping the employed alive, let them say so. Is it the CCC, which has saved so many boys from the destiny of tramps, which has improved their health and character and their value to the State? If so, let them say so.

You will be told that in some obscure town, a long way off, the PWA built a useless sidewalk and somewhere else some of its work was inefficient. This was probably true although I remember two years ago during the campaign the country was flooded with pictures of of cows walking along a cement pavement built by the PWA. A little investigation on the part of our committee proved they had hired the cows from a farmer living some miles away so as to make the pictures.

We are not asking you to believe that there have been no mistakes made. You are voting on a general issue and you may be sure that your votes will be considered and rightly considered by every politician and observer in the country as an endorsement or a repudiation of the basic principles of the Administration. He will not think that an aroused nation has thrown out experienced men because a shipping clerk sent too many oranges to Haverstraw or because somewhere in the other end of the country an unsuitable man was given a job. Your endorsement of the Administration will be interpreted, and correctly interpreted, as a further emphasizing of the fact that the American people do not wish to turn back—that on balance their interests have been better guarded by this Administration than by its predecessors. Your adverse votes will be interpreted, and correctly interpreted by the leaders of Wall Street as a sign that another "Reform Wave" has blown over and that they will soon be able to return to the happy days of their exploitation with their own friends and associates in the solemn place of public watchmen.

You are told of their experience, that they are the only party fit to govern. In 1920 they were given complete control of the richest country in the world. Neither relatively nor absolutely had any nation ever stood in the position in which the United States stood when Mr. Wilson left office and Senator Harding became President. The financial control of the planet, for hundreds of years to come, was in the hands of the New York bankers. Our producing plant was greater than that of any country in the world. The other great manufacturing nations were wrecked by war and we were untouched.

In nine years the only party fit to govern directed by

the best minds produced a wreck, the like of which was never seen in history, which almost provoked a revolution in the United States and which did much to stem the rising tide of democracy in Europe. This is their experience. These are the men who are attacking us. These are the men who want to gain control of the country. They are telling you that you are worse off than you were last year but never reminding you how much better off you are than you were when the present Administration came into power.

It comes with very ill grace that those who ran the ship on the reef should be the loudest to complain of the discomforts of a lifeboat.

What with all the campaign material plus the fact that Herbert Pell no longer was an influential Democrat, his paper was not used in the 1938 congressional campaign. That was unfortunate. It is one of the best brief defenses of what Franklin Roosevelt was trying to accomplish with his government involvement in the marketplace and his make-work projects. It was hard not to agree with Herbert Pell that people loved Franklin Roosevelt for his enemies.

4   FEW PEOPLE IN THE UNITED STATES DURING
the 1930s knew Europe as well as did Herbert Pell. He
spoke of Paris before the First World War, and of Italy
at that time—all the old order he had known personally.
He had seen Verdun, for example, first in 1913, visiting
it while motoring with a friend. What an obscure town
he and his friend thought, but interesting. They noted the
gate with the old French royal arms. Being fascinated
with the details of history, Herbert Pell than spoke of
the Verdunische Altar in Vienna and recalled that the
last marshal of France under the royal regime, Comte
Jean de Rochambeau, had received his baton at Verdun.
Pell left the town of Verdun in 1913, believing its history
was all in the past.

But then came the First World War, and the young
men of France wrote a new history for Verdun. Herbert
Pell returned in 1923. "We saw things like the *tranchée
des baïonnettes* where one of the trenches in soft ground
had closed in over a line of soldiers who were stationed
there and who were all killed by the earth collapsing over
them," he wrote. "There was nothing sticking out ex-

cept their bayonets. There was an enormous thing they called an *ossuaire* where bones of soldiers had been gathered in piles. I will always remember one marker— *Inconnu. Prénom Marcel.* All that anybody knew about him was that his first name was Marcel. . . . He was just a man who had been a man, who had had a life, and whose first name was painted on board. That was all that kept him on the edge of the fog, vaguely sticking out from the anonymity of the others. It was a pathetic sight."

It was during this 1923 trip that he saw how badly Paris had fared in the war. The war had broken the back of France. "There was a certain apathy," Pell said, "a lack of confidence, as Oliver Wendell Holmes said, 'a general feeling of mild decay.'" He had expected to find the streets of Paris empty of young men killed in the war, but instead, he saw a shortage of the older people, who had been unable to adjust to the changed conditions. And all Europe was that way: Austria pleasant but shattered, Italy oppressed; only Germany under the Weimar Republic seemed headed toward recovery. "I remember saying," Pell recalled, "that Germany had learned the lesson of the war." He added then, as much of the world added later: "Boy! Was I wrong!"

In 1926, after he had resigned as Democratic state chairman, he had visited his mother in Italy, his first trip there since the war. He had loved Italy on his previous trips— the small towns with their great churches, the friendly people, the relics of a glorious past. In this 1926 trip he spent approximately six weeks in Italy, driving over the rutted roads, visiting the scattered villages, talking to the people, seeing the cities he had learned to admire—Florence, Ravenna, Rimini, Perugia, Orvieto, and then back to Florence through Siena. Years later there would be a belief that Italy during the early years of Mussolini actually was a pleasant place for the Italians. That Il Duce had made the railroads run on time and the Italian people were satisfied. This is Herbert Pell's description of Italy in the late 1920s:

The people were afraid. They didn't dare talk. No three Italians dared converse on any political subject. Each one knew that he might be denounced and would denounce the person who talked. Each of the others knew that if he didn't denounce the fellow who talked, the other fellow would and would also denounce him for not reporting it.

I remember at one hotel there was a man of a type whom anyone would say was the most outspoken, fearless person you could possibly imagine. He was an English retired colonel who had served in the Indian Army. No class is more opinionated than retired English officers and, usually, more willing to express their opinion, regardless of who listens to it. This fellow took me out in front of the hotel in the middle of the street and whispered to me. "What do you think of *him?*" He didn't dare use the word "Mussolini" there.

I remember when we left I had gotten tickets on the train to Paris, through Cook's. I had taken a full com-

partment for myself—I had to buy two tickets to do it
—and I thought of course that I could put all my bags
in the compartment. But no, some had to go in the baggage car. I turned to the Cook's man and said, "I suppose
that's so these damn Fascists can steal it." The man
turned as white as a sheet when I said that.

I had friends in Italy whom I had known before the
First World War, and they told me what was going on.
The way the government was run was not glaringly
corrupt. It was simply domineering and utterly intoler-
ant of any criticism. There was a story I heard of a
gardener, apparently quite illiterate, who was told to
vote. He voted and, by mistake, was told he had voted
the wrong ticket. He was taken out, beaten, and kept
away for several days.

Mussolini was, like Hitler who imitated him, nothing
but a Pinkerton who refused to stay bought. He got his
first start in the employ of the big businessmen who felt
that the use of violence would prevent labor trouble.
The first work of the Fascists was attacking unions.
But . . . Mussolini did not stay bought. He later turned
on the bourgeoisie as he had originally on the unions. . . .

I think the Italian people accepted Fascism because of
a combination of apathy, selfishness, and fear. All three
worked together. The Italian government had been inefficient, as Italian organizations always have been inefficient. The people took little interest in the government. A very large number of Italians are abjectly poor
and are really more interested in three meals a day than

in anything else. That is their first thought. Ignorant people are always susceptible to fear, and the larger the group of ignorant the more fearful they become. Most of the excesses of mobs are due to fear—not all, but most.

In 1933 Pell returned to Europe. The situation had worsened. "The Austrian condition," he told a friend, "is really pitiable." He recounted then how Germany under its new leader, Adolf Hitler, was attacking Austria from every side, with radio propaganda, enormous economic pressures and the subversion of political organizations. The purpose of all this, Pell said in 1933, was to achieve the otherthrow of the Dollfuss government in Austria and the absorption of Austria into the Third Reich. "This is not being done merely for the sake of adding the few million inhabitants, and the square miles of Austria to Germany," Pell said then. "The great effect of this capture will be to advertise to Poland, and to Yugoslavia, to Denmark, and to the Baltic countries, that, although the English and the French may talk, they will not act to protect the smaller nations from German aggression."

Herbert Pell knew history well enough to see signposts from the past. "This, of course," he said of Adolf Hitler's tactics in 1933, "was the process of Bismarck. In 1864, he joined with Austria in the attack on Denmark. This divided the blame. Bismarck was much more clever than the Austrian minister and was able to show the other smaller German states that they would not do well to rely on Austria as a protector. In 1866, when he attacked

Austria, the vacillations of France showed the great German States—Bavaria, Baden, Saxony—that the French could not be counted on. This, of course, weakened 'the French party' and made it easy to achieve the alliance against France in 1870 and to organize the Empire. The situation is much the same today. The seizure of Austria by Germany would be the beginning of a process alienating from England all continental support, and leaving England alone. . . ."

Herbert Pell recognized in 1933 that another war was coming. "I believe the next war will be different from the last, even more than the war of 1914 was different from the Russian-Japanese war of 1905. There is no use discussing seriously the wonderful tales in the Sunday papers about chemical warfare, which describe the dropping of a small bomb, about the size of a human head, in the middle of Central Park, followed in five minutes by the instant and painful demise of all the inhabitants. The seriously dangerous thing is the incendiary bomb and the developed submarine; the modern underseaboat is not the delicate thing of the past. It is re-enforced and is in little danger from depth bombs. . . ."

As the years passed, Pell became more and more convinced of Germany's intentions to conquer the world. This was not a particularly popular conviction in the United States during the 1930s. The Nazis had beat up the Communists and had earned much conservative American support for displaying violence against the proper victims. While the rest of the world struggled to pull itself out of the economic depression, Germany under

Hitler seemed to leap out from it. In a book called *The Nazi Economic System*, Otto Nathan, the emigré economist, wrote: "Our horror and indignation at the insufferable brutality of Naziism, our complete rejection of all it stands for, should not obscure the *possible* importance of the economic experiments carried out under the Fascist auspices, experiments which may take on new value and significance in a different political atmosphere." Nathan, and the many who agreed with him, could not have been more wrong. Germany appeared prosperous only because it was stealing from its neighbors and from itself, from its present and more important from its future. Because he chose to watch what took place before him and because he refused to fool himself, Herbert Pell understood that. In 1936, for example, an American millionaire sent copies of a letter to a number of prominent Americans. The letter was a favorable commentary on the efficient condition that he had found in Hitler's Germany.

Herbert Pell received one of the letters and answered it. It said:

> You are quite right in saying that Germany is today in an extremely efficient condition. My only fear is that when belts begin to tighten, it will be necessary once more for Hitler to stage some sort of a coup. Whether this be the absorption of Austria, the division of Czechoslovakia with Hungary or the capture of the Danish provinces or the seizure of the Polish corridor which is Poland's only outlet to the sea, we do not know.

Eventually circumstances must lead to a clash with England. Most Germans believe and intend that the Twentieth Century shall be as definitely German as the Nineteenth was English. They believe that German ideas are the best and must dominate the world. They can not achieve this object until Great Britain ceases to be a barrier and becomes a breakwater.

Pell was speaking of a Nazi Germany he knew personally. He found there was nothing secret about Hitler's intentions. "The Nazi organization was built as openly as Grand Central Station was," he said, "with everything explained, every plan advertised." In the German book stores he saw prominently displayed a book entitled *Sporting Guide for Young Men*. The "sports" were hurling bombs and sneaking surreptitiously upon your enemy. He heard the Nazi military machine proclaim loudly its hunger for guns and demand that the public surrender butter. But outside Germany few people listened. "The Nazis assumed that we would be more interested in games, in making money, and in murder cases than we were in what was going on abroad," said Pell, "and they were right."

Herbert Pell summed up his feelings best to an old friend, Arthur N. Holcombe, a professor of government at Harvard. "Berlin, where I spent a considerable time," said Pell, "was terrifying. I felt as if I were watching a heavily armed man going mad."

As an observer of Europe in the 1930s, Herbert Pell

was undoubtedly as competent as could be found. His sympathies were quite clear: he hated Naziism. And he was a confidant of the President of the United States. It was not too surprising then that one morning in the early spring of 1937 a call was made to Herbert Pell's New York home. There was much activity in the house at that moment, as he and Olive were planning to go to England for the coronation of King George VI. They would have a good view of the event, from Pierre Cartier's rooms in the Carlton Hotel. That particular morning they were in a special hurry because they were to meet Pell's mother for luncheon. Then the phone rang. It was Jim Farley.

Would you like to go to Portugal?" he asked.

"What do you want me to do in Portugal?" Pell answered.

"Be minister there."

"All right. Yes."

"Well, your instructions will come right up."

Herbert Pell thanked his old friend from his days in New York politics, hung up and joined Olive, who still talked excitedly of going to see George crowned. "I don't think we'll be able to go," he told her. "We must go to Portugal. I'm going to be minister there."

The newspapermen came to Pell's home, which was at Hopewell Junction, to photograph the new envoy and they managed to catch a handsome shot of Herbert and Olive. Because Herbert Pell was in the country, he was dressed in what for him was a traditional country costume —knickerbocker suit, Pell's being the only knickerbocker suits extant in 1937 which would fit a six-foot, five-inch man in his middle fifties. Farley thought the picture amusing. He cut it from the New York newspaper and sent it to Roosevelt. "I thought you might like to see a picture of your new minister to Portugal," he wrote. "Note he is dressed up in his Coronation costume."

Herbert Pell went to Washington to receive his instructions and briefings at the State Department. He was brought into the office of Sumner Welles, Under Secretary of State. "There's no need," said Herbert Pell to his guide, "to introduce me to Mr. Welles. I've known him, not all my life, but all of his." Born in 1892, Welles was Pell's junior by eight years.

Welles answered: "I'm awfully glad you said that because I've just left my son, who treats me as a marvel of senescence."

Pell always had understood that a new minister spends a month in Washington learning about his new assignment, but Sumner Welles sent him right off. "The secretary will tell you all you need to know," he said, "and here are some papers."

As a young man Herbert Pell had deliberately bypassed a diplomatic career for the pleasures of the wealthy and private traveler. Now, at an age when most men consider their careers coming to an end, he was starting a new career in the diplomatic service he had once spurned. Although ministerial appointments traditionally were considered payoffs for large campaign contributions or diligent political campaigning, that was not true in Herbert Pell's case. Franklin Roosevelt, during his second term, was very much aware of the changes taking place in Europe, of the threats to the future developing there. Deliberately he picked for the foreign service intelligent persons he could trust, whose ability as observers he could rely on, and sent them to key European posts. He encouraged them to write to him, detailing to him the Europe they saw, its dangers, its convulsions and its opportunities. Portugal was such a listening post.

Pell's nomination was formally submitted to the Senate April 19, 1937. However, it was delayed several weeks by the conservative Senator Peter Goelet Gerry, who disapproved of Pell's (and Roosevelt's) liberal Democratic politics. As a Rhode Island senator, he had the right to delay his constituent's appointment. The Senate Foreign Relations Committee unanimously approved the nomination one month later, however, and the next day, May 20, the Senate confirmed the appointment without objection. Herbert Claiborne Pell was now "Mr. Minister."

In Lisbon he presented his credentials to the president of Portugal, Oscar de Fragoso Carmona, and the next day met the country's real boss, Antonio de Oliveira Salazar. Salazar then was only forty-eight years old and had been the undisputed leader of Portugal for five years. Born into a peasant family, he searched for years trying to find a career for himself; he spent eight years in a seminary studying for the priesthood, attended law school, then became a specialist in political economics. He entered government service in 1926 at the ministerial level, from where he rose to become Portugal's dictator. Like most men who insist on assuming unchallenged power for themselves, Salazar considered his motives beyond dispute. He was going to raise the level of education of the people in his country, their economic standing, their cultural attainments. The vision was glorious and grandiose. And like most dictators, he would fail. The social revolution would never take place.

To Herbert Pell, Dr. Salazar was the soul of disarming courtesy. They talked casually for a few moments. Pell congratulated Salazar on Portugal's new roads, saying that he knew from personal experience what an improvement they made. Salazar, who had been a college teacher before becoming a politician, asked Pell about Harvard. Then Salazar began speaking of his country. He acknowledged Portugal was governed by a dictator but insisted that his government was only a quasidictatorship. He insisted that the country was run on a democratic basis and described his own work as keeping abreast of the interests of all the people of the nation and making certain that the government responded to those interests. Salazar praised the industriousness and the ability of the Portuguese people. Pell described Salazar as "a very young looking man on the thin side, but not skinny and," Pell continued, predicting accurately, "he gave the appearance of endurance." (Salazar did in fact endure as dictator until 1969.)

Herbert and Olive Pell found Lisbon a beautiful city. It was built on the sides of very steep hills so that the second floor of their house was on a level with their garden. Directly opposite their front door was the Belgian legation, and the Belgians entered their own garden through the legation cellar. In every house the windows with southern exposures looked out over the house opposite and down into the harbor. From a little loggia at the top of the American legation, Herbert and Olive could see the entire Lisbon harbor and the plains beyond about thirty kilometers away—hills crowned by the ruins of the castles of Sosimber and Palmila. With this vista a backdrop, they dined every evening in the loggia as long as the summer sun lasted to give them light.

Officially there was little for Pell to do his first year in Portugal. "Every Friday," he said, "I would write a letter to the Secretary of State: 'Sir, I have the honor to enclose a copy of the official journal. I am, respectfully,' There was nothing more to do until the next Friday when the same letter had to be signed again." Because he was a habitual tourist with a real interest in the people and the country where he was—no matter which people and which country—he spent much of his time traveling. "I really saw Portugal," he said, "and knew more about it than most Portuguese did."

He found few American interests in Portugal. There was little shipping, an occasional tin mine owned by an American, and a few oil people; no American he met there had been in Portugal more than seven years. In contrast, he found a large English colony whose members not only had been in the country for generations but also appeared to own much of it—"the cloth works, the cotton weaving plants, the street railroads of Lisbon and that kind of thing." Pell found the English conceited about their longevity in Portugal. One of them spoke of a family firm in Portugal dating back to the early 1800s. "You don't have anything like that in America, do you?" asked the Englishman.

Herbert Pell pulled a package of Old Gold cigarettes from his pocket and pointed to the words on the side saying "P. Lorillard and Company, founded in 1760." The Englishman looked taken aback when Pell said: "That is my family business."

Time in Portugal during those few remaining years before the outbreak of the Second World War had little meaning. It was like living in the last days of a dying civilization at the moment before it is engulfed by a future one. People moved slowly, worked without ambition and felt no compulsion to act otherwise—even on the official level. One afternoon Pell was in the country having tea with the Italian minister when he received a rush message from the legation. The Portuguese foreign minister would appreciate Pell's paying a call that very afternoon at five o'clock. Pell hopped into his car and rushed back, arriving at the Foreign Office thirty minutes late. He was shown into the minister's presence immediately; the minister had waited a half-hour beyond his department's closing time for Pell to appear. "I came in, of course, full of apologies," Pell said, "expressing my great regret at having kept him there. He honestly had no idea of what I was apologizing about. I had wasted half an hour of his time, yes, but what of it? He would have wasted half an hour of mine with an equal lack of consideration and would have thought nothing of it."

The Portuguese could not accept that they might be playing a crucial role in the coming years. "Portugal was like an old maid who had inherited a fortune, unaccustomed to courtship but enjoying it," said Pell. They "bargained about every possible point, were coy here and there, took about three and a half years to make the concession for the use of Lisbon as a port of call for American airways." The point here was that transatlantic aviation was coming and the European nation that moved most quickly could benefit greatly from it. "I remember explaining to the Portuguese foreign minister that if they once started a straight line between France and the United States, or Great Britain and the United States, it would be the end of any thought of a regular line to Lisbon," Pell recalled, "but that if Lisbon started in and became a great junction for airplanes from all over the world it would probably remain so, much as Liverpool remained so important for so many years as a British seaport. The first two big English shipping lines across the Atlantic were the Cunard and the White Star both of which went from Liverpool to New York and Boston. The result was that traffic from America to England was normally channeled through Liverpool. Liverpool banking houses, insurance and various businesses concentrated there kept that trade for a very long time." The American airplanes ultimately did come to Portugal, but about two years later than they could have if the Portuguese government had acted with more efficiency than it did. The arrival of aviation probably did more than anything else to keep Portugal out of the Second World War. Because of planes to and from Portugal, it became the place where both sides observed each other and met clandestinely, and the point from which both sides surreptitiously entered the other's territory.

While in Portugal, Herbert Pell was very much aware of the civil war going on in neighboring Spain. He reported to the State Department that he was not commenting on that war in his dispatches because he did not wish to cut in on anyone else's territory. But the answer came back that he should report all that he could, because the department was interested in gathering all possible information about the Spanish Civil War. "So I got some news which I tamed down a great deal because I knew they wouldn't believe it back home if I told them all I really knew," said Pell. What he did report was that there were five thousand German aviators in Spain who were rotated back to Germany every three months, giving Germany twenty thousand aviators a year experienced in flying fighter airplanes. He also reported that about seventy thousand foreign troops were fighting in Spain on Franco's side.

"I had a quick letter back," Pell recalled, "saying that this was nonsense. The best information that they could get from the British was that there were five thousand Italians and a negligible number of Germans. As a matter of fact, my figures were just about half of the truth, but I knew they wouldn't swallow more."

Pell even then was finding that it was impossible to persuade State Department officials to accept what was contrary to what they believed. Although he couldn't convince the State Department, Herbert Pell had no doubt that war was coming. Once in Portugal he was talking to another diplomat about the European situation and used the phrase "When the war breaks out."

"Surely, your Excellency," said the other man, "you mean if the war breaks out."

"No," Pell insisted, "I said when."

"Do you think then that war is inevitable?"

Pell answered slowly: "Not at all, but I am certain that it will not be avoided."

He also understood that Europe after the war never would be the same as Europe before the war. He wrote his brother, Clarence, suggesting that Clarence send his son to Europe for "a last look." Herbert Pell's own son, Claiborne, wrote asking for money to make another trip to Europe, and Herbert sent it to him with the same idea— that Claiborne should take a last look at the old Europe.

In 1939, Claiborne, now twenty-one, came to Europe. He crossed the Atlantic on a Polish ship and found himself by the Danzig harbor. With a couple of young companions, he got into a rowboat and began moving about the harbor taking photographs. The Germans, who were building submarines in Danzig, became very upset and arrested young Claiborne. Herbert Pell told the remainder of this story with some pride:

Apparently knowing that there are just three things that are believed of every American in Europe—one, that he is crazy; two, that he's a first class shot with a pistol; three, that he's rich . . . Claiborne played on the first. He managed to convince the Gestapo that he thought these installations were art museums. He was left, however, in the Gestapo filing room and he amused himself looking over the files a little before he was released.

Herbert Pell and his son had a last summer together in prewar Europe. They drove through Italy from Naples to Paris. Herbert Pell remembered the route without using a map although he had not made the trip for twenty-five years. "We had a very good time driving up," Herbert Pell recalled. "I showed my son Italy. We stopped to see places, and I never allowed him to spend more than an hour at a time in a museum so that he really got interested. We came up through France, then we went over to London." The father was doing what he enjoyed most—visiting the old museums and the churches and other buildings, telling their stories, spending a last few months with his son. It was a summer to be repeated over the next several years by millions of families, parents garnering a last few weeks with their children knowing that if their children survived the coming war, they no longer would be childlike, knowing that the price of war was, in the least, the loss of innocence.

Herbert Pell wrote for Franklin Roosevelt a description of the Italy he saw during this trip. It read:

Italy was much changed since I had last seen it. . . . The gaiety and noise to which I was accustomed were entirely absent. There were no excited groups talking vigorously and no singing. In spite of some definite and obvious improvements, the people did not impress me as either being well off or as happy as they had been in the past. I am told that they are thoroughly dissatisfied with the idea of the Germans on their border and that the majority of Italians do not like the idea of the Rome-Berlin axis. When I was a boy one of the most popular phrases to chalk was "Death to the Germans" and this traditional attitude has not changed very much.

One of the things that most shocked me was the signs painted on almost every wall; the belligerent phrases extracted from Mussolini's speeches are displayed in enormous letters and it a rare thing to be out of sight of at least one: "Believe, obey, fight"—"Italy fears no one"—"The plough opens the land but the sword defends it." These and similar phrases are plastered all over the countryside. A rather amusing detail was that we saw a few people cheering Hitler and the Germans but all of these were along the railroad line and visible from the trains, placed there on the assumption that it was not worth bothering about the few Germans who had money enough to travel by automobile. We did not see a single one of these signs of friendship out of sight of the railroad.

There were many reasons why a man like Herbert Pell was repelled by Naziism. It was the denial of the free spirit he admired. The war he saw coming would destroy the Europe he knew and loved. Also, Naziism reflected an arrogance that he always had hated. It was a triumph of militant ignorance over inquiring intelligence. He also was repelled by it because of its basis in racial superiority. Pell himself was part of a snobbish class in America. Its servants were Catholics, the tradesmen in town were Jews, and Negroes never were seen. And that was the understanding of things the members of this class had grown up with and learned to live by. But none of the racial or religious prejudices had rubbed off on him, or on many of the others he had grown up with, such as Franklin Roosevelt. Pell was a snob, it is probably fair to say, but his snobbishness was based on ability and individuality rather than on arbitrary standards. These men who emerged from the Gilded Age were secure and confident enough that they did not need to support themselves by indulging in arbitrary prejudices. Although Pell chose his associates carefully, he chose them from every walk of life. Some, like his close friend Jerry Mahoney, originally of his New York political days, had come from the East Side tenements. Others had come from the Hudson River estates. Pell rejected all notions of racial or ethnic superiority and particularly enjoyed puncturing the pomposity of his wealthy acquaintances on the subject. In the early 1930s there was much furor in the United States over immigrants and persons with foreign-sounding names. Herbert Pell wrote a magazine article in 1934 about it:

These impulses of culture and fashion are very powerful, but we must remember that they come from the

top. It is absurd to say, as do so many of our contemporaries, that the old American stock is being overwhelmed by wicked foreigners and that our old standards
are being slowly washed away. In the first place, the
farther back we go in the commercial history of the
United States, the worse we will find conditions. The
men who speculated in the warrants of American revo-
lutionary soldiers, knowing perfectly well what their
eventual value would be, were not Slavic immigrants.
The men who twenty years ago wrecked the New
Haven Railroad were as Nordic as Nordic could be. The
new blood is a very poor excuse.

In writing once to Claiborne, Herbert Pell commented
that the white race—in no matter which country—always
has a feeling of superiority. "Wherever the Negroes work
they have the same handicaps that women suffer
from . . . ," he said. "They are not expected to do as
well as white men. Very few people will employ a woman
doctor or lawyer. An extraordinary small number of
women have by their own merits reached high positions
in business. They are watched for errors and any errors that
they may make are blamed on their sex, whereas the mistakes of men are blamed on the individual. . . ."

He continued: "Of course any minority is bound to be
in a disadvantageous position. In the first place every member must suffer to a certain extent for all the faults of
any of the others. This is a great and terrible load. The
tendency of any majority group is to consider its own

qualifications those of its leaders and to judge every minority group according to its most discreditable or at least most conspicuous members."

Claiborne Pell recalled his father's emotions toward Naziism in the late 1930s. "A lot of Americans were not as disapproving of the Germans as they should have been in those days," Claiborne Pell explained. "I can remember the climate at the time, and Dad really was such an egalitarian and liberal. The whole thing, not only the cruel treatment of the Jews but the whole thing, used to absolutely horrify him. It made him feel history was going into reverse."

Herbert Pell was firmly convinced that Hitler's behavior through the late 1930s would ultimately lead to a general world war, although many Europeans and more Americans discounted that possibility. "I have watched international affairs for about fifty years and have never observed a single statesman whose course could be prophesied more accurately than could that of Hitler. . . . Hitler's whole policy has been perfectly clear, and from the time he increased the army to the present day, every step has logically and inevitably followed the preceding one."

Late in September, 1938, Prime Minister Neville Chamberlain and Adolf Hitler came together to give weakness and vacillation a new name—"Munich." At that time Pell was in London with his son and was astonished at how the normally reserved English seemed so open in their delight that war had been averted. Shortly afterward, in Portugal, Herbert Pell dined with Francisco Giorgio and Vera Mameli, the Italian minister and his wife, both his close personal friends. Over the wine the Mamelis spoke freely to Pell. They spoke of England's eminence in the world coming to an end. They described Chamberlain as a great man because he had the courage to acknowledge his defeat. England, they said, had learned not to interfere with the military powers of Germany, Italy and Japan. They spoke of the disintegration of the British Empire, of how England could not maintain communications with her soldiers scattered in Gibraltar, Malta and Palestine and of how India would become a source of weakness for England rather than of strength.

Pell reported this dinner conversation to Secretary of State Cordell Hull and closed his letter by passing on the conclusion of his Italian friends: "The capital of Europe will be Berlin rather than London."

Of the Munich conference, an English government outsider said to the English people: "You were given the choice between war and dishonor." Then Winston Churchill continued: "You chose dishonor and you will have war." Herbert Pell believed much the same thing. In a long report to Franklin Roosevelt, he said:

It is political pettifogging to deny the basic contention of Chamberlain . . . that the peace of Europe is worth any price that is asked. We can not give too much permanently to prevent war but a truce may well be too costly. The price paid at Munich is cruelly apparent. The Germans received practically everything they asked for and within a few days of the time they wanted it.

I was in France during August and in England during the early part of September. In both countries I found the people hateful of war but prepared to meet the issue, morally ready and united to an extent that may not recur for some time. I was tremendously impressed by the courage and determination which I saw and heard. From the highest to the lowest in both France and England, the people were ready to march to a task that they loathed. A combination of even and red would only occur on the roulette wheel once in four times and I do not believe that the psychological preparedness of two great nations will coincide much more frequently. The feeling in foreign countries was strongly behind the English and French.

Then Pell raised an issue that in 1940 and 1941 would greatly trouble Franklin Roosevelt and that the President would try to solve by the development of the lend-lease program. Said Pell:

The situation today is different from that of 1914. Then Great Britain and France had enormous holdings of American securities which could be converted into cash; they had unimpaired credit, and free access to the American money market. Today their investments in the United States are very much less, their credit is not too good and the law of the United States denies them access to the American market. Unless they can appeal to the sympathy of a great part of the American people it will be impossible for them to use the American manufacturing plant as readily, or as anywhere near as readily, as they did in 1914. This will put an almost ruinous burden on their own resources. . . .

Pell continued:

In most other countries the prestige of Great Britain and France has fallen tremendously. In Portugal the Italians and the Germans somewhat more modestly look on the Munich conference as a great victory for the dictators and a crushing defeat for England. They seem to think that they can without real danger continue indefinitely to nibble at the strength and prestige of Great Britain. The so-called guarantee of the integrity of the remains of Czechoslovakia is generally considered to be a mockery. They could not or would not defend it nor provide great assistance to it but they are ready to guarantee it after stripping it of its military power. This of course is nonsense. . . .

The real question is not what [Chamberlain] left at Berchtesgaden and Munich but what he brought back. Has he bought a gold brick?—that is the question. Will Hitler use his increased strength to demand even greater concessions within a year or have they crammed him so

full that he will forever hate the sight of food? My
observation of small boys at Christmas parties leads me
to the conclusion that a surfeit seldom kills.

The result of these conferences will be either an almost fatal loss to Great Britain or a great triumph.
Which you think it will be, depends on your opinion
of Mr. Chamberlain's appraisal of Hitler's appetite. . . .

There can be no doubt that Chamberlain bet the future
of the British Empire on Hitler's integrity and before
making any permanent judgment we must await the
event.

Herbert Pell concluded: "I think he will lose."

Franklin Roosevelt appreciated this kind of frank report. He answered promptly, wrote briefly about the congressional elections at the beginning of November, 1938:
". . . while the State of New York did very well on the
whole, we lost in a good many other States because,
frankly, our officeholders and our candidates had not
measured up." He then discussed the contents of Pell's
letter. "You are right about the European situation," he
said. "Our British friends must begin to fish or cut bait.
The dictator threat from Europe is a good deal closer to
the United States and the American Continent than it was
before. . . ."

Beginning the next year Franklin Roosevelt began the
slow process of building up the military posture of the
United States. He called for fifty thousand airplanes, a
huge army, a gigantic lend-lease program, and spoke of

making the United States the arsenal of democracy. He demanded a draft, enlisted Republicans in his cause, dropped old friends who did not agree with him about the looming threat and wooed old enemies who did. He risked himself politically and, ultimately, sacrificed himself physically because of the danger ahead. He was capable of understanding the danger because of his broad background, his sensitivity to the political currents of the world, and, finally because stationed in the diplomatic outposts of the world there were friends like Herbert Pell, professional diplomats like William Bullitt, George Messersmith and others on whom he could rely for sharp appraisals of what was developing in Europe.

In the summer of 1939, Herbert Pell had returned to the United States for a visit. He saw some old friends and went to the dentist ("which is always the first thing that any diplomat does coming back"). He explained that "the English diplomats have a tremendous advantage here because if there is anything the matter with their teeth they just take them out and wear their Sunday teeth during the week and send the others back to London to be repaired. We have to accompany ours."

In New York City he was staying at the Knickerbocker Club and he was awakened one morning by the valet there and informed that the German air force had bombed Warsaw to begin the Second World War. Civilization had caught up with the cataclysm waiting just ahead of it.

Pell drove to his Upstate New York home at Hopewell Junction. While there he telephoned a friend's house to see who was there. Only the President's mother, Sara Roosevelt, was home. Herbert Pell dropped by to see her and she made him iced tea. Like many people Herbert Pell was in awe of Sara Delano Roosevelt. She was the only person, for example, who could make him drink iced tea, which he detested. He once mentioned that to Franklin Roosevelt, and the President replied: "Yes, I was afraid of her, too."

Over their tea Pell and Mrs. Roosevelt had a pleasant chat, about the countryside, their friends—the ordinary talk of two old acquaintances with mutual concerns. There would not be time for many such conversations in the future, not for the mother of the President of the United States or for the diplomat in that President's service. In a way the visit, probably on the wide front porch of the Hyde Park home overlooking the Hudson River, was a saying good-bye to a life that had been. All over the world that day people were making such farewells.

After the war declaration, Pell took a Dutch boat back to Europe. He spent some time in England, then went to Paris. It had been forty-four years since he first came to this city with his parents and bicycled along the Champs Élysées and browsed through the bookstores. He had come back many times; like all those who come to Paris with an open heart and the time to savor the city, he loved it. As with Gertrude Stein, America was his country but Paris was his hometown. The night life that intrigued so many Americans had never attracted Pell; rather, he was fascinated by the Louvre, Notre Dame, the small bookstalls where one found a seventeenth-century work as easily as a modern one. It was to these bookstalls he had first gone as a young boy forty-four years earlier and it was here he returned. "I had no idea that Paris was going to be taken," he recalled. "I'm not a magician, but I knew it would be a long time before I got to Paris again so I went around and bought everything I could want. I would take a taxi to the various bookshops and buy anything that I could see that I thought I would want. I pulled books out of the shelves with both hands, filled the cab up."

Portugal had been a sleepy post, a window on the European world but not a part of that world. The Luftwaffe attack on Warsaw had changed that. Lisbon became a center of intrigue, a passageway between Europe and the United States, a militarily strategic spot as well as the floodgate through which the mass of European refugees passed. Herbert Pell returned to his post in Lisbon as the floodgate opened. "People from every country came along in all stages of discomfort and poverty," he recalled. "I have seen women who walked hundreds of miles through the fields at night because they were so afraid of the soldiery that they hid in the woods during the daytime, never daring to go on the roads. I have seen men and women who had suffered danger, torture and pain coming from all parts."

He found that he liked most of these refugees. "They were of all nations and all religions," he said, "and almost all of them were very nice. They tried to help each other." They all had trouble on their journeys from the war areas to Lisbon. "There was nobody," said Pell, "who crossed Spain in comfort. Nobody ever did cross Spain in comfort, but during the war it was worse." It was Pell's job to

assist these people—to find them visas and usher them
aboard one of the small boats—built for a hundred and
fifty passengers but carrying more than two hundred—
on their way to the United States. In most cases it was
a satisfying task, but there were many delays and many
exasperating times. A few of the refugees were wealthy
or had been, and could not understand why the American
legation did not jump to fulfill their wishes. One man,
angered because he could not get a visa immediately,
asked if he could send a cablegram. Pell answered that the
man could send as many as he wished to pay for through
the facilities of the American legation. The man then pro-
ceeded to send the following message: "Dear Cordell,
please tell the Chief that I will not be able to get over
there on the plane next Thursday because the American
minister here will not help me to get on board. I am, your
old friend,——" but the man still had to wait his turn
for a visa.

On another occasion a man explained that he should
have a visa quickly because he was an old school friend
of Herbert Pell, the American minister. The man went on
with a long description of his early relationship with Herbert Pell, how they had grown up together and gone on
sprees together. And, the man concluded, the legation
flunky sitting in front of him better snap to and produce
a visa immediately unless he wished to anger his boss, the
minister. The "flunky" was, of course, Herbert Pell, who
had never seen the man before in his life. That man too
had to wait his turn.

Lisbon also was a distribution point for Red Cross packages to English prisoners of war being held in Europe. Unfortunately many of the packages from the British Red Cross were lying on the docks being soaked by rain and eaten by rats. There was an international agreement that Red Cross packages should cross a country at the expense of that country's government. Portugal was willing to ship the packages across her territory, but Spain balked at assisting the British in any way. The problem then was to get the packages to Geneva, where the Swiss had agreed to see they were distributed properly. Pell's idea was to ship them in trucks, but he was informed that a convoy of trucks could not make the journey between Lisbon and Geneva; the roads and wartime conditions were too much for them. Claiborne, then twenty-two years old and recently graduated from Princeton, was visiting his father at the time. He determined to prove the trip could be made. He acquired an ambulance contributed by Ambassador Anthony J. D. Biddle, converted it, loaded it up with extra gas and Red Cross packages and made the trip, arriving in Geneva just before Christmas, 1940. (Ultimately the packages were sent from Lisbon to Marseilles by coastal boat and then taken by Swiss train to Geneva. Apparently it was easier in Lisbon to acquire boats than it was to acquire one hundred trucks complete with spare parts.)

Another problem was the Azores Islands in the Atlantic, owned by Portugal. "The nation which can use them as a naval and air base," Pell reported to Roosevelt, "commands all access to the South Atlantic. It is not only vital that they should not get in the hands of Germany . . .

it is to the world's interest and to ours that the United States, which will have to succeed England as the dominant naval power of the world, should command these islands." Herbert Pell was more correct than he knew. At about the time he was urging the American acquisition of the Azores, Adolf Hitler, so William L. Shirer reports, was "occupied with the question of the occupation of the Atlantic Islands with a view to the prosecution of war against America at a later date." The German navy rejected the idea of occupying the Azores, explaining that it did not have the power to do so. But Hitler continued to see the Azores as an embarkation point for an air attack against the United States.

Pell believed the Azores could have been acquired as a possession of the United States. Certainly he believed that the people there were willing to change overseers, at least according to Franklin Roosevelt. During World War I, Roosevelt, as assistant secretary of the Navy, had visited the Azores. As he later recounted to Pell, a group of people there offered to start a revolution and make Roosevelt president. When Herbert Pell told that story, he chuckled and added: "I had less political ambition than Roosevelt had, and I probably would have been glad to take it."

Being an American minister in a neutral country presented certain problems. One problem was an American admiral who arrived in Lisbon and attended a luncheon with the British ambassador. To observe diplomatic courtesy, the Americans then had to invite both the British and the Germans—at different times—to pay calls on the admiral aboard his ship. There were times, however, when diplomatic protocol was ignored. In June, 1940, Benito Mussolini declared war on England and France. The declaration by Italy was a tawdry act, almost embarrassing in its baseness. Mussolini obviously believed that the Allies were finished and he wanted to move in and pick up some of the spoils. The day after the declaration by Italy, Herbert Pell appeared at a diplomatic gathering in Lisbon wearing the purple rosette of the Officier de l'Instruction Publique, the only French decoration he possessed at the time. Although wearing it was against American law, he did so because he wanted to show publicly his sympathies for France.

He visited France in 1940, after it had fallen to the Germans; briefly, for it was a painful visit. "For the first time since my visit in 1895, and there have been many in each of the four succeeding decades," he wrote, "I left France without regret." He continued:

Outwardly of course there was almost no change—the most conspicuous is the small number of automobiles on the roads. Gasoline is allotted to the people in very small quantities—even doctors are limited. . . . All along the road we saw the country people bringing in the vintage or working in the fields to all physical appearance as if nothing had happened. Olive wanted some chocolate so we stopped at grocery shops in several towns but could get none. The shops were open but badly stocked.

I remember seeing men playing football who after a blow would continue playing without any consciousness of what they were doing, or any recollection of it afterwards. France was like that. Although the appearance of life went on, it was impossible to fail to see that all of the motions were gone through in a daze. Conversation was made up of clichés and catch words like stockbrokers discussing prohibition—words and phrases not necessarily without meaning, but uttered completely without thought.

Even in the short time we were in France, I began to see the return of rational consciousness and a painful thing it was. . . . People began to realize what had happened to them and what had been taken from them by a group of Frenchmen, who, if they did not desire and engineer the defeat, have at least not hesitated to profit by the alien system they have imposed on their own people.

It is evident that the present French government is ready to turn France into an agrarian hinterland of manufacturing Germany if it can continue romantic, pseudo-aristocratic rule for the benefit of its own members. Back to the land and farm-grown virtues are lauded in almost every copy of every newspaper. The ideals set before the young are muscular bodies ready for labor and atrophied minds receptive of orders—reproduction is the whole job of woman. Apathy, gravidity and obedience have succeeded liberty, equality and fraternity.

The city slicker is held up for obloquy; the industrial worker is a thing of shame.

Every paper is full of authoritarian propaganda; every moment before the awakening of a dazed people is being used to consolidate the control of a shoddy elite. This is the desire of Germany and this is the desire of the present rulers of France.

The Nazis manifestly hope to surround Germany with a group of satellite agrarian customers for German manufacturers. They represent a military people and care little for the things of the intellect and of the spirit. These can be left to the French with the contempt with which the Romans left art and matters of taste to the Greeks as sissified things unworthy of the consideration of a nation of governing he men. . . .

As realization returns to the French, the first sign of awakening is the understanding that all their hopes are bound up with British chances of victory. At first there was some bitterness caused by the fact that the English effort did not begin until the famous last Frenchman had disappeared. This fooling still continues but they realize that their cause and hope are nevertheless in British hands. . . .

I walked a good deal about the streets of Aix-les-Bains and as is my habit observed with some attention the offerings exposed for sale in the booksellers' windows. Aix is a first class but neither pre-eminent nor large watering place. There were four or five bookshops which offered in their windows a most interesting lot of books of memoirs, history, politics or science. What a remarkable contrast to the shops in similar places in other countries. It seems to me that it will be impossible to regiment and stultify a people so receptive of such reading. A Frenchman who knows the history of France can never be a slave.

It is impossible not to pity the unfortunate Pétain. I was his civilian aide when he visited Newport in 1932. Even then he seemed to me to be a feeble and tired man. His career rose to such a height and it seemed that he was then finishing it in honor and in ease. In the last years he has run a fearful and undignified race. Snatched from the comfort of pleasant and earned retirement to eat dirt as the symbol of his country at the Fascist court of Franco, he was carried to the center of all the world's attention to kiss the rod of Hitler as it drew blood from his country—the emblem not of defeat but of surrender. . . .

In this period Herbert Pell fiddled with the idea of returning to politics. His granduncle, Duncan Pell, had been lieutenant governor of Rhode Island and a founder of the Newport Reading Room. In Rhode Island there was interest among Democrats in running Herbert Pell for governor—he always had been active in Newport affairs and had once been offered the nomination for state senator there—but the movement did not pick up adequate support; he would have been pitted against the popular J. Howard McGrath. About this time he offered his Newport home, really an estate, to the city without cost for use by the city as a high school; he had not really lived in it for several years, since his appointment as minister. For inexplicable reasons, which may have involved a Republican city government's not wishing to accept a large gift from a prominent Democrat, the city turned down his offer. The house eventually was given to the Catholic diocese for use by the Sisters of St. Joseph as a Catholic girls' school—St. Catherine's Academy.

Very early in 1941 Herbert Pell was reassigned from Lisbon to Hungary. He and Claiborne flew to the United States with a brief stop at Bermuda. He immediately went to Washington for instructions. No longer was he to be at the window of Europe. He would be inside the house.

He left pessimistic. "This war," he told a friend, "has done to Europe what the thirty-year-war did to Germany. It will be the year two thousand before Europe is again the intellectual center of the world. It will surely take thirty years or more to reestablish the mental life of France, and more than that to set up again the great German universities. . . ."

Nor was he optimistic about the possibility of lasting peace. "It must be obvious to the meanest intelligence that civilization cannot go on if we are to be burdened with alternate periods of twenty years preparation and five years war," he wrote to another friend. He equated war with the plagues of the Middle Ages and believed that the same energy used to attack disease should be used to eliminate war. "Wars do not come by accident," he wrote. "They are not phenomena of nature. A group of doctors fighting against typhoid would investigate and try to purify the water supply of the affected district." Later Herbert Pell would try to purify the water. That would come after Hungary.

5 ROOSEVELT WAS WILLING TO HAVE HERBERT
Pell go either to Hungary or to Egypt and Pell preferred
Hungary. This time Senator Gerry made no trouble for
Pell when it came to his Senate confirmation, and Pell was
ready to return to Europe in February. He went by the
State Department to pick up his tickets and other para-
phernalia as well as his instructions. He anticipated because of the war situation—much of Europe had been
taken by the Nazis, and Hungary was waiting to be swal-
lowed with the other nations—that he would be briefed
on what was expected of him and on what he should
watch for particularly. "But," he said, "there was absolutely nothing." He did take his oath of office and then he
was allowed to impress his commission as minister with
the great seal of the United States. He first tried the seal on
a blank piece of paper and then he casually placed the
impressed paper in his pocket to keep as a souvenir. A
State Department functionary quickly informed him that
every imprint from the seal had to be either destroyed or
officially preserved. Herbert Pell's difficulties with the de-

partment would grow from this bit of trivia to matters of more seriousness.

Before returning to Europe he spoke to a gathering at Newport. "The United States has the choice," he told them in February, 1941, "of two terrible alternatives. Both imply danger. The great difference is that one must be taken or the other will be thrust upon us. . . . We can either take the leadership of the world and during the rest of our time and the time of our children and children's children be the great leading nation of the world or give some illustration to history of the fact that sordid and lazy selfish cynicism engendered by decadent privilege and easy life before crystalized in the phrase, 'After me, the deluge.'"

February, 1941, when Pell made those comments, was the month a six-foot, two-hundred-pound Japanese navy admiral arrived in the United States. His name was Kichisaburo Nomura and his confidential instructions informed him that the Japanese must obtain carte blanche in the western Pacific from the United States or the United States would be attacked. That was the month also when Roosevelt's lieutenants in the Congress were struggling to achieve passage of the Lend-Lease Act. Without passage of that program to supply arms to England, Adolf Hitler would control the Atlantic, the pathway for him to the United States. There was very little time remaining for the United States to make the choice of which Pell had spoken.

Perhaps because it was Europe during a war or perhaps because Herbert Pell was not now the kind of person who could throw a few things in a bag and be off, the trip to Budapest became a project. His boat brought him to Lisbon. He believed it best to keep his means of communication and transportation under his own control and decided to make the journey between Budapest and Lisbon by car —three cars. There was a station wagon he had purchased in New York and had sent over, a limousine and a truck to carry gasoline and spare parts, each vehicle with a chauffeur. The limousine carried Pell, his secretary and a friend of Olive's. Olive herself was waiting for the convoy in Berne. Rather than return to the United States with her husband, she had stayed in Europe because of an illness.

Traveling through Europe by automobile then always was an adventure and it was more so in wartime. The first delay was at the Spanish frontier at Badajoz, where the Pell flotilla encountered some Spanish customs officers. Spain had a rule then, fostered by its oil industry, that any oil crossing the nation had to be kept sealed; the purpose was to force people to buy Spanish oil and gas. Pell could not agree to that because he needed the fuel he had brought along for use by his vehicles. While the situation was being smoothed out, his party had to stay at Badajoz overnight. He was told not to worry; the Portuguese ambassador had made the same overland trip a few months before on his way to the Vatican and had been held up only three days. Overnight, all right, Pell thought; three days, no.

He believed he understood the Spanish people; he had visited the country often enough. "The Spaniard is proud, noble, disagreeable, cruel, and very dignified," he explained, "but there's absolutely nothing that he won't do for a cigarette. Offer any Spaniard that you're dealing with—at that time at least—a cigarette and he'll fly at it like a hungry orphan at an eclair."

The next morning Pell tested his theory. He offered a cigarette to the customs guard. After the guard had sucked a few puffs out of it, Pell turned to him and asked: "Do you like it?"

"Oh, yes, señor," was the answer.

Pell became as gracious as he could, and that stretched back many years to his growing up in Tuxedo Park; he could be very gracious indeed. "Will you do me the honor," he begged, "to accept a box, two boxes, a carton?"

Pell explained later: "We opened Spain up that way."

After passing the border the next day on their way to Madrid, the cars drove for a while and then stopped for a picnic lunch by the side of the road. A Spanish farmer on a donkey passed and Pell offered him a white roll he had brought from Portugal. The man accepted it but explained that he did not plan to eat it then. First he must take it home to his son, who never before had seen a white roll or white bread. "The general poverty in Spain is perfectly hideous. The people are miserable," Pell commented, recalling that 1941 trip. "In the middle of this town is a church big enough for a first class city, ornamented inside, usually with poor taste, but with a huge display of gold— probably an accumulation of precious metal important enough to buy the entire town—and with a priest who was always fat. I've seen very few skinny Spanish priests. . . ."

But the Spanish guards were no problem compared to the difficulties the Pell convoy encountered when it tried to leave Switzerland and cross Germany on its way to Budapest. The problem was not that a diplomat wanted to cross Germany; in 1941 that was still possible. But the usual crossing was by train. To cross by automobile was to be unique and for a German bureaucrat to approve anything not covered by regulations was to risk censure. "There wasn't a clerk in the German Foreign Office," Pell said, "who didn't know perfectly well that there was some Nazi standing behind him who would like to get his job." The days began to add up and Pell finally produced another ploy. He telephoned the American *chargé d'affaires* in Berne and in an angry voice lectured his fellow American on the right of an envoy of a neutral country to passage to his post. The telephone lecture was brief, directly to the point and blunt with rage. Also, it had not been directed to the American *chargé d'affaires* at the other end of the telephone line but to the German functionaries who were listening in on the conversation. It was a means of speaking sharply to the Germans while preventing them from responding. (Later Pell apologized to the *chargé d'affaires*, who told him that apologies were unnecessary; he had understood Pell's plan perfectly.)

Threats of calling in international lawyers succeeded and Pell was given permission to drive across Germany. He wished to go by way of Munich and Salzburg. Why? the Germans wanted to know. Pell explained that he

wished to stop at Munich and sit briefly in the Franziskanerkeller and drink beer and then continue by way of
Chiemsee, which was, he explained to the Germans, one
of the most beautiful places he had ever seen in his life. The
Nazis had a fetish for shunning weak sentiment and refused to accept it in an American. He was routed another
way.

Occasionally the roads in Germany were so bad as to
be near-impassable. At one point the road forked and in
desperation Pell had his chauffeur take the better of the
two roads. After several kilometers, Pell's car passed a man
on the road. Pell had the car stopped; he asked the man if
he was on the road to Innsbruck. The man shook his head,
slowly from side to side. This wasn't the road to Innsbruck,
he said. Rather, it was the Fuhrer's private road to
Berchtesgaden. Pell turned around.

Later that same day, Pell asked directions of a second
man "as you do without particularly looking at him." To
Pell's surprise, the man answered in French. He was a
French prisoner of war. Although it was the middle of
winter, the prisoner wore a summer-weight coat. He was
doing road work under German orders. Pell talked with
him for several minutes and found out that many of the
man's companions had died. He did not have to explain
from what; his cold and hunger were evident. Pell offered
him tins of cocoa, chocolate, coffee, cigarettes. The watering of the man's mouth could be seen in his eyes. But he
said he could not accept anything. The German guards
would take it from him as he passed through the gate.
Pell suggested he hide the cans under his clothes. "He had

thinned off to such an extent," Pell recalled, "that he was able to carry without attracting any attention about three kilos of chocolate and a full carton of cigarettes hidden away in his garments where the flesh had been when he was captured."

When he arrived in Budapest, Pell wrote a report on his trip through Germany to Secretary of State Hull. "There is no use underestimating the strength of the German military machine," he said. "I am told that a steady line of big motors drove through Budapest day and night at high speed, almost entirely without accident (I only heard of three). I have looked at these cars and have talked about them to mechanics; they are strong, well built and quite capable of standing up under rough usage. The coordination of the various parts of the army seems to be perfect—tanks, armored cars, aeroplanes, foot soldiers, all appear at the moment when they are needed. It is the old Confederate principle, 'git thar fustest with the mostest men.' The relation between the officers and men are very different than they were in the old imperial army. The spirit of the soldiers is enthusiastic and they at least seem to be well fed." His conclusion, if not heartening, was realistic. "Neither the German army nor anything else is unbeatable," he wrote Hull, "but it certainly will take a lot to beat them."

Before Pell had left Washington he told President Roosevelt: "Look for another place for me pretty soon as there is likely to be trouble." Actually it did not take much prescience to realize that Hungary soon would be involved in the war, and so would the United States. In the

United States that realization could not be accepted by
Charles A. Lindbergh, the daring aviator turned rabid iso-
lationist, or by Senator Burton K. Wheeler, the pro-Roose-
velt Democrat turned Roosevelt-hater, or by many others.
But people who understood Europe, who appreciated the
forces of history and who could rise above their prejudices
knew what was coming.

Because he did not anticipate having much time in Hungary, Pell decided to make his living quarters in the Ritz
Hotel, which was on the Pest, or flat side, of the Danube.
He secured six rooms with a balcony overlooking the
square. He and Olive redecorated, putting in an imitation
fireplace and covering the hotel furniture with white slipcovers. They did not do it elaborately, just sufficiently to
give it their own touch.

Naturally, Herbert Pell found a club to join in Budapest.
This was the Nemzeti Casino, or National Club, the best
club then in Hungary. He lunched there several times a
week and found its reputation well earned. Hungary then
was occupied by German troops, including many German
officers who lunched at the Nemzeti Casino. Not wishing
to embarrass anyone, Pell always sat down at an empty
table rather than with any of the Hungarians at their tables.
Invariably, however, first one Hungarian, then another,
still another, and finally one more came to his table, asked
to join him and then sat down. Shortly, Pell had to choose
a larger table for his luncheon. "This had nothing to do
with my personal charm," Pell said later. "It was partly a
desire for information but mostly, I think, a wish to advertise their opinion. Manifestly, a man walking up to the

American minister and joining him at the table was flaunting his opinion of Germany."

Hungary's problem at that time is seen on a map. It was a small country bordered on the east by Rumania, which was bordered in turn by Russia. On Hungary's west lay Austria and Czechoslovakia, occupied by German troops. Adolf Hitler then had to have Hungary; it would be a barrier for Russia, if Russia chose to attack Germany, and could be a pathway for Germany if Germany decided to attack Russia. For the Hungarians to have risked German military power appeared foolhardy. Also, in the beginning at least, the Hungarian regent, Admiral Miklós von Nagybánya Horthy, had some sympathy for Hitler's anti-communism and cooperated with the Germans in hopes of acquiring Hungarian lands taken earlier by Yugoslavia. The result was that in 1941, when Herbert Pell came to Hungary, he came to a German satellite presided over by Admiral Horthy but ruled by German bullets. "It was," Pell said, "a very unsympathetic alliance."

Even he did not realize how unsympathetic an alliance it was. Howard Travers, a foreign service officer, had been stationed in Budapest for six years and had come to know Admiral Horthy, and Count Teleki, his prime minister, and to admire them both. They understood that their nation was in danger and were, Travers was certain, pro-American. They gave Travers their confidence. On one occasion the Regent told Travers of having been ordered to meet Hitler. "Travers," Admiral Horthy said to the American, "the world has changed when the Regent can be ordered around by a damned little corporal."

On the morning of April 2, 1941, when Herbert Pell was still in transit, the Regent told Travers that Hitler was becoming more and more demanding, that he insisted that the Nazi army be allowed to enter Hungary to "protect" it from Yugoslavia. Late that night, actually 1 A.M. the morning of April 3, Count Teleki telephoned Travers and asked him to come over. "When I saw him," Travers recalled, "perhaps half an hour later, I hardly knew him. He was a beaten man. He was in very bad condition, very emotional and with great difficulty said, 'Travers, the rumors that the Regent mentioned to you are true and at this moment Nazi troops are entering Hungary—O God, what can I do. It is my country. I have tried and failed.'" Shortly after Travers left him, Count Teleki committed suicide by shooting himself in the head.

Two days later Great Britain severed relations with Hungary, and the United States legation was charged with handling the remaining British business in Budapest. Travers went to the British minister to place the facilities of the American legation at his disposal. The British minister answered: "What a shame that the British Empire had to have your country represent it. You are a gang of cowards with no guts and yellow to the core, just bloody cowards. Now get out!" All in all, Budapest was no easy post.

Pell had arrived in Budapest in April but had to wait several weeks before being formally presented to Admiral Horthy. There had been a mix-up. The man who all his life had subscribed to the rule that gentlemen dress properly on all occasions, who always moved with everything he needed—even if it required three cars to cross war-ravaged Europe—this man had come to Budapest without his formal morning clothes. He did not have a cutaway coat with which to be presented at court! Travers inquired discreetly of the Regent if Pell could be presented wearing a business suit, but the reply was a blunt "no." Admiral Horthy maintained the position that although he could be ordered around by a "damned little corporal," he still was considered the ruler of his country by his people and the presentation would be proper or not at all. The cutaway must be sent for.

Finally, on May 19, Herbert Claiborne Pell, formally attired in cutaway coat, presented his credentials as American Minister to Hungary to Admiral Horthy at the Royal Palace. Despite the brouhaha over the coat, Horthy was very anxious to meet Pell for several reasons. He believed that ultimately the United States must rescue Europe from Hitler. Horthy had known and admired Franklin Roosevelt during and immediately after the First World War; Horthy had been admiral of the Austro-Hungarian fleet when Roosevelt was assistant secretary of the Navy. Horthy knew that Pell was a close friend of Roosevelt's and considered him a means of bringing the plight of Hungary to the attention of the President and the American people. At the presentation ceremony, Horthy told Pell of his violent dislike for Hitler and the Communists and said that neither was to be trusted.

Pell responded sympathetically to the situation in Hungary. "The Germans exploited Hungary," he reported. What Germany had done to other nations, she was now doing to Hungary. "It should be remembered," he said, "that Hungary was one of the few countries in Europe that exported wheat but when we were in Hungary there was practically no wheat or bread available to the Hungarian people." Some Hungarians tried to hide some of their wheat crop for themselves, but they were unsuccessful. "The Germans knew a great deal more than the Hungarians did about what was going on in Hungary and how much wheat was being grown," Pell said.

Shortly after Pell arrived in Budapest, a new German minister also arrived, a man named Dietrich von Jagow "in many ways a boorish little fellow." Von Jagow was from a prominent family in Germany but had always been considered the black sheep. Coming into Hungary as the German minister automatically made him also the black sheep of the Budapest diplomatic community and he did nothing to overcome that designation. He violated diplomatic protocol, not in a way to demonstrate his independence but rather in a manner to show his ignorance. The diplomatic custom then was that a new minister announce his arrival to his colleagues with a formal letter written in French. French had evolved as the language of diplomacy and its usage was standard. Von Jagow compiled with protocol sufficiently to write the note but did so in German rather than French. Pell answered in French. The Chilean minister responded in Spanish and it was rumored that the Egyptian minister answered in Egyptian. The responses illustrate why one language was necessary.

Von Jagow paid an official call on Pell one August afternoon at five o'clock. Tea was ready when Von Jagow entered, clicked his heels and saluted with a loud "Heil

Hitler." He sat down on the edge of a chair, did not drink, eat or smoke. "Some one more accustomed to good society," said Pell, "had evidently told him that he must stay at least fifteen minutes. He kept continually looking at his watch and when the time was up, he sprang to his feet, saluted and left." Pell, who appreciated good manners, considered Von Jagow's visit "a very ungentlemanly performance." Von Jagow's wife never paid the required courtesy call on Olive Pell. Pell said he never knew whether this was because Von Jagow feared his wife's own bad manners or because he feared her good manners would put him to shame.

Von Jagow, after his courtesy call, was determined not to concern himself any longer with the American minister —formally, that is. The Germans were, however, very interested in Herbert Pell's household and they determined to find out as much as they could. And that was a great deal, for what the Germans lacked in courtesy, they made up for handsomely in craftiness. As Ladislas Farago has pointed out, "There was hardly a British or American diplomatic outpost throughout the world, even in places as exotic as Afghanistan and Nepal, that was not under intimate observation by at least one German agent." They had a line into the British embassy's mailroom in Lisbon, a female agent in the British legation in Chile, a "Cicero" in the bedroom of the British ambassador in Ankara, and they also had a spy in Herbert Pell's suite at the Ritz. She was a young, attractive woman hired to work as a maid and to help with the serving when the Pells entertained. She occasionally cleaned in Herbert Pell's study and found that he kept a complete file of letters to him from President Roosevelt and others, and also carbons of his letters to the President, to his son Claiborne and to other relatives and friends. The maid believed she had stumbled onto a gold mine; the Germans would pay handsomely for this, she was certain. All she had to do was contact them. She did not have to worry; the Germans contacted her.

For some time after Pell's arrival in Hungary, the Germans in Berlin had been hearing of his great popularity. Not only were there the luncheons at the club which attracted so many Hungarians, but also many prominent Hungarians paid social calls on the American minister and his wife while ignoring the Germans. The Nazis interpreted this as it was intended—as an affront to the Third Reich and to the representatives of Adolf Hitler. A formal protest was filed with the Hungarian foreign minister in Budapest. He shrugged his shoulders over the Nazi complaint. What could he do, he asked, if private citizens wish to call on their friend the American minister? Rebuffed and made to look somewhat silly by that answer, the Nazis in Berlin ordered their Budapest henchmen to keep a constant watch on the Pells. The hope was that the Germans could catch the Pells in some indiscretion that would force the Hungarian government to expel them. Hotel employees were paid to report every movement Herbert and Olive Pell made. Whenever they left the hotel, they were followed by German agents. And the Germans began to seek out Hungarians who knew Pell and who might be persuaded to spy on him. One of these was the maid in the Pell apartment.

She had been hired because she knew how to dust and serve, but her real talent was adding up money. She told the Germans what she had access to and they realized they had stumbled on an espionage agent's dream. Soon her occasional pilfering was not adequate for the Germans. Whenever the Pells were out, an agent came to their suite. With the maid's help, he opened the Pell files and took the documents to the maid's bedroom, where he photographed them in quantity before returning them.

The material seemed invaluable. There was the correspondence between Roosevelt and Pell, dating from 1937; many of Pell's reports to the State Department, as well as his private letters. Of course the tone of the letters was disconcerting to the Germans who read them. Herbert Pell frequently spoke critically of the Nazis and of what the Nazis were doing to the nations they occupied. There was a long letter commenting on Charles Lindbergh, then much admired by the Nazis because of his efforts to keep the United States out of the European war. The comments were not flattering: "Lindbergh has attempted to hoodwink and deceive his own generation . . . well-schooled in promoting his own public image . . . his mentality will lead a certain social class to believe that it can control and use him for its own goals. . . ."

In a letter to Claiborne, read by the Germans, Herbert Pell expressed the hope that England would not declare war on Hungary. "There's a large group of people here," he wrote, "who want to impede Germany's war efforts and they would be imprisoned or at least restricted in their work should war break out." The Germans read on. "The U.S. legation was the center of anti-axis sentiments," said a memorandum by Pell. "I was able to get books, which the Germans were eager to keep from circulating, and have them passed on from hand to hand until they fell apart from use. The New York papers, although six weeks old by the time they reached Budapest, informed me about events the Germans managed to keep from the public. While I stayed out of active politics, I offered some practical suggestions and arranged discussion meetings to encourage the Hungarian government. A very able Hungarian described our legation as 'their last ray of civilization.' "

The Germans read on. There were no plans, no embarrassing revelations. Rather, all the venom Herbert Pell had for the Nazi system which had spilled out in his letters to Roosevelt, all the horror he felt at what the Germans had done to occupied lands—the shock of the French, the prisoner of war on the road in Germany, the critique of the German bureaucracy—was shown to the Germans. And they did not like it. They had bought a pig in a poke. "After careful examination of the Pell material received to date," said a German memorandum, "the Foreign Ministry regrets to conclude that the letters of the former American Minister Pell contain nothing of interest. . . . Since the letters contain little except a categorical refutation and rejection of the National Socialist and Fascist ideologies, it is considered inadvisable to bring them to the attention of the Reich's Foreign Minister."

The great espionage coup was a bust.

Although Pell now was fifty-seven years of age, he still was a man of great strength. He had an opportunity to demonstrate it in a minor incident that was much talked of in later days. On a Friday in August he and Olive had gone to pay a formal call on the Regent and Madame Horthy at Godollo, where they lived during the summer. Pell was, of course, dressed in his errant formal diplomatic costume—striped trousers, cutaway coat, top hat. On the way back to Budapest, the Pell car came upon a car that had been in an accident. The man and woman who had been driving in it were uninjured and the car appeared undamaged—except that it had turned over on its top and its wheels were spinning in the air. A couple of Hungarian soldiers had stopped and stood staring helplessly at the car. They flagged down Pell's car and asked him to send a wrecker out from the city. Six-foot-five-inch, two-hundred-and-fifty-pound Herbert Pell emerged from his limousine. Learning that the only problem was an upside-down car, he said that correcting that did not seem like a great challenge. With skeptical soldiers helping him, he thrust his shoulder against the car, shoved, and the car flipped over so that it stood upright. The man and woman who had been driving it got in, turned on the ignition and to their surprise found that it worked perfectly. They drove away. Herbert Pell gave a wave of his hand to the astonished soldiers and joined Olive in their car for the return to Budapest.

One of Pell's first problems of the war in Eastern Europe was in Yugoslavia. In the wake of the German capture of Belgrade, the Yugoslavian capital, there was an outbreak of typhus in that city. Pell's job was to get the one hundred or so Americans safely out of the capital before they were struck by the epidemic. "The only way you could do that was to send a boat down the Danube," he recalled. That would cost several thousands of dollars and he cabled the State Department for authorization to spend the money. The answer came back that according to State Department records a railroad ran between Belgrade and Budapest and the Americans should be evacuated by train because it was cheaper. Pell was aghast. The railroad had not existed for some time. What had not been destroyed by the Germans had been seized by them for military purposes; it was completely unavailable for civilian use. A boat was the only escape route for the Americans in Belgrade, and a decision had to be made quickly. It was early spring and the Danube boats still were in drydock. Getting one ready required several days of preparation. Pell ordered a boat, guaranteeing to pay for it out of his own pocket. He then cabled the State Department a second time, explaining the railroad situation and asking again for authorization to use a boat, repeating that it was a necessity. "That of course meant the expenditure of government money and the assuming of responsibility," Pell recalled, "so they did as they always do, they had a conference of otherwise unoccupied clerks who checked the thing over and over, and in about ten days sent a notice that it was all right to go ahead." By the time the notice came, the boat already was on its way out of Belgrade and the Americans were safe. Some years later Pell recalled that incident:

> If I had waited for the authorization to come ... a lot of them would have died of typhus, all of them would have been living in discomfort and danger, but nobody could have criticized me. I was a servant of the government. I had stated the case to the government, and if I had just waited until the government, in its own good time, chose to decide, there could have been no complaint by anybody. Of course if they had had a Minister there that didn't have the money in his pocket, he couldn't have done it. That is a fair illustration of their [the clerks'] distrust of their own representatives, especially when it comes to money.

In years following, Herbert Pell continued to have difficulties with the State Department and he never could get over the suspicion that the department was, in reality, a group of "otherwise unoccupied clerks" unprepared to assume responsibility.

During the summer of 1941 he made a quick trip to Vienna. He had known Vienna well in the years between the wars and had been welcomed to its society. In 1928, during a lengthy visit, he went to dinners where the host announced that the assembled group would dine in German or in English or in French—whichever language interested the host that night. And from that moment on, the entire dinner conversation would be in the language chosen. Speaking a second or third language, said Pell, "is taken as part of the necessary education of any man with the slightest claim to cultivation" in Europe. Pell also recalled that the business of languages could be carried to extremes. Hungarian aristocrats did not like Austrian aristocrats, and the ill feelings were reciprocated. The troubles were ethnic, political, social and probably too deeply rooted to be remembered. When a member of Hungarian society came to Vienna during the time between the wars, he did not have any hesitation about speaking German to such persons as taxi drivers, sales clerks and the like. But when he went out in society with persons of his own class, he refused to speak German. In return, the Austrian member of high society refused to speak Hungarian. Thus it was necessary for them to meet on a neutral ground, such as French or Italian.

When Pell went to Vienna in this summer of 1941, he found it dead. The city never had been the carefree, Strauss-waltz, champagne-bubbling town of fiction. But it had been a pleasant city filled with people, cars, bright shops along the Karntner Strasse. This time the Karntner Strasse was almost completely empty. The shop windows were bare; the people had disappeared. Perhaps in Vienna, more than anywhere else, the Germans had succeeded in draining away the life to leave only the corpse. "I left with an old lady we knew there," said Pell, "a kilo of tea, one of coffee and one of chocolate. She was as grateful as if I had given her diamonds." Pell had been given food coupons for three days, but he stayed only one. He used up his three days' worth of coupons "and I was not overfed."

Much of the Nazi bestiality still was to be learned. The revelations of Buchenwald were still in the future. But enough was known even in 1941 to realize that the German system was built on the traditional concept of dictators: take away from the many to support the few. In the United States it still was difficult to accept that the Nazis could act so brutally; Anne Morrow Lindbergh and other isolationists wondered in print if perhaps there might not be something of value to be gained from the Nazi system just as the respected liberal economist Otto Nathan asked if the world could not learn something positive from Nazi economics. But to those who saw it and especially to those who, like Pell, knew well that Europe had been before Adolf Hitler had begun to suck its life juices from it, it was very evident that Naziism offered nothing for the future, that it represented history shifting into reverse.

One August day Herbert and Olive Pell drove out to St. Margaret's Island with a friend, Baronness Imre Jeszenszky. There was a polo tournament there, culminating in a game between the Hungarians and Italians. The Pells and their hostess were walking along the path behind the grandstand when they were called by Madame Istvan Horthy, the daughter-in-law of the Regent. She asked them to sit in her box, which they did. They could see the Regent and the Italian minister sitting together a short distance away. The minister looked glum because, Pell correctly assumed, his team had been defeated by the Hungarians. The Italian minister grew angrier when the Regent left him and walked to his daughter-in-law's box to chat with the Pells. The Regent talked for some time and smiled for a photographer who took his picture with the Pells. At a time when Hungary was supposed to be a satellite of Germany, the paying of so much attention to the American minister was construed as a slap at Germany and Italy, as certainly the Regent intended it to be.

The next month the Regent asked the Pells to come down to dinner at Godollo. It was a family dinner, with the Regent and Madame Horthy, their son Istvan and his wife and the Pells. "It was a very pleasant little party," Pell recalled. "After dinner the Regent played bridge with his son and daughter-in-law and me; my wife and Madame Horthy sat and talked until it became time to leave." Olive was still painting and the Regent and Madame Horthy agreed to sit for her. The evening seemed to be an average gathering of people who liked one another and appreciated one another's company. And, yes, the Regent made clear, he and his wife would be happy to dine with the Pells at their apartment in the Ritz some evening. Just a normal relationship, except that in wartime nothing can be normal.

A few days before the scheduled dinner party at the Pells's, Herbert Pell was taking his usual evening stroll along the Danube when a car drove up with the Hungarian chief of protocol. He was greatly agitated and insisted that Pell come to the Foreign Office immediately. Once there, Pell learned that the Regent was unable to keep his dinner engagement at the Pells's apartment. "It was manifest," Pell said, "that the Germans objected to any such sign of friendliness to the United States." Although the Regent's refusal to come to dinner was, technically, a snub, Herbert Pell understood it was dictated and shrugged it off. He believed the incident actually hurt the Germans in Hungary and called it an illustration "of the ever present tactlessness and stupidity of German officials." He explained that if the Regent had come to the dinner party, a very few people would have known about it or cared. However, he said, "the open demonstration that the German state was able so to overawe the Hungarian government that it could force the chief of the nation into a position of such discourtesy, kicked up on all sides a great deal of indignation so that in the end German unpopularity was much increased." The Regent remained a friend of the Pells, however, until his death in Portugal in 1957; in fact, the Pells did what they could to help the Horthys in their impoverished years of postwar exile.

A picture of Herbert Pell as a minister of the United States was drawn by Franklin Mott Gunther, the American minister in Bucharest, in a letter to Franklin Roosevelt. "Last week, . . ." he wrote, "I visited Budapest. . . . I found the Pells in great form. Bertie is already a popular figure with his leonine head and giant stature, and the Buick station wagon in which he generally drives about unfailingly collects a crowd. They are both much liked and appreciated and the fact that he is an old friend of yours loses nothing in the telling among the Hungarians. . . . Olive is most talented. I saw two portraits painted by her . . . which are absolute 'knockouts.' She seems to have the great gift of converting to canvas a person's most charming, albeit fleeting, expression. As Ruskin once remarked, 'For a hundred people who can talk there is only one man who can think; but for a thousand who can think there is only one that can see.' Bertie likes it there. . . ."

Gunther was a good friend of Laszlo de Bardossy, who had become Hungarian prime minister and minister of foreign affairs. "As soon as he knew that I was in Budapest," Gunther wrote the President, "he asked me to come to tea and I found him alone. We talked for about an hour over the teacups. He began by expressing his liking for and appreciation of Bertie. . . ."

Herbert Pell never could forget his relationship to his numerous cousins who were part of the clan; keeping up with and advising them, assisting them at times, were part of the responsibilities he felt strongly. And even while minister to Hungary he took time out to write a young girl, a second cousin, a chatty letter of news about himself and of their mutual relatives. Then he asked her to let him know how she was getting along at school, saying that both he and Olive are "always very glad to get your news and to hear what is happening to you." He urged her to pay attention to her schooling. "The time may very well come when you will not be able to have a stable and horses," he wrote, "but you will always have access to a public library."

And he wrote to his mother regularly. In one letter he talked of Olive's painting—"for the benefit of winter charities organized by Madame Horthy . . . her hand has

(12) In 1937, President Roosevelt asked Herbert Pell to be minister to Portugal. They are shown on the front porch of Roosevelt's home in Hyde Park a few days before Pell left to assume his new post. Standing is Mrs. Olive Pell, Herbert's second wife, and sitting with them is Edward Perkins, treasurer of the New York Democratic State Committee. (FRANKLIN D. ROOSEVELT LIBRARY)

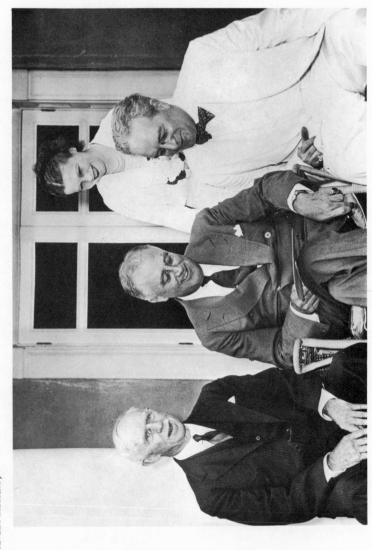

(13) Pell and Roosevelt chatting on the front porch of Pellbridge, Pell's New York home near Hyde Park, where F.D.R. had stopped by to wish his friend *bon voyage.* (SENATOR CLAIBORNE PELL)

(14) Herbert Pell began his ministerial duties in Lisbon with a formal presentation of his credentials. (SENATOR CLAIBORNE PELL)

(15) The new minister at work in his office. (SENATOR CLAIBORNE PELL)

(16) Hosting one of numerous state functions, Herbert and Olive Pell await the arrival of guests in their garden. (FRANKLIN D. ROOSEVELT LIBRARY)

Herbert Pell

Wendell Willkie

LISBON
HARBOUR

(17) Lisbon was a window on the holocaust developing in Europe, and the pace of activity quickened for Herbert Pell in the 1940s. Here he is shown with Wendell L. Willkie, just defeated by F.D.R. in the 1940 election and now on a European mission for him. (SENATOR CLAIBORNE PELL)

(18) From Lisbon, Pell was transferred to Budapest and received Hungary's declaration of war against the United States. He is shown at his desk in the American legation there. (SENATOR CLAIBORNE PELL)

(19) After his experience with the War Crimes Commission, Pell retired. He lived for a while at his New York State home, Pellbridge, then resumed his European travels. (SENATOR CLAIBORNE PELL)

(20) This black and white silhouette, done earlier in his life in Paris, captures his characteristic dignity and refinement. (SENATOR CLAIBORNE PELL)

(21) In his seventies, Herbert Pell attends a formal ball in London with his wife, Olive. (SENATOR CLAIBORNE PELL)

(22) Herbert Pell tried to pay as much attention to the upbringing of his grandson, Herbert C. Pell III *(left)*, as he had to that of his own son *(right)*. (SENATOR CLAIBORNE PELL)

(23) A few years before he died Herbert Pell said of himself: "I have been well served by the world, and by fortune, and I retire with confidence in the future of my country and of mankind. There is nothing I can do more except to shake hands and say that I have had a very good time — which I certainly have. (SENATOR CLAIBORNE PELL)

lost none of its skill by enforced idleness while we were in Portugal." The weather was turning cold: "As far as I can gather the climate here is very much like that of New York, although it does not get quite so cold." Social life had come to a halt because of the difficulties in moving about. Gasoline was practically nonexistent. Tires could not be found. "The dressmakers here are going in for short evening dresses so it will be possible to walk out to parties. . . ." The date of this letter was December 1, 1941.

A few days before Pell sent this letter to his mother, Russia had sent a message to England. Russia now had been at war with Germany for five months and she wanted England to offer an ultimatum to Hungary: withdraw her troops from the Russian front or else England would declare war on Hungary. Because Pell represented the British interests in Budapest, it was his job to deliver the ultimatum. He saw no value in it. The Hungarian troops on the Russian frontier were small in number. "There was one case of a cavalry regiment that disappeared," he reported, "all their horses were stolen. What happened was that the men got out and sold them to peasants on their way through the country and they continued on foot." It also was obvious that Hungary never could attack England and there was little England could do against Hungary except occasionally send a bomber over. On the other side, Hungary's real sympathies seemed to lie with the Allies, and Pell felt that the Hungarians actually were obstructing the Germans in many small ways. War, Pell argued in a cable to the State Department, "would curtail the activities of the many influential men who now work against Germany, while the pro-German elements would be strengthened." He hoped that the State Department would pressure the English into holding back their ultimatum.

His efforts failed. That Saturday, December 6, he received a cable from the American State Department to the effect that England had declared war on Hungary. He understood that he must immediately deliver the message. It was not inconceivable that England might send a group of planes over on a bombing raid, and the war declaration had to be formally delivered before that happened.

During the next few hours Herbert Pell became the man who could not declare war. Officials at the Hungarian Foreign Office knew that the war declaration was coming up. Pell himself had discussed it at great length with Prime Minister Bardossy. Knowing diplomatic requirements, Bardossy or his representative should have been on call to receive the declaration. But Pell found neither man at the foreign office. The building, in fact, was closed. With Pell was a secretary who spoke Hungarian; he alternately screamed at and cajoled a building guard, until he admitted them. The building seemed empty. Pell and his secretary wandered through the corridors looking for someone, anyone. At last, through a transom they saw some light. They knocked on the door.

Inside they found a man who identified himself as a member of the Hungarian consular service. This was his office and he lived there during the winter rather than in his apartment near the Danube, which grew so damp in winter as to be uninhabitable. They had interrupted him as he was preparing his supper, cooking a small fish over a kerosene lamp. And to give the scene a familiar touch for Pell, the man was wearing a blue-and-red-striped robe from the Racquet and Tennis Club of New York. Herbert Pell was certain of the robe's source; his brother, Clarence, once had been president of the club.

Pell explained that he was the American minister and his responsibility was to deliver England's declaration of war against Hungary. Would this man help him? In the true spirit of diplomacy the man agreed to help Pell deliver the war declaration against his own country. First they telephoned the foreign minister's home. A voice on the telephone informed them that Bardossy had gone to the opera. They called the opera. The phone rang and rang; finally it was answered by a porter. Would he look in his audience for Prime Minister Bardossy? No, was the answer. Why? Because, the porter explained, there was no audience; there had been no opera that night. Then they telephoned every theater in Budapest to demand that the audience be searched for Bardossy. He did not turn up. They called his home every twenty minutes. Finally word reached the Prime Minister that an American named Pell and another man in the Hungarian consular service were trying desperately to find him. They rendezvoused at the Foreign Office. Bardossy was in a tuxedo, a sign he had been at a party, and wore some decorations, a sign he had stopped at his home on the way to the Foreign Office. With him were four soldiers whom he apparently had picked up on the street and brought to his office to present arms as Herbert Claiborne Pell formally told the Hungarian government that England considered herself at war with Hungary. Diplomatic protocol had triumphed, thanks to Pell's tenacity and to the unknown consular official who wore robes from the Racquet and Tennis Club and cooked fish over a kerosene lamp in his office.

Shortly afterward Pell was instructed to inform Hungary that first Canada and Australia, then New Zealand and the Union of South Africa, had declared war on her. He did this without difficulty.

His own days as a neutral had come to an end also. The Japanese bombed Pearl Harbor. Hitler declared war on the United States. "I was in my office," Pell said, "and there was this screaming on the radio which was in a language and accent and at a speed that was far beyond any German of mine. Eventually they told me he had declared war on us." Germany's declaration of war against the United States meant its satellites also would declare war.

A few days after Pearl Harbor, Herbert Pell was in his Budapest office when he received a telephone call from the Brazilian minister. The Brazilian wanted to come up to see him; Pell offered to go to him. No, insisted the Brazilian, he would come to Pell's office. The two men talked informally about inconsequential things for a while after he arrived. Their conversation was interrupted when Pell was peremptorily summoned to the Foreign Office, obviously to be informed that Hungary had broken diplomatic relations with the United States. The Brazilian minister, who had known the summons was coming, then offered to drive Pell to the Foreign Office. "So I went up to receive the notice of the breaking of relations in his car with the Brazilian flag flying on the front," Pell said. "I thought that was a very nice touch of American solidarity."

When he returned to the legation, Pell immediately began to destroy codes, records, communications and other materials. There was quite a lot of it to burn and some Hungarian soldiers came to his assistance by offering a couple of flame bombs. The Americans then simply piled the material up, tossed the Hungarian bombs at the mass and waited for the destruction to be completed. The next day Pell was again summoned to the Foreign Office. Admiral Horthy, the Regent, had wanted to avoid declaring war on the United States, hoping the Germans would be satisfied with the severing of relations. But the Germans insisted on the final act. Pell recalled the scene vividly. "There was Bardossy," he wrote. "He was very much worried and this time he was actually in tears when I came up. He had tears running down his face and, just as I came in, the German minister walked out of his office in a state of rage, and Bardossy declared war on me."

The official notice from Pell to President Roosevelt is dated December 13, 1941, and reads: "The Prime Minister informed me, the American Minister at Budapest, at five-thirty this afternoon that Hungary considers war to exist between Hungary and the United States. Pell." There was no room in diplomatic cables for mention of tears.

After the war declaration, Pell finished the work at the legation and returned to the Ritz. He now had to sit and wait until he and the legation staff were returned to the United States. Hungarians came to visit him; they sent him flowers and other presents. The widespread friendship of the Hungarian people for the United States was showing itself. Whenever Pell and his wife went out, they were cheered on the streets. When Pell was restricted to his hotel suite, he believed it was because the Germans had complained of his popularity. He was wrong. Actually the Hungarians were doing him a favor. They had learned of the maid who was helping the Germans photograph his private documents. The Hungarians did not feel they could tell Herbert Pell. They were, after all, at war with his country. But by restricting him to his quarters, the Hungarians made it impossible for the Germans to photograph any more of Pell's letters.

While Pell was waiting to be sent home, the German foreign minister, Joachim von Ribbentrop, came to Budapest and stayed at the Ritz. He demanded the best suite. When informed that the best suite was occupied by the American minister, his reaction was as expected: "Throw him out." Pell was ejected, but he took his white slipcovers with him. "I would be damned," he said, "if I would have that fellow sitting on my slipcovers."

But the Germans were complaining about the Pells's popularity, and the Hungarian government felt compelled to restrict the American minister in some way. He was finally sent off for "durance vile," as he called it, to St. Margaret's Island in the Danube. During the summer, the island was a favorite vacation spot for the people of Budapest. There were hot springs, a summer resort hotel, polo games and lovely gardens to walk through escorted by friendly pheasants and peacocks. In the winter, however, it was just a cold, dismal spot. Pell told the Hungarian authorities he would go to the island only if he were properly protected. "I want two men outside my apartment at *all* times," he insisted. "I want six men in the hotel, one of whom is walking around the outside all the time, and a guard at the entrance to the island." The Hungarians, either because they wanted to appease the American or because they were impressed by Pell's commanding voice or perhaps because they agreed he needed protection, granted his wishes. He did need the protection. One night a gang of Nazis in civilian clothes carrying pistols and whips tried to invade the island, threatening to attack Pell. They were stopped by the Hungarian guards and turned back.

Moving Pell from the Ritz to St. Margaret's did not produce the results the Germans had expected. Although gasoline was virtually impossible to obtain for civilians, the Hungarians still came to visit the American minister. They walked long distances to have lunch or dinner with Pell. Many of them stayed the afternoon for a few rubbers of bridge. These were not government officials; they were too rigidly directed by the Germans to follow their own wishes. These were, instead, the prominent members of society, the businessmen, the men Pell had met at the Nemzeti Casino. They continued to insult the Nazis by stopping at Pell's table.

Pell and the other members of the American group were concerned that they would not be released, not because

Hitler feared them but because Hitler did not wish to exchange them for Germans or Hungarians in the United States. Hitler did not want European nationals returning to speak of the quality of life in America and wishing to live there. He correctly judged their sentiments. The Hungarian diplomatic delegation to the United States, for example, was shifted to Hershey, a resort town in Pennsylvania, after war broke out. Its members did not wish to return to Hungary. As a result, the Pells did not arrive in the United States until June because he had to wait until the Hungarians at Hershey were persuaded to return to their native land.

Preparations for the return for Herbert and Olive Pell and the other Americans, however, began shortly after war was declared. A special train was assembled to take them to Lisbon. Organizing the train was no small logistics problem for the Nazis. They never enjoyed being publicly ridiculed and revealed as inept. This meant that they did not want to sponsor a train carrying a cargo of diplomats if that train might break down, to the amusement of the world. They had to find, then, engineers capable of taking the train from Budapest, through Croatia, northern Italy, southern France, Spain and Portugal. They also needed several good engines to pull the train. They ultimately rounded up the proper personnel and the equipment, and the train was scheduled to leave at midnight, January 18, 1942.

The United States and Hungary were at war. No matter what earlier relationship had existed between the Regent and Franklin Roosevelt, Herbert Pell and the people of

Hungary, they were at this moment at war. Their soldiers were expected to fight each other, to kill each other. Their bombers were expected to destroy each other. And for Pell and the other Americans the last glimpse of a country for which they had had great affection was to be an empty train station on a cold January night.

But when they arrived at the station, it was not empty. Howard Travers estimates that there must have been five thousand Hungarians there to say good-bye to their friends, the Americans. Herbert Pell recalled the waiting room packed "with people of all classes, rich and poor, swell and common, all gathered at considerable risk to themselves as the crowd was undoubtedly observed by the Gestapo." These people, Pell said, had come "to bid farewell to the best of their hopes for their country." And then he added—he wrote this in the early 1940s—"I hate to think of them all as they must be now. I don't suppose that I shall see many of them alive again."

Waiting by the train was an aide of Admiral Horthy. In full view of the crowd he saluted the Pells and presented Olive with a large bouquet of orchids. In a loud voice that could be heard throughout the station, by Hungarian and German alike, the Regent's aide announced that the flowers were for Mrs. Pell and from the Regent.

The train pulled out of the station a few moments later. For the Americans on board the last memory of Hungary was of a people thrusting forward their decency at the risk of their lives. The Nazi experience meant many things to the people who lived through it or who read about it. The one thing it meant at that moment to those people aboard the train was that being decent, honorable and friendly was possible only at the risk of one's life.

The morning of Monday, June 1, 1942, the Swedish liner *Drottningholm*, gaudily painted and brightly marked as a diplomatic ship, docked in Jersey City with nine hundred and eight passengers aboard. Among these passengers was the first group of American diplomats to be exchanged since the United States had entered the war. Escorted by patrol boats, the steamer moved through the bay watched by thousands of people commuting by ferry. Despite the summer squall that morning, the commuters as well as the people on the shore, saw her bright blue and yellow markings. They watched her then because she contrasted sharply with the camouflaged grays of the other ships in the harbor which belonged to nations at war.

The *Drottningholm* carried a strange collection of passengers. Although chartered by the United States Maritime Commission as a rescue ship for Americans stranded in Europe, almost half its passengers were non-Americans; they were Europeans trying to escape from a continent overrun by Nazis. Of the four hundred and eighty Americans on board, there were some who had been in Europe so long they could not speak English. Some of the elderly Americans had not been in their homeland since childhood. Others born in Europe had never seen the United States. There were the American diplomats from Rumania, Rome and Germany, as well as Herbert Pell and his entourage from Budapest. Pell attracted attention, not only as usual because of his great size and striking appearance, but also because piled high around him on the Jersey City pier were eighty-five cases of French, Spanish and Portuguese wines. (That wine lasted many years. In 1970 Senator and Mrs. Claiborne Pell donated eleven cases of Muscatel De Setubal to a wine auction in Washington to raise money for the Washington Intergroup Youth Program and police-youth programs.)

Pell knew that the war the United States was now in would produce many changes, that the rich of which he had been a prominent member would have to surrender many of its privileges. "We will certainly be obliged to give up a great many luxuries," he wrote to a friend, "but I cannot agree with a few of my swell friends that this means the end of all possible happiness and distinction." Almost sixty years old now and having led a life others envied, Pell felt he could be somewhat philosophical. He was optimistic about the future, encouraged by what young people were doing. "A great many of the sons of my friends, and my own boy too," he said, "have joined the armed forces of the country as privates or as seamen. A good many of them have achieved promotion, also including Claiborne, and are now officers, but have done this without the exertion of any outside influence in their favor. The boys honestly seem to prefer to enter this way. . . . These boys are certainly better than we were at their age. They have a more serious purpose in life and a better understanding of their responsibility to their country."

Claiborne was typical of these young men that Herbert Pell was writing about. He had wanted to join the service early in 1941 because he realized war was coming. Like many others with a college education he applied for a naval reserve commission. He would have received it except for an eye defect. Herbert Pell wrote President Roosevelt asking that the eye defect be waived; the father was not trying to save his son from military service but to help him enter. Roosevelt answered that he made a policy of not interfering in matters of that kind. Meanwhile, Claiborne had enlisted in the Coast Guard as a seaman. Learning this, Roosevelt wrote to Treasury Secretary Henry Morgenthau, who had jurisdiction over the Coast Guard, and asked him to look out for "Bertie Pell's boy." Morgenthau checked and found that Claiborne had passed his reserve officer's commission test and soon would become an ensign. Morgenthau promised F.D.R. that as soon as Claiborne became an officer he would be assigned to a public relations unit in the United States. Both Roosevelt and Morgenthau were trying to find a soft berth for Claiborne, something that Herbert Pell had never wanted. It was something that Claiborne did not want either. He became an officer and served in the North Atlantic and in the military occupation of southern Italy. He was like many millions of young Americans at the time who had "a more serious purpose in life and a better understanding of their responsibility to their country," to use his father's words.

6 HERBERT PELL EXPECTED TO BE REASSIGNED to another diplomatic post after he returned from Hungary; he had been a minister since 1937 and his experience plus the need in wartime for good men should have brought an appointment for him. But the weeks and months went by and nothing happened. He and Olive spent their time taking care of the details of their New York home, Pellbridge in Hopewell Junction, which since the gift of the Newport home for the Catholic girls' school had become their permanent residence. They visited with old friends, caught up on gossip. But Herbert Pell was restless. The war was on and the Allies were not doing well. Claiborne was in the service. Herbert wanted an assignment. Franklin Roosevelt, his old friend and boss, wanted him in the Administration. He wrote a memorandum to his aide Marvin H. McIntyre: "Will you tell Bertie Pell that I hope to be able to see him soon and will you check with Sumner Welles about placing Bertie Pell somewhere —I want it done and done quickly. F.D.R." Sumner Welles was the wrong person with whom to check. He was then Under Secretary of State and was the quintessential bureaucrat.

Although Roosevelt made his own foreign policy aided by Secretary of State Hull, sometimes prompted by Hull, Welles ran the departmental organization, which had little to do with foreign policy. As most presidents come to realize, Roosevelt had learned that his State Department was a collection of civil servants anxious more to avoid making decisions—decisions that years later someone like Senator Joe McCarthy might question—than to serve the nation's international interest. It was over this fiefdom of bureaucrats that Welles ruled. Anything that disturbed his rule was obviously improper and dangerous. An American *chargé d'affaires* from one of the European legations returned to Washington in the late 1930s for a series of briefings and conferences. In a meeting with Welles, and in response to a direct question from Welles, this American foreign service officer predicted that Hitler would bring war to Europe. He also pointed out that the United States, if attacked by Hitler, had no weapons with which to stop the Nazis. "If they land on the East Coast," said this official to Welles, "there's nothing we can do except wave at them as they cross to the West Coast." This was a hard assessment but a proper one and, at the time, certainly accurate. It disturbed Welles and he responded by accusing the foreign service officer of being a Nazi sympathizer and ordering him rotated home. It was because of Welles and his bureaucratic colleagues that Roosevelt had selected friends like Herbert Pell for foreign posts. They told him what was really going on abroad without fear of upsetting the State Department. Welles resented this.

The reports by Pell to Roosevelt of conditions in Europe were honest accounts; they also were bypasses of the proper channels, which Welles controlled. It was because of this that when Marvin McIntyre asked Welles what job could be found for Herbert Pell, the answer was: "There is absolutely no place in the Department of State where Bertie Pell could be used."

Roosevelt was concerned but obviously could not fire his top advisers in wartime on the basis that they would not find a position for one of his friends, no matter how deserving that friend was. Later Roosevelt wrote a note to Secretary of State Hull, which has almost a plaintive ring to it. "Do you think," the President's note began, "there is some place where we could use Herbert Pell? As you know, he is a very devoted friend of the Administration."

Pell appreciated what his friend was trying to do for him and also understood the pressures on the President in wartime. The two men had known each other for many years, and Herbert Pell's admiration for Franklin Roosevelt never had flagged. Early in 1943, Pell sent F.D.R. a telegram. It said: "Read Job Twenty three, verses three four five six eleven and twelve."* The President appreciated the

* Oh that I knew where I might find him! *that* I might come even to his seat!

I would order *my* cause before him, and fill my mouth with arguments.

I would know the words *which* he would answer me, and understand what he would say unto me.

Will he plead against me with *his* great power? No; but he would put *strength* in me.

．　．　．

telegram (and also knew his Bible well). "Thanks for the reference to Job in your telegram of February eighth," he telegraphed back. "It's a comfort to know that things got a little easier for that paragon of patience in the last chapter wherein we are assured that 'The Lord blessed the latter end of Job more than his beginning. . . .'" (Chapter 42, Verse 12.)

It turned out, however, that there was a job where Herbert Pell could be used advantageously. It was a perfect slot, considering his background. His youth in Tuxedo, where he had learned standards of conduct revealing to him the tarnish in the Gilded Age, the family ties that had given him a sense of perspective and decency, the artistic sense that made him love beauty and hate those who would defile it, the travels in Europe, which had shown him exactly what it was that the Nazis were destroying, his political background, which meant he would not move among statesmen as a novice, and above all the gentlemanliness that was so much a part of him in a time when such values were losing importance—all of these combined to make him the ideal choice for the job he was now offered.

In the spring of 1943, Herbert and Olive left Hopewell Junction to spend a few days with a friend at Islesboro, Maine, then went to Boston and on to Edgartown, renewing old acquaintances. When they returned to their

---

My foot hath his steps, his way have I kept, and not declined.

Neither have I gone back from the commandment of his lips; I have esteemed the words of his mouth more than my necessary *food*.

New York home, they found a letter for Herbert from Washington. The letter was dated just before they had started on their trip; it had followed them for a time, then come back to Hopewell Junction. It read:

My dear Mr. Pell:

As you may know, there is about to be established by the United Nations a Commission to investigate war crimes committed by the Axis powers and their agencies. The Commission will have its seat in London. I should be very glad to have you represent this Government on the Commission, greater details concerning which may be obtained from the Department of State, with whose officials you may desire to confer. You would be paid a salary of $9,000 a year plus costs of transportation to and from London and the customary per diem while outside the United States on the work of the Commission.

If you are willing to accept the designation, I suggest that you arrange to call on appropriate officials of the Department of State at an early date, since it is desired that you shall proceed to London as soon as possible.

Very sincerely yours,
Franklin D. Roosevelt

There had been attempts for centuries to establish certain standards to reduce the cruelty of war. These efforts took on more serious overtones as the weapons of war became more powerful and as more people lived in cities, making thousands vulnerable to a single attack of wanton brutality. In 1880 the Institute of International Law, meeting at Oxford, England, called for "the offending parties . . . [to] be punished, after a judicial hearing, by the belligerent in whose hands they are." The institute was trying to establish the principle that a person committing an act described as a "war crime" could expect punishment, that he could not escape simply by saying that he was a soldier, exempt from normal laws, and exempt from retribution. "Offenders against the laws of war," the institute said, "are liable to the punishments specified in the penal or criminal law."

After the First World War, the victorious Allies, shocked by the needless cruelty of German soldiers, tried to formalize the rules of war. The premise was that if the German war criminals in the First World War were punished, that act of punishment would become a precedent and would serve as a warning to any who waged war in the future. Delegates from fifteen nations came together in Paris in 1919. They issued a report on March 29 saying that they had reviewed a substantial number of documents. These documents established beyond question, the delegates continued, that outrages of every kind were committed by Germany and her allies against the customs of war. The delegates accused the Germans of the "most cruel practices which primitive barbarism, aided by all the resources of modern science, could devise for the execution of a system of terrorism carefully planned, and carried out to the end. Not even prisoners, or wounded, or women, or children have been respected by belligerents who deliberately sought to strike terror into every heart for the purpose of repressing all resistance." Crimes listed included murders, massacres, tortures, arbitrary destruction of property, killing of prisoners, attacks on hospital ships, poisoning of water wells, unmotivated attacks on individuals. These comments were directed at German conduct during the First World War from 1914 to 1918.

Following its review of the German crimes, the report then recommended that "all persons belonging to enemy countries, however high their position may have been, without distinction of rank, including chiefs of states, who have been guilty of offences against the laws and customs of war or the laws of humanity, are liable to criminal prosecution. . . ." There was no doubt at the time that the delegates in their report were referring to Kaiser Wilhelm and that they were saying that the Kaiser should be tried and, if found guilty (and the delegates believed that the evidence left no alternative), he should be punished. History provides no answers to the question of whether there would have been a Second World War if out of the first had come the principle that rank does not excuse.

The Kaiser was allowed to escape to Holland, where he lived out his remaining years in peace and comfort. Why? Although the report at Paris called for his trial and punishment if deserved, the American representatives to the Paris meeting objected. Robert Lansing and James Brown Scott argued in an annex to the report that the proposal subjected chiefs of states to a degree of responsibility never before formalized in law and for which there were no precedents. The precedents, Lansing and Scott argued, are in the other direction. They then referred to an opinion by the United States Supreme Court announced by Chief Justice John Marshall. The 1812 case is known as Schooner Exchange v. McFadden and is found in 7 Cranch 116. The case had been brought before the Supreme Court by two Maryland citizens who claimed that a French warship, docked in Philadelphia, was really their merchant ship stolen from them by men working for Napoleon. The Marshall decision went against the Marylanders, saying that a sovereign of another nation and his representatives must be immune from prosecution. Lansing and Scott argued that this decision, rendered one hundred and seven years before their Paris conference, "does not mean that the head of the State, whether he be called emperor, king, or chief executive, is not responsible for breaches of the law, but that he is responsible not to the judicial but to the political authority of his country." In other words, the Kaiser could not be punished by the Allies' court, only by the German people.

It is unfortunate the other delegates apparently did not double-check Lansing's and Scott's interpretation of American constitutional law. The two men had relied heavily on Marshall's decision and they misinterpreted it. The crucial point in the Marshall decision reads this way:

It seems, then, to the court, to be a principle of public law, that national ships of war, entering the port of a friendly power, open for their reception, are to be considered as exempted by the consent of that power from its jurisdiction.

Marshall was writing in the decision of a sovereign, or his representative, of a friendly power, invited to the United States. The Marshall decision is a cornerstone of what a later time called "diplomatic immunity" but has no relationship with the question of the fate of a defeated ruler who initiated a war. The Marshall decision had no applicability to the question of the Kaiser which Lansing and Scott tried to give it.

Even in Lansing's and Scott's time the State Department—as Herbert Pell was to learn—was not particularly interested in the question of war crimes, or in punishing leaders for war crimes. Such a policy was not a part of America's history and was not accepted as a part of the present. Whatever formal reaction the United States had in the 1930s to the German attacks on the Jews within its borders was the result of actions by President Roosevelt over the hesitation of the State Department. American officials who publicly criticized the Nazis were scolded by the State Department and privately encouraged by Roosevelt. To the professional diplomats, war, with all of its barbarism, was an accepted if brutal act of diplomacy and one should not take its regulation too seriously.

Roosevelt and others, however, no longer accepted this

attitude in the Second World War. On October 25, 1941, Roosevelt told the world:

> The practice of executing scores of innocent hostages in reprisal for isolated attacks on Germans in countries temporarily under the Nazi heel revolts a world already inured to suffering and brutality. . . .
>
> These are acts of desperate men who know in their hearts they cannot win. Frightfulness can never bring peace to Europe. It only sows seeds of hatred which will one day bring a fearful retribution. . . .

That same day in London, Winston Churchill said:

> His Majesty's Government associate themselves fully with the sentiments of horror and condemnation expressed by the President of the United States upon the Nazi butcheries in France. These coldblooded executions of innocent people will only recoil upon the savages who order and execute them. . . .
>
> Retribution for these crimes must henceforward take its place among the major purposes of the war. . . .

As the Nazis were pressed by Allied forces, they became desperate and their behavior in occupied countries became even more outrageous. Roosevelt announced to the Germans that when the United Nations won the war, "It is the purpose of the Government of the United States, as I know it is the purpose of each of the United Nations, to make appropriate use of the information and evidence in respect to these barbaric crimes of the invaders, in Europe and in Asia." Then he made clear that the Nazis could not hope to escape justice as the Germans had escaped after World War I. "It seems only fair that they should have this warning," he said of the Germans, "that the time will come when they shall have to stand in courts of law in the very countries which they are now oppressing and answer for their acts."

This position was formalized in a Presidential statement of October 7, 1942, in which Roosevelt said:

I now declare it to be the intention of this Government that the successful close of the war shall include provisions for the surrender to the United Nations of war criminals.

With a view to establishing responsibility of the guilty individuals through the collection and assessment of all available evidence, this Government is prepared to cooperate with the British and other Governments in establishing a United Nations Commission for the Investigation of War Crimes.

The number of persons eventually found guilty will undoubtedly be extremely small compared to the total enemy populations. It is not the intention of the Government or of the Governments associated with us to resort to mass reprisals. It is our intention that just and sure punishment shall be meted out to the ringleaders responsible for the organized murders of thousands of innocent persons and the commission of atrocities which have violated every tenet of Christian faith.

There was another aspect to the Roosevelt declaration. Despite the disclaimers, in history there is a strong tradition that the spoils go to the victors and that those victors exact the punishments they see fit. And history is filled with accounts of the rapes and pillages those victors considered fit. But the Roosevelt declaration was saying the Allies were limiting their victory. Only the ringleaders responsible for the murder of innocents and for atrocities would be punished. It would not be a peace in which those responsible for the war would escape, as happened after the First World War. But it would not be a brutal peace. It would be a civilized peace. The task of defining the limits of that civilized peace was the job of the Commission for the Investigation of War Crimes that Herbert Pell was named to as the American representative.

His appointment was announced June 29, 1943, and Pell met that day with Franklin Roosevelt. "I told him that I expected to do what I could to see to the punishment of those who had tortured innocent people in concentration camps and had massacred citizens in the occupied countries," Pell recalled. "I realized at the time that there was no such thing as international law to cover these cases. These ideas were quite new. I told the President at the time that many people were going to sacrifice their lives in this war and that I stood ready to sacrifice my reputation."

Pell believed that the most important task was to prevent a third world war. As he wrote a friend in 1944, "The danger starts to end for us and I hope that we can arrange things so that it does not begin again later for our children." He knew enough history, American and European, to know that yesterday's soldier, be he victorious or defeated, is tomorrow's hero. From the southern side of his family he had learned of the Civil War veterans lounging around their courthouse square, leaning against the statue of their favorite Confederate general and boasting of the battles they had seen and of the glories of the Old Confederacy until every school boy's eyes glowed with longing.

"In a small German village," Pell prophesied, "the local member of the Gestapo will be the hero of every beer garden and meeting place. He will tell the young boys of the excitement of Norway, the fun of shooting Jews in Poland, or the profit of looting France. They will look up to him, if for no other reason, because he is the only person in the village who will talk of anything but local gossip. Presently along will come someone hopeful of succeeding Hitler, who will tell these boys he is ready to take the risk of Hitler's fate. He will ask these boys to join him, and tell them that by following him they can have the life of their glorious uncle who was the village hero who was honored and listened to by the entire population." It was realization of this prophecy which Pell determined to prevent.

Pell had been impressed with the work of Sheldon Glueck of Harvard, who had written extensively on the question of war trials and the fate of convicted criminals. Glueck argued that although vengeance is a base sentiment, the evocation of law and justice was legitimate, commendable and "morally virtuous." Glueck was disturbed by suggestions that the Germans not be punished for any proven war crimes on the basis that if they were excused from any consequences of their acts, they would not make war a third time. Glueck considered this "simply the old appeasement policy all over again, an attitude which has proved so tragically bankrupt through the democracies' dealings with the Fascists. It amounts, simply, to the paying of blackmail to ruthless gangsters who have seized the reins of government in foreign lands." Glueck's principal thesis was not only that the Germans should be punished but that there was ample precedent for holding the leaders and perpetrators of war crimes responsible for their acts. What it all came down to was a soldier shooting at another on the battlefield was committing an act of war for which he would not be held responsible at war's end. But when that same soldier entered a farmhouse in an occupied territory and raped the family's daughter, or killed a prisoner of war whose hands were tied behind his back or machine-gunned unarmed civilians, that soldier was committing a crime for which there were laws to punish him.

When Pell went over to the State Department to confer about his new job, he found officials there much disturbed over his appointment. The job had looked like an interesting one, and the regulars at the State Department had hoped to have it for one of their own. The State Department's old dislike for Pell still existed. His manner of appointment—the President had directed that he be given a job and recommended the War Crimes Commission—augmented this dislike, a feeling that quickly came to the surface. First, he was not permitted to ask Sheldon Glueck to become his legal assistant. The State Department insisted that one of its regulars go with Pell. Also he was specifically told that he should stay in the United States some time before leaving for England. The English had requested, he was informed, that he not be sent across the Atlantic until the commission actually was ready to operate.

So Pell remained at his country home at Hopewell Junction doing very little. He had taken his oath of office, was receiving his salary and waited impatiently for orders. He was not the only impatient one. "Why can't Herbert Pell get off for London?" the President inquired of Cordell Hull, only to be told of the English request. That request had been transmitted to the State Department by the American ambassador in London, John G. Winant, who had written in June that "Mr. Pell should not leave for London until the position is clearer."

Winant's attitude had changed by September. On the

first of that month Winant had been sent a message from
the British Foreign Office. This was the second paragraph:

The replies now received from all the governments
concerned, including your excellency's government, in-
dicate that a sufficient basis of agreement exists to enable further progress to be made. I am impressed by the
urgency of setting up this Commission without further
delay and to this end would propose that a meeting of
the Diplomatic Representatives in London of the Allied
Governments concerned should be held towards the end
of September in order to take the necessary steps to set
up the Commission and to settle its constitution and
function. . . .

That message was passed on to the State Department on
September 6. Pell still waited for his orders to travel. They
did not come.

On October 26, Winant telegraphed to the State Department:

The informal meeting of the members of the United
Nations Commission for the Investigation of War Crimes
. . . met this afternoon at the Law Courts and was presided over by Sir Cecil Hurst. At my request Allison sat
in as an observer. While there was considerable discussion about the exact purpose and functions of the Com-

mission and just what the scope of its activities should be, there was no attempt made to reach a final decision in view of the unofficial character of the meeting. It was stressed by Sir Cecil Hurst that until it had been decided whether or not the Soviet Government was to be represented and until the United States representative arrived it would be impossible to hold official meetings. . . .

At this point a State Department official telephoned Herbert Pell and told him to be ready to leave in three days. Pell said that was impossible and actually left about ten days later. On Tuesday, November 9, 1943, he was ordered to report to Brooklyn for his shots. He was then told his departure must be made in utmost secrecy. He was instructed to return to his hotel room and stand by for further orders. It was the following Sunday before an army lieutenant called for him at his hotel and drove him in an army car to the dock. More than forty years earlier when Herbert Pell had been at Pomfret, he had befriended "a fat little boy who knew nothing of school life or customs. I helped him as well as I could." That fat little boy grew up to be the troop embarkation officer for New York harbor and he was waiting when Herbert Pell's car came to a halt on the dock. This officer escorted Pell aboard the *Queen Mary* and showed him his room, a private one. "I think I was the only American who received this distinction," Pell recalled about that trip. The *Queen Mary*, of course, had been a luxury liner originally; now it was a troop ship. When Pell crossed in it, that November of 1943, it carried fourteen thousand men jammed into every corner. "Cabins ordinarily inhabited by at most two people," Pell said, "and which would not have been too luxurious for one, were occupied by between six to ten officers. The men were placed all over; a great many of them slept on the deck; the crowd was like a subway station."

As soon as the ship began to move away from land, Pell and the other passengers were informed by the ship's officers that they must be very careful about doing anything to reveal that they were on the open sea. They were directed not to throw anything overboard and not to show any lights at night. A single mistake, they were warned, would reveal them to a German U-boat. As they were being given these orders, the ship itself was moving down the bay in full view of the ferry boats crossing with commuters from New Jersey to New York. At least two hundred and fifty thousand people could not have avoided observing that the *Queen Mary*, obviously carrying American troops, was then embarking for England "That," said Pell, "was the so-called secrecy of departure." None of those people were Nazi spies apparently. The ship did arrive without mishap.

Pell naturally assumed that it would. He was, after all, a very lucky person, as he often remarked. He had been fortunate in his birth, in the society in which he developed, in having the freedom to pursue his artistic and historical interests in Europe as a young man. He had been fortunate in the 1920s to have known and worked

with men like Franklin Roosevelt and Al Smith. And
then as diplomat he had witnessed the cataclysm that forever would be a part of European history. Now he was
beginning again, on a new experience. For this he would
need more than luck. He was not to be a witness this
time, nor an acquaintance of the activists. This time he
was to be the front participant. This time he would not
be in the shadows. This time he would need the decency
he had learned as a child and the adroitness he had learned
as a man. This time he would be measured; he would not
measure others.

As the *Queen Mary* moved out a little way beyond
Sandy Hook on its way to England, the lower end of
Brooklyn and Long Island already had dipped below the
horizon and all one could see of New York was the top
of Manhattan's skyscrapers. Herbert Pell thought it an
extremely effective last view of the United States.

7   Pell had, of course, been giving much thought to what he hoped to accomplish as a member of the War Crimes Commission. It was all mixed up with the Europe he had seen as a young man and with the fact that many of his friends and relatives as well as his own son were in uniform. "I am much too lazy to bother about revenge," he wrote to a close friend a few days before he sailed. Rather, he continued, he was interested in justice and instruction "and particularly in the prevention of future wrong." Two generations had gone to war, he said, not because the German people were vicious but "because the German people allowed themselves to be persuaded that war may be a profitable enterprise." With his sense of history, Herbert Pell realized how easy it was for the Germans to have accepted such a belief. In his letter he ticked off the dates: 1864, Prussia seized land from Denmark; 1866, Prussia drove Austria out of Germany and became the ruler of that people; 1871, Prussia became the important nation in Europe. And then the war of 1914–1918, which Germany "certainly did not lose as badly as did France and England."

Since the Second World War a popular theory had grown that the Allies planted the seeds of that second war in the demands they made upon Germany after the first; that they flaunted their victory in peace to keep Germany forever defeated. Herbert Pell had a different picture of Europe after the First World War, a picture he recalled in this letter in November of 1943:

After 1918 France was shattered and never really recovered. The shock was too great. Over a million Frenchmen were killed. The French manufacturing districts were ruined. Those who went through the war were crushed. No one who knew Paris before 1914, as I did, could fail to see the difference. The buildings were more grimy; public gardens were less well kept up; the vigor and taste of the people were broken; men and women lived from day to day like ship-wrecked sailors. Germany, which was practically untouched by the war, was able to recover very much more quickly than any other country. We cannot allow this to be repeated.

He was concerned by the developing efficiency of the German military machine. In the First World War, he pointed out, the Germans were stopped before they reached Calais or Paris. In the Second World War, the Germans needed only nine months to do what they had been unable to do a quarter of a century earlier. "If they begin again in twelve years," he wrote in 1943, "it will take about nine days, which will mean the almost certain capture of England." Recalling the line he had written at the letter's beginning, he said that the only way to prevent a third world war "is to make it clear to every last German that war is the most unprofitable enterprise in the world."

Perhaps the most practical thing Herbert Pell did in connection with his assignment to London was to write his English tailor in advance and ask him to find a dozen suits of long woolen underclothes. The tailor was the only person in London who had Pell's measurements, and a six-foot, five-inch, two-hundred-and-fifty-pound man simply did not walk into a store during wartime London and find long woolen underclothes to fit him; he hardly did in peacetime. Like most persons, Pell considered such undergarments the horror of childhood and better not used again. But he was glad to have them in London. It was the coldest winter he ever experienced. The temperature actually never dropped below freezing. But the heating of the homes, a rare thing normally in England, was virtually nonexistent in the winter of 1943–44. Coal, like everything else, was shoveled into the war effort.

London shocked him. Not only were there areas, acres wide, that were nothing more than heaps of rubble left after the German bombers had passed over, but on every block it seemed there was at least one home destroyed. The war struck everywhere.

Herbert Pell described an air raid he witnessed. All persons were supposed to go to shelters, but he stayed on the street to watch it. Huge flares were dropped by parachute from the German bombers. The flares lit up the streets of London and also made an effective shield against British anti-aircraft gunners. The British gunners did fire toward the sky, toward planes they could not see and German pilots they cursed. One bomb landed in the square in front of St. James's Palace. Office building fronts were ripped off and windows broken hundreds of yards away. The palace wall was pockmarked by flying debris, and the Ritz Hotel shook as if it were in an earthquake. Another bomb struck in Duke Street. Some old brick buildings crumbled in a heap. A chimney fell, staying intact, and landed upright on the rubble. Police came quickly with specially trained dogs, which sniffed through the pile, hunting for humans buried underneath. The dogs ran to the spot where they smelled a body and scratched at the rubble until the diggers came.

That particular raid was the last one by airplane. Next came the V-1 rockets. These were fired from northern France and defense against them was virtually impossible. When they struck a building, they destroyed it and at least two buildings on either side. "Three of my comparatively small number of friends in London were killed instantly by these bombs, and probably more," Pell said. "When a person was killed no official notice was published until about ten days later when the name appeared in the death list as killed by enemy action, and a memorial service was held."

The V-1 rockets were called Doodlebugs. They could be heard and even seen as they screamed toward London. But they were surpassed in the Nazi arsenal by the V-2, which came so fast there was no indication of its approach, nothing to warn the people of London. In Pell's opinion, the V-1 rockets were the more serious threat to the English. "As you lay in bed," he said, "you heard the motors of the approaching Doodlebug for several minutes. From the inside of a room, it was manifestly impossible to gauge its direction. You simply lay and waited. After a short time the sound suddenly ceased and three or four very long seconds later, you heard the explosion, and it was only when you heard the explosion that you could have any idea whether the thing was near or far."

A friend of Pell's was killed one Sunday morning in church. The Doodlebug broke through the church walls, killing everyone except the clergymen at one end of the building and a guard at the other. "I do not think," Pell said, "that anybody but a fool or a liar can tell you that he heard these things with calm and equanimity."

Herbert Pell made a point of never going into a bomb shelter. It was not bravery as much as it was a matter of the odds he calculated. He figured the chances of his catching the flu in the crowded and poorly ventilated shelters at age fifty-nine were much more serious than the chances of being killed by a bomb. London was full of stories of narrow escapes from bombing attacks, of persons miraculously saved while those around them were killed by falling debris. Pell had his own favorite story. The War Crimes Commission was arguing over whether the bombing of a civilian center, such as the city of London, where they were then meeting, was a legitimate act of war. The commission members had just reached the decision that such an act was indeed legal, when a German bomb dropped near them, shaking the building violently, "like a tree in the wind."

Shortly after his arrival in London, Herbert Pell lunched with Sir Cecil Hurst, the British delegate to the commission and its chairman. Then in his seventies, Sir Cecil was considered a British elder statesman and a shrewd diplomat and politician. As they lunched at the Athenaeum Club, Sir Cecil consistently refused to bring the discussion around to the War Crimes Commission, concentrating instead on his garden in Sussex. He obviously was waiting for Pell to bring up the subject so that he could find out exactly what Pell's instructions were. Because of the American contribution to the Allied effort in the Second World War, no one ever underestimated the position of the American delegate to any commission. But Pell was not fooled by Sir Cecil's play. Actually he could not be. He had no instructions. Although he had been appointed six months earlier and had made himself amply available to the State Department, he had no instructions whatsoever. He was in the worst position for a diplomat; he could not act without fear that his government might accuse him of having gone too far and back away from the position he had taken.

After meeting with Sir Cecil, Pell met with other members of the commission and other persons with whom he should talk. The Chinese delegate was Wellington Koo, an old friend of Pell's. They had been at Columbia at the same time and their paths had crossed over the years. Koo believed that the commission should establish a separate panel to handle Asiatic questions. Pell lunched with the Polish delegate, who believed that the suffering in Poland at the hands of the Germans was not being given serious enough consideration. Each delegate had his own ax to grind.

Several days later Pell learned that a group of delegates to the commission were working up a formal letter to Sir Cecil demanding that the group quickly proceed to its work. Pell opposed the letter. His point was that the position should be developed in secrecy and then sprung on Sir Cecil at a future meeting. Sending an advance letter, Pell argued, permitted the opposition time to develop an answer. The letter proposal was a sign the members were restless. Although no one seemed quite certain what the commission would do, the members were determined that it be done quickly and effectively.

Although Pell had always suspected the State Department's reluctant assent to his appointment, he found proof of it two days before Christmas. He dined that night with Ambassador John G. Winant. Winant commented with regret on the lateness of Pell's arrival in London. Pell was aghast. He told of spending the entire summer badgering the State Department for permission to leave then for England, of twice making personal visits to speed his departure and of being rebuffed each time. Always the excuse offered, he said, was that Winant had recommended that his arrival in London be delayed. At one point, Pell said, he was told he might not be sent to London for half a year—all at Winant's request. Winant replied that, other than the one cable in June suggesting a brief delay, he had sent no messages asking for a delay in Pell's coming. Rather, he had called for Pell's quick arrival. For Pell it was a disturbing story, particularly because he had been sending cables to the State Department since his arrival in London, speaking of his plans and asking for guidelines for his approach to the commission's work. All had gone unanswered.

It was, of course, the spirit of Lansing and Scott at work again. War was not a moral question but an arm of international diplomacy, or so it was thought at the department's new building in the Foggy Bottom section of Washington. The "professional" diplomats there were still part of the eighteenth and nineteenth centuries, when England controlled the oceans as well as the commercial trade routes by the adroit use of her navy. The only banner under which warriors moved then was that of profits, and for the people over whom control was passed back and forth like pawns being slid across a chessboard, it really made little difference who was the ruler. No one was particularly better than another. But war had changed, even if the professionals' attitude toward it had not. Trade routes and profits no longer were motivating. At stake now was civilization, whatever sense of decency and law that Western man had inherited from his ancestors. If professional diplomats did not know this, people did. People who read in the newspapers of the senseless bombings of unarmed cities, people who read of innocent refugees strafed on a road, of the massacre of Jews and Catholics, of Russians and Poles; these people knew that this was not business as usual. There always had been those who understood that war was evidence of civilized man's failure rather than a means for his diplomatic triumph. They always had managed to muster only a quiet voice. During the Second World War, as the nightmare of the destruction of civilization almost came true, that voice became louder and never again would be quieted.

One day Herbert Pell returned to his office to find his wife, Olive, sitting at his desk. She had sailed to Portugal, flown from Lisbon to Bristol, and then come to London. Not knowing where her husband was living, she went to his office and sat herself down to wait for him. In addition to the personal happiness his wife's presence gave him, Olive was invaluable because of the entertaining required of him. Not only was she a gracious hostess, but Olive Pell had lived for many years in England and knew the English people intimately, exactly what made them tick. She brought with her a picture of Iroquois, the horse that belonged to Pierre Lorillard when it won the English Derby in 1881. It was an inexpensive print; Herbert Pell had purchased it years earlier for several dollars and had it framed. When Olive brought it to London, Herbert hung it in the apartment bathroom. Olive smiled, took the picture down and hung it in the parlor and, remarked Pell, "It was perfectly astounding to see the English looking at it." They wanted to know "What's the horse?" To which Olive answered, "It won the Derby and belonged to my husband's uncle." Herbert's stock rose quickly among his guests. The Pells were, of course, playing on the British interest in "family," the belief that respectability comes with ancestors and relatives of attainment. They won their game.

The Pells had to entertain a good deal. *The Times of London* recorded it. "Mr. Herbert Pell, American representative on the War Crimes Commission, and Mrs. Pell gave a luncheon yesterday at the Senior Officers' Club . . . a dinner party last night at the Dorchester. . . ."

Occasionally relatives or old friends, most of them in uniform, passed through London, and Herbert Pell enjoyed squiring them around the city. A cousin, John H. G. Pell (married to Olive's daughter Pyrma), came by and Herbert Pell took him to the Athenaeum Club for tea. The Doodlebugs had been particularly active, John Pell remembered, and the Athenaeum did not have a complete window left. But the waiters went noiselessly around, serving tea to guests with the same *hauteur* that had made them famous in prewar years. After tea Herbert took his cousin to show him a Doodlebug crater. A bobby stopped them. Unauthorized personnel, the policeman explained, were not permitted near the crater. John Pell recalled that Herbert pulled himself up to his full six-foot-five-inch height, thrust out his massive chest and boomed that he was "Herbert Pell, the delegate of the United States to the United Nations War Crimes Commission" and he demanded to be allowed to pass. As John Pell told it, "the bobby then collapsed and let us go by."

Herbert Pell finally received some instructions from the United States government. The first came from Secretary of State Cordell Hull. The War Crimes Commission, Hull wrote, is a fact-finding organization with the job of collecting "all available evidence with respect to war crimes with a view to identifying those responsible for such crimes and assembling the evidence and proof of their guilt." Hull said that "it is not contemplated that the Commission will be entrusted with the trial of war criminals." Hull said that "there would be no occasion for it or its members to make decisions as to how cases should be disposed of after evidence has been assembled and turned over to those charged with the duty of proceeding with the case."

The Hull letter was dated December 28, 1943. Approximately six weeks later, on February 12, 1944, Franklin Roosevelt wrote a letter to Pell, beginning "My dear Bertie." He had no hesitation about having the commission become involved in the question of what kind of tribunal should be used. "If the tribunal is composed of jurists chosen from civil life," the President advised Pell, "it is only reasonable to suppose that it would move very cautiously and might more readily lend itself to resort by the accused and his counsel to legalistic and dilatory tactics. While I do not mean to say that such a tribunal should be ruled out, I should be inclined to think that more expeditious results would be obtained, and perhaps with an equal measure of justice, if it were made up, so far as possible, of able men chosen from the military branches of the service." Roosevelt continued that "after all such people know or should know what the rules of warfare are and should be able readily to detect violations of those rules and to give proper consideration to evidence."

The implication of Roosevelt's letter clearly was that

the commission should become involved in the mechanics of seeking justice rather than only gather evidence as Cordell Hull had suggested. The President's view coincided with Pell's, and Pell naturally felt strengthened to pursue his own course even if it differed from what the State Department directed. This was another cause of developing animosity between the State Department regulars and Pell.

One factor leading to the establishment of the War Crimes Commission had been the experience after the First World War: not only was the Kaiser retiring gracefully to Holland but the German war criminals were not actually tried. The Allies had wanted to conduct their trials, but the postwar German government refused to yield the men charged with crimes. The argument was that the shaky German government would be toppled by the people angered at the turning of the alleged war criminals over to the Allies. The Germans offered to try the criminals themselves, and the trials took place before a Leipzig court. A total of nine hundred and one persons were brought before that court, of which eight hundred and eighty-eight were acquitted or summarily dismissed. Thirteen were convicted but given light sentences and even these were not served. The German people were pleased at how the "trials" turned out. The United Nations War Crimes Commission was created to prevent a similar situation from developing after the Second World War.

The commission met informally several times prior to Pell's arrival and several times in December. At a point when enough members were becoming irritated by the delays, Pell proposed that the commission was sufficiently organized to consider itself capable of doing business. That was on January 11, and on January 18 the group was operating. Pell had been put in charge of the Rules Committee, since he had been a member of the American House of Representatives and was thought to be fully informed about legislative and committee procedures. Pell did prepare the operating rules for the commission, including one that a majority vote could decide issues; most international groups required more than a majority vote. On all votes in the following months the commission was unanimous. This unanimity was the result of two factors. One was the tact and compromising ability of Sir Cecil Hurst, the chairman. The other was Pell's majority rule. It was silly for a minority to filibuster or refuse to compromise with the majority when it realized that it would lose on the final vote in any event.

In addition to the United States and England, there were twelve nations represented on the commission in 1944. Their names read like a history of the Axis attacks—Belgium, China, Czechoslovakia, France, Greece, Luxembourg, the Netherlands, Norway, Poland and Yugoslavia as well as Australia and India. Almost all the delegates were famous lawyers, jurists or persons experienced in international law—with the exception of Herbert Pell. This did not disturb him. "I could make a suggestion as a layman," he said, "and they never felt they were attacking my professional pride when they criticized or explained errors that I was making, which they wouldn't have liked to have done among themselves." If Pell did run into a legal problem he could not solve, he passed it to one of the experts. It was the best of both worlds.

When the commission first met, the discussions were general, and, to make progress, the decision was made to split into three committees. One was headed by General Marcel de Baer of Belgium; its task was to receive reports of atrocities from the various nations and classify them. Another committee was headed by Stefan Glaser of Poland; its job was to attempt to codify the international law applicable to the cases. The other committee was headed by Herbert Pell; its job was to develop a method of trying the prisoners. This Pell believed was what Roosevelt anticipated the commission would do. It definitely was not what Cordell Hull and the State Department anticipated.

The meetings were held in the law courts in a large upstairs room, each man sitting on a chair around a long table. Pell chose a seat nearest the fire—"two good hatfuls of coal put in a grate"—and was less uncomfortable than the others. When there was an air raid alert, the commission moved downstairs to one of the criminal courtrooms. Again Pell chose what appeared to be the most comfortable chair. It turned out to be the prisoner's dock.

From the outset the commission understood it was not seeking to punish for the act of war. "The only thing that we considered," Pell said, "were crimes against individuals by individual Germans. We did not think it made any difference whether a person was a member of the army, a member of the Gestapo, a civilian officer of the government, or a private individual. . . ."

Proof of atrocities was sometimes difficult to obtain. Herbert Pell explained why:

It seems obvious that if you are in a room and a group of foreigners in foreign uniforms come in, shoot at you and your companions, your only chance of survival is to fall to the ground and hope that you will not bleed to death before they've gone and that they'll think you're dead so that they won't finish the job. Clearly you cannot be able to give the identification of a particular sergeant who fired the shots as you would in civil life. You could not expect to get the quality of evidence that would be necessary to convict a boy of stealing cabbages in the suburbs—that was out of the question; it could not be done.

All we could know was that a massacre had taken place, a village had been attacked, the people in one case driven into a church, the church set on fire, and the people shot trying to escape by the soldiers. That happened in France. We could find out what regiment was there, who the German commanding officers were, and we knew that no punishments had been given by the Germans for the outrage. Therefore, we inferred that it was with the authorization of the commanding officers. As a consequence, I believe those commanding officers should have been hanged.

The first major question the War Crimes Commission had to answer was, curiously, whether Adolf Hitler and the other top Nazi leaders should be considered war criminals. In the years since the Second World War the list of crimes had grown so long—the destruction of villages, the murder of a people, the deliberate rape of a land— that one becomes hardened to so tragic a story; a tragedy not only for the people attacked—that they were the victims of such depravity—but also for those who attacked—that they were so depraved. One comes to accept the ultimate judgment made against these national leaders as the least of the punishments that should have been exacted from them. But in the early 1940s the question of guilt was unanswered and Pell and the other members of the commission resolved that it be answered in the affirmative.

Not only a moral judgment was at stake. "These people are not going to forget," Pell once explained of the conquered nationalities. "Their first demand, of course, will be for food, for housing, for clothes. But underneath that, there will be a demand for justice, and that demand will outlast everything else. There certainly will be terrific indignation; there will be a wave of cynicism over the world such as we have never seen, if we tell them to forgive their enemies, for we have promised—every responsible leader of the United Nations has promised—that the war criminals will be punished." Without assurances that the demand for justice would be met, there was a serious question whether the people of the conquered nations could continue the determined resistance, both organized and unorganized, they had been putting up. How long a Normandy farmer would fight if he believed the soldier who raped his daughter would get off with a hand-

shake was a matter of conjecture. Also, without such assurances that an orderly system for punishing war criminals, blessed by law, would come into effect after the
war, there was the dread of a massive uprising against the
Germans. That Normandy farmer and the millions like
him would see their revenge done, either in a court of
law or by themselves.

What course the commission took on the question of
Hitler's war guilt would be decided by England and the
United States. They were leading the war effort and would
shape the postwar world. No decision could be made without their consent. England was against treating the Nazi
leaders as war criminals; at least within the Foreign Office
headed by Anthony Eden that was the position. The
Foreign Office took the traditional diplomatic position that
national leaders of a warring nation were not criminals
but politicians who had lost a gamble; atrocities they had
condoned and people who had been killed were simply
part of the gamble. Perhaps they should be exiled as
Napoleon had been. In a newspaper column George Or-
well wrote of this attitude:

> Reading the discussion of "war guilt" which rever-
> berates in the correspondence columns of the newspa-
> pers, I note the surprise with which many people seem
> to discover that war is not a crime. Hitler, it appears,
> has not done anything actionable. He has not raped any-
> body, nor carried off any pieces of loot with his own
> hands, nor personally flogged any prisoners, buried any
> wounded men alive, thrown any babies into the air and

spitted them on his bayonet, dipped any nuns in petrol and touched them off with church tapers—in fact he has not done any of the things which enemy nations are usually credited with doing in war time. He had merely precipitated a world war which will perhaps have cost twenty million lives before it ends. And there is nothing illegal in that. How could there be, when legality implies authority and there is no authority with power to transcend national frontiers?

At the recent trials in Kharkov some attempt was made to fix on Hitler, Himmler and the rest the responsibility for their subordinates' crimes, but the mere fact that this had to be done shows that Hitler's guilt is not self-evident. His crime, it is implied, was not to build up an army for the purpose of aggressive war, but to instruct that army to torture its prisoners. So far as it goes, the distinction between an atrocity and an act of war is valid. An atrocity means an act of terrorism which has no genuine military purpose. One must accept such distinctions if one accepts war at all, which in practice everyone does. Nevertheless, a world in which it is wrong to murder an individual civilian and right to drop a thousand tons of high explosive on a residential area does sometimes make me wonder whether this earth of ours is not a looney-bin made use of by some other planet.

The United States State Department took the same position that the British Foreign Office did, that the heads of states were responsible only to the political authority of their own nations and not to the judicial authority of their conquerors. This was the position enunciated by Lansing and Scott at the end of the First World War. Once again the Kaiser and his associates would find their sanctuary and be punished only by the nightmares they never would have.

Pell was aware that the American argument at the end of the First World War had literally made impossible any serious effort at punishing war criminals. Believing he was strongly backed by Franklin Roosevelt, Pell determined that the same situation would not happen at the end of the Second World War. The official history of the commission reports that ". . . some British authorities visualized the punishment of leading Axis war criminals by 'political action,' as had been done in the case of Napoleon. However, the delegates in favour of the proposal for an international tribune led by the American representative, pressed so strongly for its consideration that at its meeting on 22nd February, 1944, the Commission gave authority to Committee II, the Committee on Enforcement, under the Chairmanship of Mr. Herbert C. Pell, the United States representative, to begin discussions on the subject without delay."

Why was an international court necessary? A Dutch court, for example, could try German soldiers for crimes committed in Holland; a French court, for crimes committed in France. But only an international court, a new concept in the history of war, could try those Nazis who had not ventured outside Germany. Actually, the decision

Pell had pressed for on February 22, to have his committee begin discussions on organizing such a tribunal, was the key one. From that point on, only the details remained to be smoothed out; the tribunal definitely would come into existence.

For weeks the committee members amassed precedents to build up their legal case for an international tribunal. They bargained on the structure of the court to guarantee its effectiveness and its equity. They also defined what exactly were and were not war crimes. The members worked in secret, keeping their subjects of discussion and the results of those discussions confidential. There were two reasons. The first was the traditional one of allowing the members to speak freely, with the understanding that they would not be embarrassed the next day by having their remarks printed in the *Times*. The second was more critical. "The Commission's lists of war criminals were secret," Pell explained. "This was necessitated by fear of reprisals against Allied prisoners-of-war in German hands."

The Allies did not execute German prisoners of war. Nor was it their intention, as shown by the actions of the War Crimes Commission, to try and punish German soldiers who had fought for their country; and they did not. Germany, however, took a different position. The Nazis executed American and British fliers forced down during bombing raids over German cities. "No international law of warfare is in existence which provides that a soldier who has committed a mean crime can escape punishment by pleading as his defense that he followed the commands of his superiors," declared Nazi propaganda minister Goebbels to justify the executions. "This holds particularly true," Goebbels continued, "if those commands are contrary to all human ethics and opposed to the well-established international usage of warfare." Against such hypocrisy it was indeed necessary to guard against reprisals, as Pell said.

The question of whether Adolf Hitler led the list of war criminals to be tried at the war's end continued a troubling one. To include him would be such a sharp break with diplomatic practice that the English and American governments were reluctant to do so. Drew Pearson reported Hitler was not on the list. "Uncensored reports from London," he commented in what was a typical column, "reveal that the Allied War Crimes Commission is bogged down on 'legalism,' has a bunch of cookie-pushing continental lawyers working out its program."

Sir Cecil Hurst could avoid the controversy no longer. On August 30, 1944, he held a news conference to discuss the work of the commission. He was asked if Hitler would be allowed to escape as the Kaiser had been after the First World War. He answered: "We do not intend to fall into the mistakes that were made after the last war. We know what we have to avoid." The newsmen insisted his answer eluded the question and pressed him again. Sir Cecil responded: "If the commission were asked suddenly to prepare a statement against Hitler we would do our best. We are aware that throughout this war the United Nations have been dealing with an unprecedented set of circumstances."

Do their best? Unprecedented circumstances? Did Sir

Cecil mean a case against Hitler could not be prepared? He answered: "If it were decided to put Hitler on trial, and if the War Crimes Commission were asked to provide a statement as to what he was to be tried for, a document satisfying public opinion could be produced. At the moment, however, international lawyers are not completely briefed in the case against Hitler."

The reporters persisted. Were Hitler and Mussolini, they demanded, considered war criminals by the commission or not? Sir Cecil answered: "The United Nations will decide what is to be done with them. It is not a matter for the Commission. The United Nations may decide to put them on trial, or they may decide to deal with them in the way Napoleon was dealt with after the Napoleonic wars, that is, by executive action." And then asked if the case against Hitler was complete, Sir Cecil conceded: "Yes, it is complete—in the mind of man. As to what this Commission would do if it were asked to state the case, I do not know, because at the moment it has not tackled that job."

Hitler, Sir Cecil had made clear, was not yet—August, 1944—considered a war criminal by the commission.

Sir Cecil's admission made the question of Adolf Hitler's future even more of a *cause célèbre*. What really was at stake was the future of war. Karl von Clausewitz had written: "War is not merely a political act, but also a political instrument, a continuation of political relations, a carrying out of the same by other means." Hitler had believed that, and he could believe it because he held human life in little regard. Throughout the history of the world most political leaders also had made war with little respect for human life. But the world was changing. When they understood it, the masses always had been against war made indifferently by the politicians at the expense of the masses. Fifty years before Von Clausewitz spoke of war as a political instrument, the poet William Cowper had expressed that feeling in this way:

But war's a game, which, were their subjects wise,
Kings would not play at.

But now the masses were becoming wise and they were demanding that the civilized world make a statement that warmakers are criminals. They were demanding the philosophy of Karl von Clausewitz be repudiated. This was the real issue before the War Crimes Commission. This was the issue that Pell was insisting the commission face as it struggled with the problem of exacting justice from the Germans in the postwar world.

The Allies could avoid the issue no longer. The debate led by Pell within the commission had become too much a matter of public record. The people demanded an answer. The question was put directly to Winston Churchill in Commons during the debate of October 4, 1944. Were Hitler, Goering, Goebbels and Himmler on the British and/or United Nations list of war criminals for trial? Winston Churchill answered: "So far as the British list is concerned, the parties mentioned are included."

Like most major legal decisions, this was a political one. It was a response to a popular demand for revenge, for the punishment of those who had caused so much devastation in the world. More important, it was a response to the popular demand that the civilized world brand the making of aggressive war a crime. The decision also was a logical one. If soldiers cannot be punished for carrying out orders and their superiors cannot be punished for giving orders and setting policies, then nobody can be held to account. Robert H. Jackson, an associate justice of the United States Supreme Court and also chief prosecutor at the Nuremberg war trials, said of such a possibility: "Society as modernly organized cannot tolerate so broad an arch of official irresponsibility."

After the question of whether Adolf Hitler should be tried as a war criminal, the new major question was whether the Nazis should be tried as criminals for genocide. This pertained primarily to the Nazis murder of six million Jews in Germany and occupied Europe. But that was only part of the story of their racist destruction. "It is true that in the popular mind that last [genocide] refers principally to Jews in Germany," said Pell after he had spent more than a year studying accounts of Nazi atrocities. "But if no Jew had been touched in Germany," he continued, "there are an ample number of cases to horrify the conscience of the people of the world. Catholic churches have been suppressed and monasteries dissolved, their money stolen, their newspapers suppressed, their youth organizations, Boy Scouts, and that sort of thing, dissolved. Protestant clergymen have been thrown into jail, their churches used for any civilian purpose that came to hand, and of course always their property confiscated. Labor unions have been dissolved and their money taken.

The Free Masons have been broken up and their money taken. A small number of Czechs who retained German citizenship have been persecuted on account of race; altogether there has been a very large number of people —I cannot say how many non-Jews—persecuted."

The crime of genocide, the persecution of minorities, had been a legal problem for the United States before she entered the war. The stories of the barbarities committed against the Jews began reaching the United States shortly after Adolf Hitler came to power in 1933. At one time Felix Frankfurter asked Franklin Roosevelt why he as President of the United States took no action. Roosevelt replied that as leader of one nation he could not interfere with events inside another nation. His position was legally correct. But holding that position, much could still be done: Roosevelt gave his moral support to the beleaguered minority members within Germany; he made efforts to marshal the world's diplomatic community against the Nazi atrocities; he tried to open the doors of the United States to refugees from Germany. Perhaps his greatest failing was that he did not insist that the State Department follow his lead. The bureaucrats in that department found excuses for their lethargy and inertia and blamed their inaction on protocol, and Roosevelt was not sufficiently demanding of them.

When the United States entered the Second World War, Jews of the world naturally saw the end of the conflict as the end of their persecution and the bringing to justice of those responsible for the mass slaughter of their fellows. They had reason to believe that their expectations would be realized. On December 17, 1942, Anthony Eden, the British Foreign Secretary, read a statement to the House of Commons. "I reported that, after receiving reliable information of the barbarous and inhuman treatment to which Jews were being subjected in German-occupied Europe," his own account goes, "His Majesty's Government had been in consultation with the United States, the Soviet and other Allied Governments. As a consequence, a declaration was being made public in London, Moscow and Washington, at the same day and hour as I spoke, condemning in the strongest possible terms this bestial policy of cold-blooded extermination. The Government declare that such events can only strengthen the resolve of all freedom-loving peoples to overthrow the barbarous Hitlerite tyranny. They reaffirm their solemn resolution to ensure that those responsible for these crimes shall not escape retribution. . . ."

Eden later commented that his statement had a greater impact than he had anticipated. "After Jimmy de Rothschild had made a feeling little speech the whole House rose (and stood to mark in silence its support of the declaration) on the motion of a Labour Member [W. S. Cluse]," Eden wrote. "Lloyd George said to me later: 'I cannot recall a scene like that in all my years in Parliament.'"

On July 22, 1943, a few weeks after Roosevelt had named Pell to the War Crimes Commission, the President met at the White House with Rabbi Stephen S. Wise, leader of the American Jewish Congress. In their meeting, Rabbi Wise said that information reaching American Jews indicated at least three million Jews would be killed in Nazi-occupied Europe but that other sources, particularly the Russians, estimated a higher figure. "I found that the President maintains a profound and penetrating interest in those victims of Hitler who are not able to meet him on the battlefield but must die unarmed and incapable of self-defense," Rabbi Wise said. He then added: "I find it significant that the President has just named former Ambassador Herbert Pell as the American Representative on the Commission of the United Nations to try to bring to justice those of the Nazi-Fascist countries who may be found guilty of responsibility for the foulest of all crimes of wartime, the slaughter of civilian masses."

Roosevelt's personal intention was that those guilty of atrocities for racial and religious reasons be brought to justice. On March 1, 1944, he addressed a letter to Pell which began "My dear Bertie." In it he said: "There can be little reason for disagreement on the general proposition that Germany and her satellites should be required to answer for atrocities against the Jews. I do not undertake, however, to pass on the extent of the jurisdiction of your Commission in these matters. Presumably it would extend to any cases arising during the war period, of which there are many. Those occurring before the war period, or which for other reasons may not fall within the category of war crimes, will have to be dealt with by the United Nations. I should suppose, however, that a large percentage of the perpetrators of atrocities in the pre-war period, have also committed, or have been implicated in the commission of, atrocities during the war period, and

hence will be subject to punishment as war criminals."
The Roosevelt letter makes clear that he personally believed that at least those Nazis who had committed crimes
against Jews since the beginning of the Second World War
were proper subjects for the War Crimes Commission. Pell
considered the letter a green light for him to proceed with
the demand that those responsible for genocide be tried as
war criminals. "As President Roosevelt said," Pell wrote,
"it was doubtful if our commission had the right to make
rules, but unquestionably we had the right to make recom-
mendations, which we did in my committee."

But others did not believe that the Roosevelt position
was a green light for anything and they gave Herbert Pell
the fight of his life.

Herbert Pell himself conceded that "there can be no
doubt that, according to the accepted structure of international law, what a nation does to its own citizens is its own
business. It is a purely domestic issue in which others cannot intervene." But he did not feel that "the accepted
structure of international law" was the only guideline by
which civilization can operate. "Racial and religious persecution by the Nazis was the first thing that aroused
the public conscience of the world and made the mass of
people realize that Hitler and Mussolini were something
more than comic interludes on the political stage. This
persecution had been from the beginning a crime against
humanity quite as much as against the race, religion or
parties which happened to be its immediate victims. Humanity has the right and the duty, in its own defense, to
punish the perpetrators of these crimes. Such offenders

cannot be permitted peaceably to mock the conscience of the world."

Pell believed then that genocide was a crime for which the Nazis could be punished "even though it was not foreseen in its particular nature by ancient writers." He pointed out that actually the whole concept of war crimes in the Second World War was a legal novelty. "The idea of all the earlier writers seems to be that war crimes are crimes committed by soldiers acting as individuals or at least in small groups and in which no one above the rank of colonel would be involved," he wrote. "In this war we find them used as a national policy, approved and supported by the central government." He asserted, correctly, that "this essentially changes the character of the crime." He realized that he was up against a State Department and others who argued that international law was an immutable set of principles rather than an evolving code aimed at establishing a civilized order among nations. Armed with a certain egotism, Pell countered: "You must remember that there is a tendency on the part of second-class lawyers to tell you that a thing cannot be done. They will express their regret as human beings that it is impossible, but, alas, such is the case. Their reasons will sound to the innocent layman like decisions of the Supreme Court, and as long as you don't try to do the thing and get away with it, your lawyer will never be proved wrong. This fear of responsibility is a conspicuous characteristic of almost all second-class minds." He then pointed out why international law must rise to the occasion and deal with the crime of genocide. "The refusal of adequate punishment for crimes against Axis citizens amounts in practice simply to giving the green light to anyone who wants to do a little persecuting off his own bat or to any government official who feels like ordering a massacre. You can readily imagine them discussing the subject. . . ."

In asserting that the War Crimes Commission should deal with the crime of genocide, Pell argued that every leader of the United Nations had publicly stated that such criminals should be brought to justice. Pell was not alone on the commission in believing these crimes could and should be dealt with. Two distinguished British jurists, Lord Atkin and then Lord Wright, supported Pell's contention that international law could deal with a crime against humanity and that the War Crimes Commission was the place to make that statement.

On March 16, 1944, at the meeting of his committee, Herbert Pell submitted a resolution calling for the application of "the laws of humanity" against the Nazis. His resolution had been hurriedly scrawled by him on a scrap of paper. In a strong voice, he read:

> It is clearly understood that the words crimes against humanity refer among others to crimes committed against stateless persons or any persons because of their race or religion; such crimes are justiciable by the United Nations or their agencies as war crimes.

He said that he referred to such crimes as against humanity because they are crimes against the foundations of civilization, "irrespective of place and time and irrespective of the fact whether they are or are not violations of the laws and customs of war." Not one committee member objected to his resolution. When some members pointed to difficulties in implementing it, Pell answered that war itself was a gigantic chain of difficulties.

The resolution was discussed at a later meeting with a broader representation of the commission members. Several delegates then said that genocide could not be considered a war crime. Sir William Malkin of Great Britain said he doubted whether his government was ready to include such acts in the category of "war crimes." Pell then spoke up, reiterating his previous arguments, and then referred to a statement made by Franklin Roosevelt regarding the Jews of Hungary.

While Hungary had been forced into the war on the side of Germany, the regent, Admiral Horthy, continued to give the Nazis only grudging support and attempted to retain some independence for his nation. During the war years, although German soldiers occupied his land, the Jews of Hungary, while discriminated against and abused, were left alive. They could say, as their fellow Jews in other European lands could not, "We survived." But early in 1944, Horthy tried to rescue his country from complete destruction by surrendering it to Russia. The Germans blocked his efforts and forcibly detained him—arrested is more correct—in Germany. Then nothing could save the Jews of Hungary. With a meticulous regard for detail that marks the classic civil servant, Adolf Eichmann watched over the rounding up of four hundred thousand Jews in Hungary and their deportation to Germany. There they were all killed. Franklin Roosevelt called it "one of the blackest crimes of all history."

It was to this statement that Pell referred as he addressed his fellow commission members. President Roosevelt had not made such a statement, Pell insisted, solely for propaganda purposes. The commission members then agreed that such crimes should be punished, but perhaps, they countered, under another title. Sir William Malkin suggested that the sponsoring governments be asked for their positions on the question. Sir William was directed to prepare a draft to be sent to the governments. He had it ready at the next meeting. It read:

> The Committee is of the opinion that the question of punishment of offences committed in enemy territory against enemy nationals or stateless persons on account of their race, religion or political belief requires immediate consideration. Unless other steps have already been taken or are in contemplation, with a view to such consideration, the Commission would be ready to undertake this task, if the constitutent Governments so desire. The Commission accordingly requests the Governments to state whether they desire it to undertake a study of this question with the view to making recommendations to them upon it.

This did not settle the matter. Many members of the commission were uncertain whether they wished to consider the killing of racial and religious minorities as a war crime. It was discussed at various meetings and several drafts were prepared. Finally, on May 23, according to the commission's official reporter, "As a result of the discussion in the Commission all were agreed that the Commission, in addition to covering the question of war crimes proper should also include in its scope the question of crimes against humanity, and Sir Cecil Hurst was authorized to inform the British Foreign Secretary accordingly."

Pell's success in winning the commission to his position was not a casual one. "I think I have thrown a bombshell into the Commission in the form of a proposal to take up the case of the Jews in Germany," he wrote early in April. He insisted to the commission members that "we are not simply an aggregation of lawyers' clerks, digging up precedents out of files and libraries." He argued it so vociferously, so winningly and, at times, so indignantly that ultimately the commission came to agree with him.

Shortly after first making his proposal to the commission in March, Herbert Pell wrote Secretary of State Cordell Hull reporting on what he had done. He first quoted Roosevelt's letter of March 1 in which the President said that "Germany and her satellites should be required to answer for atrocities against the Jews" as his authority for framing the proposal. Pell continued that others might suggest that another body should deal with the genocide issue. "We must realize," he told Hull, "that there is no other organization in the world which can take up this question seriously and effectively. If the War Crimes Commission does not consider these offences, they will, almost certainly, go unpunished. I do not believe that it would be a wise policy to let them go, and to leave a large section of the world, intensely interested in this question, feeling that it had been mocked; that its indignation had been aroused and its assistance obtained by mere propaganda."

The formal communique from Sir Cecil Hurst, as chairman of the commission, went out on May 29. It said that the commission believed that the crimes committed against Jews by Nazis were proper subjects for the commission to take up and requested instructions from the sponsoring governments. Such instructions did not come. Neither the United States State Department nor the British Foreign Office considered the question of genocide and the existence of the War Crimes Commission significant enough either to advise their delegates to proceed in the course they had mapped out or to reverse it. They had plenty of reminders. Every day the newspapers reported evidences of new atrocities; still no reply came.

On August 28, 1944, an American official in London named John Pehle sat down and wrote a letter to the Acting Secretary of State, Edward R. Stettinius, Jr. Pehle was aware of the situation Herbert Pell was facing in not receiving any instructions from Washington and warned Stettinius that unless action was forthcoming a number of Nazi criminals would escape. Pehle even framed a draft cable for Stettinius to send. Arthur D. Morse in his chronicle *While Six Million Died* reports that "all Stettinius had to do was add his signature. But the future Secretary of State was not willing to act so hastily. Some days later

James Mann of the War Refugee Board cabled from London complaining that Pell had 'as yet received no instructions directing him to urge the Commission to treat as war crimes those crimes committed by one Axis state against its own nationals or against the nationals of another Axis state. . . . Time is most important and I strongly urge that every effort be made to have instructions on this point transmitted to Mr. Pell at once.'" Mr. Morse reports: "The plea was in vain."

The American State Department was not alone in its indifference. On October 4, 1944, more than four months after Sir Cecil Hurst had formally communicated to the Foreign Office regarding the crime of genocide, Anthony Eden was asked in Commons what would be the fate of those guilty of such a crime. Although he had condemned the treatment of the Jews the year before in Commons, Eden hedged on punishment. "Crimes committed by Germans against Germans, however reprehensible, are in a different category from war crimes, and cannot be dealt with under the same procedure. The government have the matter under consideration, but I am not in a position to make any further statement."

He was then told by an irate member that "murder in cold blood of anti-Nazi Germans in Germany is just as criminal as the murder of anti-Nazis of other nationalities elsewhere." Eden answered: "Other means will have to be found of dealing with them." However, he suggested no other means.

In 1942 when he had spoken about the plight of the Jews murdered by the Nazis and had promised that "those responsible . . . shall not escape retribution," the entire House of Commons rose in silence to show its support of his position. No one rose to support him this day.

As long as there was no public announcement from the War Crimes Commission—its members were awaiting instructions from their governments—no assurance that a legal process had been developed, the genocide continued. Why the diplomatic bureaucracies of the United States and Great Britain refused publicly to endorse the work of the commission can only be a mystery. Nora Levin in her book *The Holocaust* and other students of this period have totaled up incident after incident where the slightest effort by the Allies might have saved thousands of Jewish lives, where one signature might have allowed hundreds of Jews to escape from the world of the concentration camp— but these were not forthcoming. Part of the cause probably was an anti-Semitism that existed in both the American State Department and the British Foreign Office. The anti-Semitism allowed early mistakes in minor matters and those early mistakes forced the bureaucrats to solidify their positions rather than admit early error.

But it was more than minor prejudice. Harold L. Ickes, who served as Secretary of the Interior throughout Franklin Roosevelt's Presidency, believed the State Department was "a conglomeration of ambitious men consisting mainly of careerists who, because they are career men, feel no obligation to follow Administration policy. I believe that, in substance, it is undemocratic in its outlook and is shot through with fascism." That was true also. The career men had been in office before Roosevelt and they believed they would be in office after him. As a result, they felt no pressure to pay attention to his policies.

But it was more than that too. Basically it was the ineptitude of the bureaucrat in the Foreign Service. The earliest and most intelligent warnings about the danger of Naziism had not come to Roosevelt from the members of his State Department but from his personal friends and his political foes who traveled abroad and believed that the President should be informed of what was happening in Europe. It was not the State Department that advised and encouraged Franklin Roosevelt to marshal the forces of the free world against the tyranny of Naziism; it was the nonprofessionals. The State Department did not have a vision for the shape of the world after the war's end; Franklin Roosevelt and Winston Churchill framing a statement almost extemporaneously at the Atlantic Conference created such a vision—"their hopes for a better future for the world." Franklin Roosevelt relied on Herbert Pell and other amateurs because he could not rely on his professionals. This is a realization that has come to succeeding presidents; eventually they develop their own small staff of foreign policy advisers in the White House and ignore the bureaucracy in Foggy Bottom as much as possible.*

* Arthur M. Schlesinger, Jr., reports that President John F. Kennedy often concerned himself with the problem of annexing the State Department to the United States government and "used to divert himself with the dream of establishing a secret office of thirty people or so to run foreign policy while maintaining the State Department as a facade in which people might contentedly carry papers from bureau to bureau."

This ineptitude, more than antisemitism and more than the casual concern with the democratically elected President's policies, caused the diplomatic bureaucracy to ignore the modern question of how to deal with the crime of genocide. Ultimately someone had to make a decision on the question. But no official in a responsible position within the State Department wished to make such a decision. A decision eventually is judged right or wrong and no one was willing to make a decision that might someday be judged as wrong. There was no need for anyone to do so; the careers went on and the promotions came and the regular increases in pay and the retirement money came without a risk being taken.

And so in 1944, when the world was unable to avoid any longer facing the horror of Nazi barbarities, the United States State Department refused to send the American member of the War Crimes Commission any instructions. It refused to take a stand.

Herbert Pell, without instructions of any kind, took the position that he should continue along the lines that he understood President Roosevelt favored.

In December he returned to the United States. Claiborne was marrying Nuala O'Donnell, and the occasion would be a good time to visit the President and discuss the commission's work. Pell anticipated being in the United States only a few days; Olive stayed in London.

On December 11, Pell had wired Roosevelt that a crisis was developing within the War Crimes Commission, referring to the genocide question. Pell said he had reported this to the State Department but also wished to bring it directly to the President's attention. Three days later the President asked an aide: "Will you try to work him [Pell] in for a half hour next week?" On December 27 the aide sent Pell a wire telling him that the meeting would have to be postponed for several days. On December 30, Pell was informed that the meeting was set for twelve-thirty Tuesday afternoon, January 9.

On Friday, January 5, a story was sent from London to *The New York Times* that Sir Cecil Hurst had resigned as chairman of the War Crimes Commission and that Herbert Pell was expected to be elected to succeed him. On January 9, when Pell was being ushered into the President's office, the early edition of the Washington *Star* already was on the streets with the story that when the War Crimes Commission next met there was "very little doubt" that Herbert Pell would be elected chairman. The prediction seemed safe. Because of the leadership in the war effort given by Great Britain and the United States, one of their representatives obviously must head the commission, and it was Pell's turn. Also, he was well liked on the commission and had given it much leadership. No problems existed on the American side, apparently. Before going to the White House, Pell had stopped off at the State Department to check with an official there whether anything had happened to delay his return to England. "No, nothing," he was told.

At the White House session, Pell reported on what had been happening within the commission, how he had worked to make genocide a crime under the commission's review, and also that he expected to be elected chairman of the commission on his return. Roosevelt agreed with everything Pell said he had been doing. And as Herbert Pell left his old friend, soon to be sworn in for his fourth term as President, Roosevelt said: "Good-bye, Bertie. Good luck to you. Get back to London as quick as you can and get yourself elected chairman."

Before leaving Washington, Pell dropped by the State Department once again. He wanted to say good-bye to the new Secretary of State, Stettinius, and also to check on his traveling arrangements. The official he had seen earlier in the day was waiting for Pell and abruptly informed him that he could not return to London. Congress had refused to appropriate funds for his salary. Pell said he would go without a salary. That, he was informed, was not possible. Pell asked the official if he had been aware of this earlier in the day when Pell had met with him. The official acknowledged that he had been.

"Why didn't you tell it to me before I went over to the President?" Pell demanded.

"It was none of my business to tell you that," was the reply. "In any case, you're the President's appointee and not mine."

The reason Pell was not informed before seeing the President was that getting to see the President in wartime was a monumental achievement. The demands on Roosevelt's time were exorbitant; his meetings were rationed strictly. The State Department officials knew that Pell was seeing Roosevelt that Tuesday afternoon. If they had told him earlier he had been ousted from his job, Pell obviously would have used his meeting with the President to demand a reinstatement and undoubtedly would have secured it. However, months now would be required for Pell to secure another interview with the President and by that time his ouster would be accomplished and the commission's work would have gone on without him.

There was no question that Pell was bounced. Later that day Secretary of State Stettinius telephoned the White House. When he could not reach the President, he left a message with Grace Tully, Roosevelt's secretary. She wrote a memorandum for Roosevelt that the Secretary of State had seen Pell, informed him that no funds were available for his return to London. "The Secretary fears that Mr. Pell will insist on seeing the President again," she wrote, "so he asks that Pres. turn the whole thing over to him [Sec of State] to handle. The secretary says they will have to assign an Army Officer to carry on the work at least until June when the Congress may appropriate the necessary funds to take care of Mr. Pell's salary, etc."

The last line, the reference to June with its possibility that Pell might be reinstated, was at variance with the impression given Pell at the State Department. He had been told he was permanently dismissed.

The matter of money was an efficient technical maneuver by the State Department. The original funds for sending him abroad had come from the President's emergency fund. But that fund had been restricted by Congress so it could finance no activity more than one year. After the first year, funds would have to come as a regular appropriation by Congress. When the State Department appropriations bill was before the House, it included thirty thousand dollars for Pell's assignment. That money was dropped when the bill went to the Senate. In a House-Senate conference committee the question of what to do about the thirty thousand came up: Drop it as the Senate did or appropriate it as the House did? The committee asked the State Department for advice. When the department showed little interest in the money, the conference committee dropped the thirty thousand dollars. Pell was out of a job.

Perhaps if Herbert Pell had been more willing to cooperate with the State Department establishment and tone down the commission's work, he could have avoided being ousted. But that was not his way. He was not a bureaucratic infighter. He had never learned the skill and in 1944 did not see any reason to begin.

Meanwhile, the story of the troubles the commission had been having with its sponsoring governments broke in the news media. The day after Pell's ouster, a development still unknown to the general public, John MacCormac of *The New York Times* reported from London that Sir Cecil Hurst had resigned as chairman, not because of ill health as had been thought, but because the British Foreign Office had ignored the commission's work and Sir Cecil had reluctantly concluded that nothing was going to be done. The story reported that the commission had asked Foreign Secretary Anthony Eden on two occasions about establishing an international tribunal to try the Axis war criminals and also had asked about trying the Axis leaders for the crime of genocide. Both communications had been ignored. The story revealed: "Why the Foreign Office behaved 'as if we [the commission] were representatives of

some British colony,' as one member expressed it, is now
known." The fault appeared not to lie with Eden, who
had become too busy to deal with the problem of war
criminals, but with various of his assistants and aides who
had been appeasers of Hitler in the past and wished to make
their present positions consistent with their previous ones.

The British newspapers were on the story also. On January 14, a Sunday, one paper reported that "the Foreign
Office has dumbfounded members of the United Nations
War Crimes Commission by rejecting their recommenda-
tions that an interallied court be set up in London for the
trial of Hitler and the heads of the Nazi and Fascist parties
for their war crimes." Despite the pronouncement in October by Winston Churchill that the Nazi leaders would be
considered war criminals, the Foreign Office was developing an official position that the Axis leaders should be
dealt with by political means. This meant by exile. One
English newspaper, *The Morning Advertiser*, reported on
Wednesday, January 17:

Why has the Foreign Office apparently come down on
the other side? It has been suggested that if the cases
of these men were argued before any kind of Court,
those in the dock might endeavour to have prominent
British statesmen brought to the witness box to give
evidence for the defence. This evidence would take the
form of quotations from past utterances praising the
prisoners, and in some cases extolling the virtues of
Fascism and Nazism. This, it is suggested, would be

extremely embarrassing to those responsible for these utterances whose reputations might be ruined by a parade of such unsavoury skeletons in public. . . .

And so that was how it would all turn out. In England a desire to retain reputation blocked development of perhaps the one potentially positive accomplishment of the whole conflict—a worldwide declaration that the resort to war for political ends was a crime itself punishable before the people of the world. And this blocking was aided by the lethargy and pettiness of the American State Department.

Pell had made no public comment about his firing, hoping to meet with President Roosevelt and reverse the decision. But the President was preparing for his trip to Yalta and had no time for his old friend and appointee. The telephone message from Stettinius had suggested the ouster was only temporary anyway. But the word of Pell's firing began to circulate in Washington. Newsmen asked about it, and the State Department decided to issue a statement.

As happened all Pell's life, a face from his past appeared. Back in 1903 a young Herbert Pell and another man Joe Grew had a dramatic meeting. It was in the winter and the lake at Tuxedo Park was filled with skaters. One young lady skated across the lake to Dinsmore's Cove and practiced skating there until twilight. Suddenly realizing it was dark, the girl turned toward the clubhouse and raced across the lake. In the middle of the lake the ice gave way. She frantically grabbed an edge of the ice and shouted for help. Farther up the lake Joe Grew was skating with a young lady when they heard her cries. While his partner went for assistance, Joe Grew sailed to the rescue. Unfortunately he was a rather big man and instead of aiding the hapless young lady, he fell in also. Meanwhile, at the skate house, Herbert Pell was about to take off his skates when he heard cries for help. According to an eyewitness, "He suddenly gave a leap like a frightened stallion and set off madly across the lake with great sweeping strokes. . . . Bertie swept up shouting, 'Am I needed?' and promptly fell in." Fortunately some others came with ropes and ladders, and all three were pulled out of the lake—the girl who had fallen in first, and the two heroes who had failed so spectacularly to rescue her.

On January 26, 1945, Joe Grew was Acting Secretary of State Joseph C. Grew and he read the following announcement to the press:

I am sorry this morning to have to announce that on account of the failure of the appropriation recommended by the Department of funds to cover the salary and expenses of the Honorable Herbert C. Pell as American member of the United Nations War Crimes Commission, it will not be possible to return him to London. I have expressed my personal appreciation and the appreciation of the Department to Mr. Pell for his work on the Commission and our regret that on account of the failure of the appropriation, his services cannot be continued. . . .

There will be no diminution in the interest of activity of this Government in the general subject of the punishment of war criminals.

Bertram D. Hulen reported in *The New York Times* from Washington the next day that inquiries about why the funds were not appropriated "only deepened the mystery." However, he wrote as if he knew the answer, reporting that "Mr. Pell was largely instrumental in inducing the commission, as chairman of its important Committee on Methods, to recommend that the jurisdiction over crimes should be extended to cover acts by Germans and Hungarians against their own people, including such racial minorities as the Jews. He also was identified with the policy of having Hitler and other war criminals tried by judicial process and not disposed of by political decision." The inference was plain in his story that Pell's advocacy of those measures had earned him his dismissal.

There is a general rule about being fired in Washington. The person ousted is supposed to take it in good grace and keep quiet about it. That was the tradition; no one dared shoot back at persons he had been at school with, sat next to in a legation office for years or played golf with at the Chevy Chase Country Club. The two persons, the one fired and the one doing the firing, might have to work together again and certainly would meet at social events, so it was best not to cause any serious friction.

Herbert Pell, however, had no particular ambitions for

a career. He was over sixty. He had been a *bon vivant*, a politician, a modest writer of political articles including some diatribes, a diplomat and finally an important member of the United Nations War Crimes Commission. He did not have to worry about further honors. Nor was he concerned about any difficulties in his social life, being one of the senior members of American society.

"It is nonsense," he stated publicly, "that the reason for not returning to London is lack of money. I have offered to serve for nothing." He continued that the reason for his firing was that officials in the State Department disagreed with his view that the War Crimes Commission should take jurisdiction over crimes of genocide.

And when he spoke in public, he spoke to the press. Ever since the war had begun, the Allies had been playing games with the question of war guilt. Their leaders—Roosevelt and Churchill—said one thing, but their bureaucracies, the American State Department and the British Foreign Office, refused to go along. And they weren't pressured to because while the statements of the leaders had made news, nobody had paid much attention to the actions of the bureaucracies. But the firing of Pell and his subsequent remarks—he talked to any reporter willing to listen—made the issue front-page news around the world. No longer could the incongruity be avoided.

The Jewish groups in the United States naturally protested the firing of Pell. Telegrams went out to the major congressional figures asking that funds for his job be restored. These groups had many lines into the White House;

Roosevelt always had enjoyed wide Jewish support in his elections. And not only the Jewish groups were concerned. The Second World War had touched every American home—a life interrupted, a husband or son killed—and now, according to what Herbert Pell was telling the press, we would all shake hands when it was over and forget about it.

Grew felt compelled to say that something more would be done when the war was over. On January 29, three days after his statement publicly acknowledging that Pell had been fired, Grew issued another statement. He insisted that the State Department had every intention of pressing for the appropriations to finance the position of an American delegate to the War Crimes Commission. He acknowledged that the Pell incident "had caused a great deal of speculation to be published with regard to this Government's position on the punishment of war criminals." He then explained what the American stance was. "Our position," he said, "has been repeatedly stated by President Roosevelt, Secretary of State Stettinius and others. It is unchanged today. It is the policy of this Government that the Axis leaders and their henchmen who are guilty of war crimes shall be brought to the bar of justice. We in the government have a definite program which, I can assure you, is comprehensive and forthright."

If ever there had been a question about the ineptitude of the State Department, it was answered by the manner in which Pell had been fired. The department found an obviously trumped-up excuse; nobody with any sophistication concerning Washington, especially the reporters writ-

ing the stories, believed that the department could not
have wrangled thirty thousand dollars out of Congress if
it really wanted the money. Ben W. Gilbert of the Washington *Post* reported that "a member of the House Appropriations Committee which trimmed the appropriation
last month recalled that the State Department did not press
very hard for the appropriation. . . ."

The department's ineptitude was further demonstrated
by its discourtesy to Pell. The impoliteness further alien-
ated him and encouraged him to fight. Finally, by its bad
phrasing of statements, the department was thrown on the
defensive. Just what were its intentions toward the Axis
leaders?

In London the remaining members of the commission
realized they had an opportunity. For more than a year
they had been trying to do something but had been ignored
by their sponsoring governments. Publicity surrounding
the Pell firing meant they could not now be ignored. The
story was hot. They sought out sympathetic reporters.
The New York Times of January 30, for example, carried
a story from London that the commission members were
"puzzled" by the State Department's dismissal of Pell. The
story then said: "It was Mr. Pell who proposed that crimes
committed by the heads of States against their own nationals on grounds of race, religion or politics should be
within the commission's scope, and that an international
tribunal should be established to try major war criminals
of the Hitler-Himmler category." The suggestion was im-
plicit that the commission believed Pell had been fired because of these proposals. And then the commission mem-

bers bore in harder. According to the friendly *Times* story:

> Some members of the commission felt certain that the coincidence of Mr. Pell's dismissal with the refusal of the British Foreign Office to accede to the commission's request to call a diplomatic conference to establish an international tribunal was more than an accident. They concluded that London made representations to Washington that the trial of Axis leaders before a court would be unwelcome.
>
> It is certain that the Axis leaders could produce approving statements made before Munich by British statesmen. It is asked whether even more embarrassing evidence in documentary form might not make its appearance to discomfort the Conservative party, which must soon go before the country in a general election, and, perhaps, to the embarrassment of relations between Britain and her Soviet ally. To this and not to legal technicalities is ascribed the reluctance to punish major war criminals by a judicial process which has been long observed here and now seems to have spread to Washington.

Herbert Pell himself never had shunned publicity, but he also had rarely been front-page news as he was this week. He seemed to enjoy it. In New York City he issued a statement to the Associated Press outlining a plan for a vigorous prosecution of war criminals. "It is better that half a dozen innocent German sergeants should hang today," Pell began his statement, "than that millions of equally innocent people should suffer in twenty-five years." He made clear that punishment should be extended "far down the line" to include the entire membership of the Gestapo "which is a volunteer organization, which nobody is forced to join." At stake, he continued, was "not a matter of revenge, but of justice." He continued:

There can be no doubt where the demands of justice lie. In Europe and Asia there are millions of people, more than all the inhabitants of New York, Illinois, and California together, who have died as a result of this war. There are in Europe 300 million people—more than twice the total inhabitants of the United States, crying for justice. . . .

He concluded:

The judgment of our descendants in forty years is more important than political expediency, or articles in law journals in 1950. We owe peace to our children, and on this debt, we dare not default.

Pell's position on the trial of German leaders after his own dismissal has been described variously in the years since. Basically he was asking that any responsible German leader and all those who had volunteered for terrorist groups like the Gestapo be considered possible defendants in trials of war criminals. Any person actually tried would be one against whom evidence was brought. "All those in any way guilty of outrages should be punished . . . ." is the way he expressed it.

Meanwhile the State Department continued to come under attack. In an editorial entitled "The Pell Affair," the Washington *Post* accused the department of not trying very hard to obtain the thirty-thousand-dollar appropriation. It then said:

The real point at issue between Mr. Pell and the legal lights in the department is whether the persecution and wholesale murder by the Nazis of German Jews and other racial minorities in Germany are crimes which the United Nations have a right to punish. Mr. Pell took the position that they have such a right. . . . And his position is by no means unique. On March 24, 1944, President Roosevelt declared: "All who knowingly take part in the deportation of Jews to their death in Poland or Norwegians and French to their death in Germany are equally guilty with the executioner. All who share the guilt shall share the punishment." . . . But apparently the President did not make the point clear enough to certain well-entrenched functionaries in the State Department. Thumbing their books on international law, they found no precedent for the procedure which the

War Crimes Commission advocates. They hold that crimes against humanity perpetrated on German soil are within Germany's domestic jurisdiction, that crimes perpetrated on United Nations territory are to be punished by the individual United Nations governments. But, lacking precedents, these experts favor delay, apparently, until more volumes can be thumbed.

Changes were coming, however. In London the publicity gained by the members of the War Crimes Commission in the wake of the Pell firing had effect. The public had been aroused, and the government felt compelled to make a statement. In Commons, on January 31, a government spokesman said that although crimes such as genocide were in a different category from war crimes, the British government would make all efforts to see that those guilty of such crimes did not go unpunished. The statement continued that when the Allies controlled Germany and the other Axis nations, the authors of such crimes would receive the punishment they deserve. *The New York Times* story from London about the statement said it "brought cheers to the members of the War Crimes Commission. One of them pointed out that this was something Mr. Pell had fought for since last March."

Even in Washington the pressure resulting from the Pell firing became too much for the State Department to ignore. Acting Secretary Grew, on February 1, issued a statement on the Pell affair. The first had announced Pell's dismissal. The second had described the State Department's "good intentions" on January 29. This third statement recalled all the Roosevelt speeches promising punishment for atrocities against Jews. It then said that plans were being worked out to implement the Roosevelt promises.

I wish, however, to state categorically [said Grew] that these proposals are as forthright and far-reaching as the objectives announced by the President, which they are intended to implement. They provide for the punishment of German leaders and their associates for their responsibility for the whole broad criminal enterprise devised and executed with ruthless disregard of the very foundation of law and morality, including offenses, wherever committed, against the rules of war and against minority elements, Jewish and other groups, and individuals.

Herbert Pell had won. This Grew statement was followed seven months later by an agreement signed by Robert H. Jackson for the United States, (then Earl) Jowitt for Great Britain, Robert Falco for France, and I. Nikitchenko and A. Trainin for the Union of Soviet Socialist Republics and including this paragraph: "There shall be established after consultation with the Control Council for Germany an International Military Tribunal for the trial of war criminals whose offences have no particular geographical location whether they be accused individually or in their capacity as members of organizations or groups in both capacities."

Herbert Pell had been dismissed by the State Department, but he had turned that defeat into victory. The precedent had been established. Making war no longer was merely a political act but a crime for which the world would exact punishment. And the excesses of war, for which the Germans then seemed to have a penchant, also were crimes against humanity, for which punishment would be demanded.

There were several accolades. From London, Olive cabled him: "You are fighting good fight and will win. Love." René Blum, the Luxembourg minister in Moscow and a former member of the commission, wired his country's legation in Washington asking it to convey to Pell "my best regards and congratulations for his marvelous work for international justice." And the commission itself, in the only action of its kind, unanimously voted Pell its thanks "for the great services which you had rendered as one of its members" and also expressed its regret that "you have ceased to attend its meetings." For a short time he was a *cause célèbre* as numerous groups and influential Americans realized that because of Herbert Pell's insistence, a result of the Second World War would be the statement that war was a crime and no longer an excuse for bestiality.

Herbert Pell hoped to see Franklin Roosevelt again. He wanted to explain personally what had happened and he still wished to serve his old friend. He wrote a long letter to Roosevelt, detailing the developments and asked for a meeting. On receiving the letter, Roosevelt read it carefully and discussed the matter with Secretary of State Stettinius. Roosevelt then suggested that Stettinius and Pell get together to settle their differences.

Pell again asked to see the President and he received a reply on April 7, 1945, from Stephen Early marked "Confidential." The letter explained that the President was leaving Washington for a few days' rest prior to his departure for the United Nations conference in San Francisco and would be unable to see Pell in the near future. Early did not say where the President was going.

Pell did follow Roosevelt's suggestion and asked for an appointment with Stettinius. He received a telegram: "Will be glad to see you Thursday April 12 three forty five pm." That afternoon—April 12—Franklin Delano Roosevelt died at Warm Springs, Georgia.

8　Herbert Pell's days in politics were over. The Second World War ended. The boys came marching home, his own son among them. And the process of learning to live in peace began. He had his home at Hopewell Junction, with its surrounding land, which in 1946 he offered to the United Nations as a permanent homesite. But the U.N. chose New York City. He donated his collection of books from the romantic period in French literature, a total of six hundred and eighty-four volumes, to the Library of Congress. He had been collecting these books since his first trip to Paris as a young boy. He had had them bound, had catalogued them and had preserved them. His son, Claiborne, remembers how Herbert Pell "took great pride in how books were bound and how they were cared for." Books always had been one of his great pleasures and Herbert Pell believed that such pleasures never should be treated in a slovenly fashion.

Honors came his way. In 1948, Czechoslovakia awarded him the Order of the White Lion 3rd Class "for your outstanding and most valuable cooperation with the

Czechoslovak Delegation during the investigation of war crimes of World War II." For his work on the War Crimes Commission, he was made an Officer of the French Legion of Honor and Commander of the Crown of Belgium. He earlier had been awarded the Grand Cross of the Portuguese Order of Christ and had been made Grand Officer of the Crown of Oak of Luxembourg. And, in 1960, Italy conferred upon him the rank of Officer in the order of Merit of the Italian Republic. He enjoyed receiving these honors, of course. Vanity never had been one of his deficiencies. But more than these and the other decorations, more than that the trail of aspiring politicians who came to be photographed with him because they believed he was an "important" figure from the past, more than all this, he enjoyed the satisfaction of having led a decent and interesting life. "Since I left the Commission," he said in the 1950s, "I have lived at Hopewell Junction, New York, quietly looking at the world from which I am, at least as far as any real activity is concerned, completely retired. I look back over a varied life of no very great accomplishments, but passed in different conditions and different times at a period when the world was changing very fast."

He also supported his old friends. This was a habit he had learned in his youth at Tuxedo Park also, that you defend your friends when they are attacked. The case in point was a charge by Senator Joseph McCarthy in 1950 against John Carter Vincent, a State Department employee. Two decades after the McCarthy era it is difficult to remember his frightening power. But he was enormously popular in his heyday, and one answered him only at great personal risk. Pell wrote to the "letters to the editor" of the New York *Herald Tribune;* the column was his only means then of securing a public forum. Pell spoke of his fifteen-year friendship with Vincent and said to accuse Vincent of disloyalty is "an irresponsible and reckless falsehood of a type too often made by politicians considerate only of immediate and personal gain." Pell then accused McCarthy of a "grossly dishonorable" act in attacking Vincent.

Early in 1952 he considered returning to politics as an elder statesman to support Dwight D. Eisenhower for President. "It would be absurd to suggest," he said, "that the man who made Patton and Montgomery work as a team is not a politician and a good one." But a massive heart attack which he barely survived kept him from any active political activity that year. His disenchantment with Eisenhower began almost as soon as Eisenhower was inaugurated.

And of course he was very interested in family. This also was something he had learned from the Gilded Age, that a man watched over and took care of his family. And as he approached his seventies, Herbert Pell found himself the leader of the Pell clan in the United States. There were several dozen Pells scattered across the country and they joined together in an informal Pell Family Association with Herbert Pell as chairman of the board. For him it was more than an honorary title. Several younger Pell cousins were helped through school through the generosity of Herbert Pell. His correspondence indicates he preferred they be unaware of his assistance. Many of the younger children of his cousins or nephews received chatty letters from him. "Dear Cookie," began one letter to a young teen-aged relative at Pomfret. "I am not at all sure whether this picture interests you or not. It is the Pomfret School Baseball Team of the Spring of 1901. Thirteen to seven means that they beat Groton for the first and I believe the only time, by that score. . . ." He closed the letter as he closed many of his letters. "Let me know," he wrote, "at any time if I can be of any use to you." He saw being of assistance part of his responsibility.

But like most elderly men he took his primary joy from the fact that his son and daughter-in-law were making him a grandfather four times over. Claiborne was now in the Foreign Service and he and Nuala were living in Europe most of the time. "I have just gotten your letter and am full of interest in the increase of the inhabitants. Make it a girl this time," Herbert Pell wrote Nuala in 1949. He continued: "I really try to think constructively about the life these children will lead, and what can be done for them, as I tried to do in the case of Claiborne. There is, in a certain way, more fun in looking sixty or seventy years beyond my time, than in just looking over the horizon as I do in your case.

"Of one thing I am quite sure," he wrote his daughter-in-law, "and that is that we know so little with certainty of what will be the circumstances of their lives that we do well to let them enjoy themselves as much as possible. Give them as much pleasure and as little pain and grief as we can. Sometimes they bother us and annoy us or even humiliate us, as we bother, humiliate and annoy God in Heaven, but we would do well to follow His example— be as nice to them as possible in the full knowledge that it is more important to keep their love than decrease their ignorance which will wear off naturally in due time. It is unfortunate that few people, while they still have much left, realize the consolidative and curative value of time."

When Herbert Pell turned seventy in 1954, his family wished to have a gathering of relatives for him. He acknowledged that there were a few of his relatives he would like to see, but he did not want a grandiose party. "I have had a very happy and pleasant life," he explained, "but I see no reason to stage a festival at the entrance of my last decade."

He still enjoyed life in his seventies, but he began to have reservations about the role he should play. He recalled that "a great many years ago, Olive's grandfather, Mr. John Bigelow, an extraordinarily wise old gentleman, was asked what he thought about giving the suffrage to boys of 18—this was long before women's suffrage, and he said he didn't think it would make very much difference, but that he would support taking the vote away from men over seventy. I am well over seventy myself, and quite agree with him. Almost all my contemporaries cast their vote either by habit for one party or another, or are influenced by past conditions, habits and modes of thought. I think that we should be allowed to live, but not to interfere."

Being Herbert Pell, he naturally lived well. He kept an apartment in a Paris hotel and a suite at the Ritz in London.

He had a car with a chauffeur in Europe at all times. He also advised his younger friends on the proper steps they should take to make their way in the world, which came down to recommending a proper tailor and a proper club to them. To a nephew going to London in 1955, Herbert Pell suggested a particular tailor. "A coat and trousers cost forty pounds which is about $112," Pell said. "This seems high, but the cost per wear is a great deal lower than clothes bought in America. All of my clothes come from him, and the newest suit that I have is 1945, and some are much older."

To another young man coming to New York, Pell advised that "you can join any club, but a poor selection will make a great difference in your future life." Pell recalled that when he had joined clubs himself almost half a century earlier they "made very much more careful selection among the candidates than they do today." He then ran down the long list of organizations he was associated with. "I joined the Union Club at twenty-one, the Knickerbocker at twenty-six. . . . My father, my grandfather, my uncle and all of my cousins belonged to these or similar organizations. Many of them were governors or club officers. I have had a certain experience in other parts of the world. At the present moment, I am a member of the Athenaeum in London. I have just resigned from the Travellers in Paris, which I joined in 1908 and have been a temporary member of some of the best London Clubs. My father was a founder and a governor of the Tuxedo Club, and a governor of the Union; my brother was president of the Racquet Club. Altogether

I really feel that I know the subject." He then advised the young man to join the Racquet Club: "Most of the best young men in New York belong to it." He added: "No club today gives any prestige, but it is a nice thing to have one."

And he was, of course, still insistent that ladies and gentlemen dress properly. In 1958 he crossed the Atlantic on the *Queen Elizabeth* with Olive and his grandson Bertie. They took their meals on the verandah grill on the top deck.

Rightly or wrongly [Herbert Pell said of this experience], this is supposed to be sweller than the main dining room, but I have never in my life seen such people as our fellow passengers. I have not led a narrow cloistered life, associating only with the more ornamental. It is more than forty-five years since I first entered active politics in the Unites States. I have known people of all classes from all parts of the country, and from a good many parts of the world, but I have never even seen photographs of people like those on the *Queen Elizabeth*. Dirty, fat and fuzzy men in mussed brown shorts and illustrated shirts, on which were depicted flowers, racehorses, mermaids, starfish, almost anything that the most vulgar imagination can think of, wandered around the deck, accompanied by women also dressed in shorts, the length of which varied inversely to the breadth. I remember once in the dining room looking around. Of course I cannot move my neck as I used to, but twisting it almost to the degree of pain in each direction, I saw that Bertie and I, one twelve and the other seventy-four, were the only men in the room wearing cravats and jackets. Of course these people got off at Southampton or Cherbourg, but I do not see them or their like in the streets of London or in the pictures that I see from Paris. It is hard to say where they go, but I really wish they would stay there.

He took a lively interest in his grandchildren. Whenever he traveled to a new place, he made a point of sending them postcards. His eldest grandson, Bertie—Herbert Claiborne Pell III—recalls that "over the years we saved up about three or four hundred postcards of different places he'd visit in Europe and he'd write on the back what the place was, why it was important and that he missed us."

As he had watched closely his son's upbringing, Herbert Pell paid great attention to his grandchildren. He once sent a book to his grandson Bertie about the "bloody games in the arenas of the Roman Empire." Herbert Pell told his grandson that "the book contains nothing that is essentially opposed to common sense and it suggests throughout, what is too evident, that low and brutal tastes in a population become greater and greater. A boy, even though he might have a good taste for wine, if he goes among a lot of whiskey and cocktail drinkers, will get to like whiskey and cocktails; at first, perhaps, through affectation of what he considers to be manliness, which is at least at first as ungenuine as is the pretence of his friend who talks about vintages."

Bertie recalled years later that "it was apparent to me that my grandfather had a tremendous, an even more than paternal interest in my finishing school and going on to college and finishing college and the same for my brother, too, and our becoming thoroughly educated. I think that that might possibly be because he didn't finish college and maybe regretted it a little bit, and he was very strong, very strong-willed about wanting us to finish college. . . . My whole interest in school, my interest in history, any interest I have in people, my interest in painting—I have a degree, a bachelor's degree in fine arts from the Rhode Island School of Design—is entirely due to him because he would take me into museums and we'd look at these paintings and we'd analyze the paintings, and he'd sit there and he'd say why this painting was good, why it was bad; then he'd ask me why it was good and why it was bad. . . . He wouldn't like to see more than ten or fifteen paintings in an afternoon. He said if you see too many paintings, you won't get anything out of it. . . . If you see a whole lot of things, he said, you won't remember a thing about what you've done. Perhaps that got me interested in painting."

Herbert Pell very much enjoyed these times with his grandchildren. On his trip to Europe in 1958 he had Bertie as his guest in London for two weeks. "I gave him doses of the sights of London cut down to infant size, about half a teaspoonful at a time," Herbert Pell wrote. "We went a couple of times on the river," he continued, "which

I had done almost thirty years before with Claiborne, but this time fortunately we had a motorboat."

He took his grandchildren on tours of Europe during the summer—not the "tourist tours" but his own specially charted trips. Bertie recalled that "we'd stop in France some place and get up in the morning about nine o'clock or so and he'd eat a leisurely breakfast till about ten o'clock. We'd be leaving, getting underway and we'd spend about two or three hours touring on to the next point and he would have carefully mapped it all out beforehand. He had these trips mapped out months before we even got out of school in June. He'd know what the next stop would be and he had it all set up so that he would know where we would be on a particular morning or an afternoon, what part of the countryside we would be going through, and he'd tell us—maybe this was why he knew the history so well; I almost think he prepared for it in a way. We'd stop for lunch in a restaurant and continue on in the afternoon. If the castle, or the place looked interesting enough we'd actually get out and walk around, go and look at it. . . ."

As the 1950s neared their end Herbert Pell seemed a contented man. The books had been given away. The homes had been closed. All his affairs were in order. His son, Claiborne, after a hard-fought primary, was elected senator from Rhode Island in 1960. Herbert Pell was extremely proud of his son's achievement. To a certain extent it was also his own achievement. He had instilled in his son the value of a good education and of gentlemanly virtues.

Herbert Pell had much confidence in his own son and grandchildren and in other young people and in the future. "I am not and never have been afraid of the future," he said. "In that, I am the true American. Whatever else Americanism is, and you're hearing a great deal of talk about it, Americanism is not cowardice. It is not a slavish adherence to precedent. It is not, above all things, looking back to a golden age that is forever by. This country didn't become what it is because it feared the future."

In early June of 1961 young Bertie Pell finished his semester at boarding school and crossed the Atlantic to spend the summer with his seventy-seven-year-old grandfather. The two Berties, grandfather and grandson, and John Collins, the chauffeur-valet, drove for several days in a station wagon through England. They stopped at Bath, several other places, and took the ferry to France. They drove to Paris, down to Italy, across to Switzerland and then to Germany. In Bavaria they stopped at King Ludwig II's fairy-tale castle Neuschwanstein. Herbert Pell ordered the car to be left at the foot of the hill and walked up to the castle with the chauffeur and Bertie.

Neuschwanstein was the kind of story Herbert Pell relished. Only twenty-four when he began construction of his castle, Ludwig undoubtedly was insane even then. The operas of Richard Wagner held him spellbound and on one floor of his castle was a rocky cave, modeled after the cave in Wagner's *Tannhauser*. In the courtyard the king galloped in the dark of night pretending to be a Wagnerian hero. Building his dream castle left the king bankrupt and nearly destroyed Bavaria. When he was forty-one years old Ludwig tried to raise more funds for his building by selling his kingdom. He was declared insane and a regent took over his rule.

It was a pleasant visit and a charming story as told by Herbert Pell. But it also was a hard climb to the top of the castle, which Herbert Pell insisted on seeing. He was puffing badly. But he seemed to recover rapidly when they rested. And there was no difficulty apparent when they started the drive for Munich. They had lunch at a little roadside restaurant. When they arrived in Munich, Herbert Pell lay down for a while. Late in the afternoon he and young Bertie went to his favorite beer garden, the Franziskanerkeller. "He really enjoyed himself," young Bertie recalled. "We were sitting there and we had our arms linked with people and we were drinking steins of beer. I never saw him do it, but I heard that he had been prodigious in the amount of beer he could consume. But it wasn't anything exceptional that afternoon."

From the beer garden they walked to a nearby restaurant. After dinner, about a block and one-half from the hotel, they were crossing an intersection when Herbert Pell said, "Hold it." He grabbed his grandson for support. Then he collapsed and slid to the street. A heart attack had killed him.

He had lived a long and pleasant life. He had come to know, love and believe in his grandchildren. He had no regrets; he considered his life complete.

A few years before he died, he wrote these lines, which serve as his epitaph: "I have been well served by the

world, and by fortune, and I retire with confidence in the
future of my country and of mankind. There is nothing
I can do more except to shake hands and say that I have
had a very good time—which I certainly have."

Sources

The chief sources for this book are the papers of Herbert C. Pell—including his oral history project at the Oral History Research Office at Columbia University; the collection of his personal papers including newspaper clippings, letters, memoranda and other writings in the possession of Senator Claiborne Pell, and his papers at the Franklin D. Roosevelt Library at Hyde Park; the interviews with the persons listed in the Acknowledgements in the front of this book, and the Roosevelt papers at Hyde Park.

In addition I have found the following published materials particularly helpful:

ADDAMS, JANE, *Twenty Years at Hull-House*, New York, 1910.

ALLEN, WILLIAM H., *Al Smith's Tammany Hall*, New York, 1928.

AMERICAN HISTORICAL ASSOCIATION, "What Shall Be Done with the War Criminals?" Washington, D.C., 1944.

AMORY, CLEVELAND, *The Last Resorts*, New York, 1952.

——, *Who Killed Society?*, New York, 1960.

ASTOR, WILLIAM WALDORF, "Report to the Executive Committee of the Tuxedo Club," New York, 1888.

BARR, LOCKWOOD, *Ancient Town of Pelham*, privately printed, 1946.

BARTLETT, RICHARD A. (ed.), *The Gilded Age: America, 1865–1900*, Reading, Mass., 1969.

EDEN, ANTHONY, *The Reckoning*, London, 1965.

FEINGOLD, HENRY L., *The Politics of Rescue*, New Brunswick, N. J., 1970.

GARNER, JAMES W., "Punishment of Offenders Against the Laws and Customs of War," *American Journal of International Law*, New York, XIV (1920), 70–94.

GLUECK, SHELDON, *War Criminals—Their Prosecution and Punishment*, New York, 1944.

GREW, JOSEPH C., *Turbulent Era*, Boston, 1952.

HALE, NATHANIEL CLAIBORNE, *Roots in Virginia*, privately printed, 1948.

HEINRICHS, WALDO H., Jr., *American Ambassador*, Boston, 1966.

HUTHMACHER, J. JOSEPH, *Senator Robert F. Wagner*, New York, 1968.

ICKES, HAROLD L., *The Secret Diary of Harold L. Ickes*, New York, 1953–54.

JAMES, HENRY, *The American Scene*, New York, 1967.

JOSEPHSON, MATTHEW AND HANNAH, *Al Smith: Hero of the Cities*, Boston, 1969.

KEND, EDWIN C., *The Story of Tuxedo Park*, privately printed, 1937.

"Lorillard and Tobacco," a brochure published by the P. Lorillard Co. on the 200th anniversary of the company, New York, 1960.

McALLISTER, WARD, *Society As I Have Found It*, New York, 1890.

MAUGHAM, FREDERIC H. (Viscount), *U.N.O. and War Crimes*, London, 1951.

MORSE, ARTHUR D., *While Six Million Died*, New York, 1967.

MOSCOW, WARREN, *Politics in the Empire State*, New York, 1948.

——, *What Have You Done for Me Lately?*, Englewood Cliffs, N.J., 1967.

"Officers, Members, Constitution and Rules of the Tuxedo Club," New York, 1928.

PELL, HERBERT C., *America and Its People*, New York, 1969.

——, *Glimpses of English History*, New York, 1967.

PELL, OLIVE BIGELOW, *Belinda*, New York, 1968.

Pelliana, Pell of Pelham, privately printed. Oct. 1963.

POST, EMILY, "Tuxedo Park," *The Century Illustrated Monthly Magazine*, New York, Oct. 1911, p. 795.

PRINGLE, HENRY F., *Alfred E. Smith—A Critical Study*, New York, 1927.

ROOSEVELT, FRANKLIN D., *The Happy Warrior—Alfred E. Smith*, 1928.

RUSHMORE, GEORGE, *The World With a Fence Around It*, New York, 1957.

SCHLESINGER, ARTHUR M., JR., *A Thousand Days*, Boston, 1965.

——, *The Crisis of the Old Order*, Boston, 1957.

——, *The Coming of the New Deal*, Boston, 1959.

——, *The Politics of Upheaval*, Boston, 1960.

SCOTT, JAMES BROWN, AND LANSING, ROBERT, "Commission on the Responsibility of the Authors of the War and on Enforcement of Penalties," *The American Journal of International Law*, New York, XIV (1920), 95–154.

SHIRER, WILLIAM L., *The Rise and Fall of the Third Reich*, New York, 1960.

TAYLOR, TELFORD, *Nuremberg and Vietnam: An American Tragedy*, Chicago, 1970.

UNITED NATIONS, "Agreement . . . for the Prosecution and Punishment of the Major War Criminals of the European Axis," London, 1945.

——, "Punishment for War Crimes," New York, 1943.

UNITED NATIONS WAR CRIMES COMMISSION, *History of the United Nations War Crimes Commission*, London, 1948.

UNITED STATES CONGRESS, "Punishment of War Criminals" (Hearings before the Committee on Foreign Affairs, House of Representatives, 79th Cong. 1st Sess., March 22 and 26, 1945).

WARNER, EMILY SMITH (with HAWTHORNE DANIEL), *The Happy Warrior*, New York, 1956.

INDEX

Addams, Jane, 2
Albion, Robert G., 136
Aldrich, Nelson, 35, 50–52, 141
American free enterprise, Bell's pessimism about future of, 141
Americanism of Pell, 329
Amory, Cleveland, 2
Anti-Saloon League, 82, 120
Anti-Semitism, 298
Appearance of Pell. *See* Personal appearance of Pell
Art, Pell as student of: visits to museums, 58–59, 65–66; purchasing of works of art during European travels, 64–65; as associate of Charles Loeser in Italy, 65–66
Athenaeum Club in London, 272, 324
Azores Islands, Pell's recommendation for U.S. acquisition of, 199–200

Balls for formal presentation to society in the Gilded Age, 41; prestige of Tuxedo Ball, 41–42
Bardossy, Laszlo de, 230, 232, 235
Beard, Charles A., 34
Berlin, Ellin: on the fantasy world of society, 48; on snobbishness of old families in society, 68–69; on the Gilded Age, 69–70
Biddle, Anthony J. D., 199
Bigelow, John, 323
Bigelow, Matilda, 74–75. *See also* Pell, Matilda Bigelow
Bloch, Maurice, 104
Blum, René, 317
Books: Pell's pleasure in, 7, 319; donation of collection to Library of Congress, 7, 319; Pell's

collecting of, in his European travels, 64
Bowditch, Ernest W., 10
Brogan, Denis, 153
Bryan, William Jennings, 3, 123
Bullitt, William, 195
Business community: Pell as scourge of *laissez-faire* business world, 4; disparaging attitude of Pell toward, 36; young Pell learning about, from Nelson Aldrich, 50–52; questioning of ethics of, by young men like Pell, 52; time of unchecked *laissez-faire*, 52–53; attitude of Pell toward, 101; Pell's fight against, 145; Pell's article in magazine *Yankee*, quoted, 145–46; Pell's dispute with General Electric Company, 148–51; Pell's discouragement over the years with standards of, 151; Pell quoted on ethics of, 153; Pell as "radical," "Socialist," or worse, in eyes of, 154

Capitalists, industrial, and "doctrine of self-interest" in the Gilded Age, 1–2
Chamberlain, Neville, 190–91
Churchill, Winston, 191, 252, 285, 299, 305
Claiborne, Annie Emily Magdalene (grandmother), 8
Claiborne, William C. C., 5–6
Cleveland, Grover, 156
Clubman, Pell as, 59, 67–69, 324; Travellers Club in Paris, 59, 67, 324; prestige clubs of New York, 68, 324; exclusiveness of his clubs, 68–69; Metropolitan Club in Washington, 83–84;